Having None of It:
Women, Men and the
Future of Work

Having None of It:
Women, Men and the Future of Work

Suzanne Franks

Granta Books
London

Granta Publications, 2/3 Hanover Yard, London N1 8BE

First published in Great Britain by Granta Books 1999

A CIP catalogue record for this book is available from the British Library.

1 3 5 7 9 10 8 6 4 2

ISBN 1 86207 164 0

Typeset by M Rules
Printed and bound in Great Britain by Mackays of Chatham plc

To Emma, Hannah and Benjamin
and all their working futures.

Contents

Acknowledgements

The research for this book over the past two years included numerous interviews with a wide range of women – and quite a few men – from dauntingly sophisticated sixth-formers to some of the highest achievers in their field. Many of the interviewees are identified in the text; others, where I have just used a first name, are disguised, but I would nevertheless like to record my gratitude to them all in giving up their time to talk, often about intimate and sensitive matters.

The following people were particularly important in compiling the research: Susan Harkness, of the Centre for Economic Performance at the London School of Economics, who gave invaluable assistance in providing and interpreting statistics on all aspects of women and the labour market; Carolyn Yates who conducted a large number of the interviews with great diligence and efficiency, and whose background in television research was invaluable in sifting and refining large amounts of information; and Clare Delap, now at the Institute for Public Policy Research, who also did some interviewing as well as providing more general research across a range of topics.

Roxanne Glick gave me the idea for this book in the first place when she said that women's lives today will one day seem like those of the dinosaurs. In writing the book insights, assistance and comments have come from all kinds of angle. Some people prefer not to be named, but I would like publicly to thank Caroline Elton, Brenda Bloch, Andrew Franklin, Veronica Wootlif, Susan Spindler, Judith Osborne, Rosaleen Hughes, Michelle Rosen, Sara Nathan, Iris Kalka, Ceredwin Roberts, Corinne Westacott, Vicky Barrass, Josephine Warrior, Patricia Hewitt MP, Sue Owen, Giulia Scannavini and Debbie Gower. A number of people kindly commented on parts of the manuscript including Rosine Perelberg, Chris Giles of the Institute for Fiscal Studies, Una O'Brien, Shelagh Diplock (former director of the Fawcett Society), Clive Wolman, Donald Franklin and David Goodhart.

I am grateful for the assistance I received at the Fawcett Library (thankfully soon to be rehoused from its shabby basement into new splendour) and the Bodleian and Social Studies libraries in Oxford. The staff at the Office for National Statistics showed enormous patience in answering endless queries, and I have had critical computer assistance from Jerry Nettleton who helped me out of some deep holes. With Jerry's encouragement I lurched – rather than surfed – around the Net, which has been a fantastic help in writing the book. Although still not as confident or proficient as my eleven-year-old daughter Emma, I retrieved information and communicated with people all over the place. On some occasions I became so engrossed and excited by it, I started to feel an anorak sprouting on my back.

I would also like to acknowledge the help and support of my agent Felicity Rubinstein and to thank the delightful staff at Granta, most especially Frances Coady, who is in my view probably the closest thing there is to a dream editor. Finally I would like to pay particular tribute to the assistance given by my mother Hedy Franks, who did not have the same opportunities as me, my father Felix Franks, who has always been an inspiration, and my husband John Bowers whose wide-ranging knowledge of labour law has been an invaluable resource, in addition to his help and succour in so many other ways.

Introduction

Half a Revolution

Why do the gurus always get it wrong? We were once reliably informed that by the end of the millennium we would inhabit a world of higher productivity and also greater leisure. The future was supposed to bring in an era of flexible employment and with it a society where paid working hours would cease to dominate adult existence, both financially and in terms of identity and status. Part-time work would no longer be marginalized as second-best, and the traditional divisions between men and women would readjust as both sexes shared time and responsibility at home and at work. Instead of the much anticipated blurring of lines whereby work would become less central to personal identity, and both men and women could achieve a new understanding of caring and leisure, the status of paid work has risen higher than ever in relation to unpaid activity and so has the compulsive attitude towards work as the defining characteristic of social worth.

And there were similar mis-predictions about women's role in the workplace. In a generation young women's expectations have dramatically altered, and most young women live quite different lives to their mothers. Yet the comfortable but inaccurate forecast that the admirable rising achievements of young women would inevitably work their way through the system, enabling them to reach the top in substantial numbers was a wishful dream. Certainly women have learnt all the values of the workplace but they are still not accepted there. They remain almost invisible in the boardroom but much in evidence amongst the tea-making grades. The often-cited 'feminization of work' has confused the fact that many girls are doing well at school and starting out on the first rung of their careers on equal terms with boys, with the highly selective media myths of women conquering the commanding heights of the economy. Yet what it really means is armies of low-paid women in service industries. For the vast majority of women work has not brought 'liberation'; they work in segregated, low-paid, part-time jobs, because average families need a second wage – a tedious reality far removed from the glossy magazine image of working women.

The revolution in work has coincided with the revolution in women's aspirations. Women's public lives have been transformed, and they have been encouraged to embrace work, just at a time when the workplace is going through its own frenzied transformation and work has coincidentally become more unwelcoming to everyone. The result of the changes are deregulation, rising workplace inequality, longer hours, and greater pressures for the smaller numbers of full-timers, combined with insecurity and uncertainty of life for the growing periphery of temporary workers and part-timers, where women are of course over-represented from lecturers to cleaners. It is as if women's enhanced expectations were out of sync with wider change in the labour market. By the time they were poised to join the workplace *en masse* the conditions and rules had made it an unrecognizable and constantly changing environment. Women arrived at the party too late. Of course there are people at work who, if they can make the grade and offer infinite availability, are doing very nicely indeed – but not too many of them are women, and very few are mothers.

In most analyses of what is happening to work the male pattern of work and the male workforce are the norms. Women are usually an afterthought, but the gurus of work purr reassuringly that women are ideally suited to the new working order and that the contemporary workplace needs women's particular contribution. It all sounds like a promising match. The transformation of the labour market and the nature of the modern workplace are supposed to harmonize with women's rising expectations, because women are good at balancing many roles, or because they like part-time work, or because they are good at serving and being nice to people. These observations tend to focus on a narrow, almost abstract, view of the relationship between women and the workplace, but they remain oblivious to the wider context and they fail dismally to take account of where major obstacles might occur.

For a new generation of women, not surprisingly, the old discourse of liberation is regarded as boring: we need to find fresh ways of saying things against a different economic and political landscape – because the revolution in women's expectations and in their public participation is still only half completed. The nature of the labour market has been transformed, women's public identity has been transformed, but the expectations of home and work have changed very little as women eagerly entered the workforce. Whilst women have found an identity beyond childbearing, men have not found an identity beyond work. Despite change every-where else, expectations of mothering and who does what behind the privacy of the domestic front door have hardly altered at all. Women might be off doing all sorts of other things, but at home they are doing the same as they always did: scrubbing floors, making supper and wiping tears. The invisible unpaid economy that makes paid work possible is still a woman's world – and in a bottom-line economy where everything is perceived in terms of financial value, its status is lower than ever.

Even on the left the goal of an equal society has dropped off the agenda. The dominant belief now is in equality of opportunity, not of outcome. So the credo goes that so long as the system makes sure there is fairness at the outset, it does not matter if the market allocates winners and losers. Yet there will never be a level playing field between men and women, if male identity remains unal-tered and unpaid work continues to be shuffled off onto women. In a market system where unpaid work is invisible, there is no incentive for men to change their identity to encompass low-status, financially worthless activity. Moreover, an insecure, rapidly changing workplace is an inducement not to change one's life patterns, but to cling on tight to what there is. So, as women are invariably at the bottom of the pile, in an era of widening divi-sions between winners and losers they are in danger of being left still further behind.

Men who choose or would like to take more domestic responsi-bility are treated as freaks. Meanwhile millions of men are *real* losers in an economy that has stopped manufacturing things – those laid off in their millions from the traditional blue-collar heavy industries. Somehow the plight of these men who have been caught out in economic restructuring has been confused with a crisis in male identity. Women have transformed their lives and found a new identity not instead of, but in addition to their old one. As soon as there is any suggestion that *men* might also change a little or expand their identity into new areas, we hit panic mode: there is talk of crises, of men as victims, and the grumbling of a backlash against women in work. The prospect, let alone the reality, of change brings shudders and warnings about how powerful women are destroying men. Even erstwhile ardent feminists like Fay Weldon blame women for reduced sperm counts and argue bizarrely that what we really need is more unequal pay between the genders![1] No one explains how a handful of women in senior jobs plus a growing number of low-paid service workers threaten to emasculate society, but they conclude (rather like the Promise Keepers in the United States) that if women would go back home, then the world would return to the way it always was, crime would reduce, families would be healed, and we would all be happier.

If work brings salvation whilst conditions at work become tougher, politicians need to understand that that other convenient political icon, the family, will start to falter. Some families will fall apart through stress, in others children will fail to thrive, and some potential families will never get formed because women have decided it is not worth it. So long as the link between these issues is officially overlooked, so long as individuals are left to find their own solutions to the difficulties, and so long as this dislocation is treated as invisible or a problem for individual women, it is not a political issue. And yet these contradictions are felt today in nearly every home and workplace – only the lucky few can construct private solutions because they have sufficient control, resources, luck and emotional literacy to reconcile the various conflicts. Public discourse promotes the ludicrous stereotypes of the juggling superwoman, the perfect mother from the fifties or the wimpish new man. Elsewhere these matters are rarely addressed in anything but the gushing tones of personal confession or worthy but inaccessible academic analysis. In writing this book I have tried to steer a reasoned case somewhere in between.

The disjunction between the various shifts – in women's expectations, in the operation of the labour market, and in the patterns of home – is causing enormous concern. Because each of them operates according to quite different priorities the result is unbearable tension. On a political level there is little or no attempt to reconcile these tensions. One agenda exhorts us all to believe in the wonders of flexible labour markets, portfolio lives and transferable skills, while another howls about the destruction of the family and the need for more and better parenting. A third agenda talks exclusively about women's advancement and the desire for greater fulfilment. The crucial interrelationships and inevitable contradictions between these issues are rarely considered. The political rhetoric prefers not to see the possible inconsistencies. Meanwhile there is growing anxiety across Europe and Japan about the population imbalance – an ever-growing population of elderly people but fewer children – as over one in five women opt out of mothering and families become smaller. But there is no official recognition that the declining birth rate might just have something to do with the absence of adequate communal support for parenting.

We are in the midst of a social revolution in which girls' rising expectations have coincided with furious change at work and a static world at home. The interests of women who may want to gain more autonomy, of government that believes in the power of deregulation, and flexible labour markets whilst hoping to curb the benefits and the pensions bills, and the unchanging need of children for stability do not coincide. The research for this book made clear to me over and again that these overlapping and often conflicting issues can only be reconciled through urgent public acknowledgement and genuine political debate. We need a much wider understanding that tries to reconcile women's role in the world, the nature of the modern workplace and the enduring needs of children, so that instead of all or nothing, a sensible balance of working and caring is available for everyone. My intention is not to present a gloomy analysis full of pessimistic conclusions or to ignore the ways in which horizons for many women have expanded, but to explain the crucial interrelationship between these profound social changes and to reinterpret for a new generation how the personal is still political.

1

Great Expectations

Across the developed world, girls are getting ahead. In education they now perform better than ever before. As their exam results leave their male contemporaries lagging behind, more and more girls are entering higher education, and the range and quality of job opportunities for young women are increasing. Young women are identifying with work and achieving success; girls' aspirations and expectations are greater at the end of the twentieth century than at any previous time. The message is 'anything boys can do you can do better'.

At the beginning of the century, in 1902, when a new school curriculum was being discussed in England and Wales, the conclusion was that girls' education should be linked thoroughly 'with the chief business of their lives', that is, as housewives and mothers. It was only with the power of the suffragette movement, around the time of the First World War, that the idea emerged that girls' education, at least for a select few, might have a direct occupational outcome. Mass secondary education for girls in the UK did not arrive until nearly halfway through the century, with the 1944 Butler Education Act.

Girls have always shown promise in primary education. For years after the Butler Act the eleven-plus results had to be secretly 'interpreted' so that there were enough boys to fill the grammar school places. Girls were performing so much better than their male contemporaries that without such an adjustment many grammar schools would have had a majority of female pupils. It is in the later years of secondary schooling that girls have shown such marked improvement over the last twenty years. By 1975 girls aged sixteen were achieving equal results with boys: 24 per cent of each sex gained five O levels. Twenty years later, 49 per cent of girls had five or more GCSE (A–C) passes, but only 40 per cent of boys reached that level. This is a substantial divergence, and girls have even overtaken boys in science subjects, which were for so long seen as strictly masculine territory.

At A level the picture is more complicated because of the need to compare across all subjects, but the general drift is the same. More A levels are being taken, but girls' improvement is correspondingly better than boys'. In 1995, according to the results in England, 24 per cent of girls gained at least three A level passes, compared to only 20 per cent of boys. Two years earlier girls had been only 2 per cent ahead. In Scotland the difference is even greater: over one third of Scottish girls who left school in 1995 achieved three or more Highers (the equivalent of A levels), but only one quarter of boys reached the same level.

Girls have finally achieved the equality in education that was one of the five original demands of the women's liberation movement. It is nearly thirty years ago, in 1970, that modern feminism was launched in the UK at a conference at Ruskin College, Oxford, which laid out five goals for the so-called second wave of women's emancipation. The other four – free abortion on demand, safe, reliable and free contraception, equal pay, and twenty-four-hour nurseries – are still unrealized.

In a generation, educational stereotypes have changed. It used to be girls who feared being identified as too studious or clever. Scholastic attainment was considered unfeminine. Today it is the reverse. It is girls who are associated with hard work and a serious attitude towards school. For some boys it is not cool or macho to work hard at school, because that is what sissies do. Teachers notice that boys in secondary school 'can tend to drift. They fail to come to grips with what the job market now requires, where a basic education is a necessary, if not sufficient, condition.' In stark contrast, teachers note that it is girls who have become ever more serious about their education and career prospects. In 1997 when the Industrial Society questioned 10,000 young people about their prospects, they confirmed a pattern of ambitious, realistic girls in contrast, to boys who were far less inclined to plan and prepare constructively for their working future.[1] Sixth-form girls today are well aware of how their attitudes differ from those of the boys around them. 'Boys are much more laid back, they don't worry too much. You can see it walking through the common room. Girls seem much more concerned about the future and more determined, they tend to plan more ahead and work towards goals, and boys tend to let it happen,' says a London sixth-former. 'Girls have a lot more focus now,' 'Boys don't work as hard and don't like to be seen to work as hard,' 'We're focusing on our new identity and they're losing their old one,' commented others.

In some schools the gap has become a chasm: in several education authorities in 1997 the difference between boys and girls at GCSE was already over 15 per cent. In one South Yorkshire comprehensive in 1996, 51 per cent of girls gained five A–C GCSE passes, compared with a mere 15 per cent of boys. When subjects are streamed according to ability, the bottom sets in many schools are invariably full of boys.[2] The far slower rise in boys' attainment has prompted reports and panic. In 1996 the Secondary Heads Association published a handbook entitled *Can Boys Do Better?* And Ofsted, responsible for school inspection, issued a joint report with the Equal Opportunities Commission on the growing educational gender divide, urging schools to focus on low-achieving boys.[3] It also predicted that in some of the best-run and best-managed schools the gulf between boys' and girls' achievement would increase even further. Even though the standards of all pupils might rise, girls seemed able to take correspondingly more advantage than boys of inspiring teachers, a more settled, stable environment, and all the other things that Ofsted praised in the best schools.

The story does not end there. More boys than girls leave school with no qualifications, and fewer boys than girls go on to some form of education and training at sixteen. When the Robbins Report on the expansion of universities appeared in 1963, only one quarter of undergraduates were female, and even in the mid-seventies girls were only one third of the undergraduate population, but by 1995 slightly over 50 per cent of undergraduates were women. Girls overall achieve better degree results, although boys are still to be found at the extreme ends of the spectrum, more likely to do exceptionally well or exceptionally badly. So whereas boys continue to gain more first-class honours degrees at university, once firsts and upper second degrees are grouped together girls are still performing better, except at Oxford and Cambridge.

Professor Bernard Rosen at Cornell University studied the achievements of schoolgirls in the UK, the US and Italy over twenty years and published his findings in *Women, Work and*

Achievement: The Endless Revolution, in 1989. He concluded that 'the educational and occupational expectations of girls have risen to the point where the differences between the sexes (in this respect) are becoming negligible'. These high expectations mean that 'girls are raising their sights and aiming for high occupational targets, confident that they can score as many bulls-eyes as boys . . . adolescent girls have on average similar competencies, achievements, values and perceptions as well as educational and occupational expectations'.[4] They have also become equally subject to parental exhortation and encouragement. The old double standard in many families which accepted that it was valid to educate sons better than daughters has gradually disappeared and it has become unacceptable to most parents to expect less of girls than of boys.

Many other studies confirm the extent to which girls have gradually come to identify with work and feel the need to succeed in work as a primary goal. In the 1970s Sue Sharpe interviewed Ealing schoolgirls for her book *Just Like a Girl*.[5] Twenty years later, she returned to conduct similar interviews and discovered that girls in the nineties leave school with a much greater attachment to the idea of a working life and developing a career. According to *The Can-Do Girls*[6] – a 1997 report which interviewed 3,000 teenagers about their attitudes and expectations – there has been a dramatic change in young women. Instead of the traditional pattern where little girls did very well but lost their confidence and drive when they reached the rocky shore of adolescence, the reverse is happening. Provided there is sufficient encouragement at home, the report concluded, adolescent girls are now assertive, motivated and positive about their future.

The American writer Naomi Wolf famously described this change in young women's perceptions as the 'genderquake'.[7] The fashionable think-tank, Demos, took up the concept to show how the values and aspirations of young women have shifted towards those of men. According to Demos surveys, young women aged under thirty-five score highly on the trend of 'androgyny'. They value risk, adventure, ambition and personal fulfilment but not necessarily through childbearing. Pat Dade of the research institute Synergy has provided much of the evidence for the genderquake research, by examining values and goals across the spectrum of age and gender. He believes that the profile of young women today is like that not of contemporary young men, but of men twenty-five years ago, because these young women exhibit 'self-confidence, optimism and the attitude that the world is their oyster'. According to his and other studies, young men today have a more pessimistic outlook than women. They have a gloomier view of their future and as a group seem less driven in their desire for academic success and career.

These changes have also affected girls' views on motherhood. For an ICM Research survey in 1996, young women were asked to imagine what, looking back on their deathbed, they would most regret not having done in life. Not having children ranked fifth in order of priorities, after having a successful career, a long and stable relationship, travelling the world and making loads of money.[8] According to a survey by the National Council of Women, *Superwoman Keeps Going*, only 13 per cent of women of childbearing age think that children are necessary to being fulfilled.[9] This is a huge generational change and in conversations with adolescent girls who have sufficient educational and social advantage the message is constantly reinforced that fulfilment through employment and independence are crucial. Marriage and children fall much further down their list of priorities. The first concerns are 'a good job', 'supporting myself', 'independence', 'success in my field', and 'doing something worthwhile'. Where young women are offered career opportunities and routes to fulfilment beyond childbearing, they will take them.

The majority of young women who choose motherhood at an early age do so because little else is on offer. They are overwhelmingly from backgrounds where expectations continue to be severely limited. As soon as an alternative is available, girls are tending to identify with historically male goals beyond solely childbearing. So clear is this link between poverty of expectation and early motherhood that in August 1997 the government started looking at ways of using poor school test results to identify potential teenage pregnancies. The government spokesman explained that 'girls who do not achieve after the age of 11 are most likely to become parents in their teens'. And conversely it appears that ambition is the best form of contraception.

The new sense of ambition and acceptance of work as central to young women's lives is reinforced by the instability both of modern marriage and of the wider labour market. Historically the strict division of labour in marriage meant that women would happily give up paid employment if their husbands could afford to support them; they made that decision on the basis that, barring emergencies, they had a cast-iron future. Today no one can be certain that they will be looked after through marriage or cohabitation. There are no jobs for life. A woman could suddenly find her partner unemployed and herself as the main breadwinner or family provider.

And if job security is a global problem, one of the most dramatic rises of all is in the insecurity of a spouse within a marriage. As the potential for marital breakdown heads towards 50 per cent, anyone intending to find a lifetime meal ticket through marriage is choosing a shaky occupation. In the United States the grim category of 'displaced homemaker' has gained currency – to describe the wife who devoted everything to husband and family, only to be left poverty-stricken and insecure when she is discarded for a newer model. After many years of domesticity and no employment experience outside the home, she is truly stranded. The majority of divorces may be initiated by women, but the very concept of married life for women as a secure alternative lifestyle to paid work is rapidly disappearing. The message today is that at some stage everyone needs a means of earning a living, unless they are content to live on benefit. At the very least, work could be a necessary evil.

For young women with the highest expectations and best opportunities, the desire to obtain good results and find a good job has become imperative and relentlessly exceeds the basic need for economic security. In fact the pressure to succeed and achieve can become almost obsessive. Headmistresses at some of the most academically prestigious girls' schools are alarmed by the plague of anorexia and other eating disorders affecting clever and ambitious girls.[10] Such disorders are often seen as symptomatic of girls' constant striving for self-discipline and perfection. According to one researcher who has studied middle-class schoolgirls, 'for a lot of them it was unthinkable to get less than straight As . . . everything else – relationships especially – was subordinated to education'.[11] It seems unimaginable that only a generation ago education and academic success hardly mattered for most girls from comfortable backgrounds, whose expectations were of a brief spell of work until marriage and children. Today even those few involved in the archaic society ritual of coming out as débutantes are concerned that charity balls do not interfere with school exams, whilst the teenage supermodel is busy doing homework between assignments.

Girls with sufficient education no longer opt for the stereotypical vocational training and careers. They are not only widening their scope of choice but also gaining a stronger foothold in those areas where they had previously only a modest representation. When Dr Wendy Greengross wanted to study medicine in 1943 she chose University College Hospital, London, because it was one of only three places in the UK that accepted women as medical students. 'Women were nurses not doctors, so we were encouraged to behave like pseudo-nurses.' Dr Elizabeth Shore recalls how when she wanted to study medicine all the London teaching hospitals still had a 20 per cent quota on women. Oxford would only take ten female medics a year, and there was a special quota interview for women entrants.[12] In 1996 for the first time, more women than men entered medical school. At the University Hospital in Wales 125 female first-year students were admitted and only 68 male students.

The Law Society reports that women have outnumbered men admitted to the profession since 1991. In 1995/6 52 per cent of newly qualified solicitors were women. Nearly 40 per cent of the new intake of chartered accountants are women, a proportion that has increased over 10 per cent in the last decade. One third of the City's annual graduate intake is female, and there are similar trends across the professions. The traditional university milk round, which large employers or City institutions use to recruit graduate entrants, has slowly become gender-blind. Women have started to venture successfully into other areas that were previously out of bounds. Yvonne Kershaw was the first woman to pilot a Boeing 747. Karren Brady is the Managing Director of Birmingham City Football Club. Women have entered the Fire Brigade and been taken on by breweries to run pubs. They have become oil exploration engineers and joined the construction industry. Bovis Construction has female graduate management trainees.

Women entering the professions are only part of the picture. There are wide (and indeed widening) gaps between women able to reach the highest levels of educational and professional entry and those who have more restricted prospects. However, even amongst those with few opportunities – school-leavers at sixteen and eighteen with limited qualifications – girls are performing better than boys. They are more likely to get jobs, even if these are stereotypically female jobs, and they are far less likely to find themselves unemployed than men of the same age. Even when they are unemployed, according to a Policy Studies Institute report, they are likely to benefit more than men from government job placement schemes. Both Job Clubs and the Job Interview Guarantee showed substantially higher rates of success for women than men in securing new employment.[13]

Fewer and fewer jobs today require the physical strength that was always a man's unique selling point. The invention of the forklift truck alone displaced countless unskilled men by eliminating the need for many of the basic tasks of humping and shifting heavy loads. Meanwhile the majority of new jobs that have been created are in areas where women have traditionally worked: answering telephones or pounding keyboards. And most new jobs are within the service sector where women have always been in demand – being nice to people. So even those women who have fewer educational attainments are more likely to find employment, albeit in low-status and underpaid positions, than men of the same age and qualifications.

The gender gap in unemployment is widest of all between young – especially unskilled – black men and women. The achievements of black women relative to black men in both education and employment are especially astonishing. Some economists see black women as the leading edge of what is happening to the rest of society, at least amongst lower socio-economic groups. Not only are black women's employment rates so much higher than black men's but they are much closer to achieving wage parity than the rest of the population. (According to one survey, black women now earn more than black men or white women.[14]) In the US too the pay of black women has gained on that of black men by fifteen percentage points more than the pay of women in the population as a whole. And twice as many black women as black men graduate from college.

The better educational performance and enhanced employment prospects of young women have increased expectations dramatically and produced rising self-esteem and optimism. It is as though a new generation has been given visas to travel in a foreign country – the world of work – and their behaviour is similar to the stereotype of some new immigrant groups: keen to take advantage of new opportunities, hungry to prove themselves, to overcome discrimination and to get ahead. Interestingly some of the top educational (but not employment) indicators are from women who themselves are from ethnic minorities. A higher proportion of Indian, Chinese and Asian women aged between twenty-five and twenty-nine are educated to degree level or higher than of white women of the same age. In this meritocratic area the disadvantaged group from within the disadvantaged group does best of all.

There are many separate explanations as to why young women over the last twenty-five years have experienced such a transformation in their achievements and attitudes: from the pill to the growing weight of coursework assessment in exam results. Yet none of these innovations by itself explains the revolution in expectations. The underlying and fundamental change is the mainstream acceptance of the feminist message that girls should and could achieve within the public domain. Even if the actual word 'feminist' is no longer used by the rising generation, as Carmen Callil the founder of Virago Press has pointed out, these ideas have become part of the water supply. Once the inhibitions (as much internal as external) were removed, young women took advantage of the opportunities and gradually raised their expectations and ambitions so that their attitudes naturally became more similar to those that had traditionally been associated with men. They exhibited the same identification with work and articulated an ethos of individual self-fulfilment – in complete contrast to the ancient view of women's destiny as servicing others. In popular culture in the late nineties this ethos became packaged as 'girl power'. So just as women now in late middle age find the goals and lifestyles of much younger women unrecognizable, the reverse is also true. Young women say that they cannot imagine making the same self-sacrifices and compromises that characterized their mothers' lives. These south London sixth-formers sum it up:

'I don't know how my mum does it – I couldn't think of anything more boring. My mum had a really good job and she decided not to go back to work until I went to secondary school, and the job she's got now in comparison to the job she had then . . . is just stupidness really. As an individual she's lost her sense of herself. And when she tells me about herself then when she worked, she seems like a completely different person.'

'My mum left school when she was 15, worked for 10 years, met my dad, left and a year later had me. My life is going to take a totally different pattern, I want to go to university, I do want the education that is going to enable me to live my life the way I want. I want to have more than she did, I need more to fulfil my life to make it satisfying.'[15]

Ambitious girls are impatient both with their mothers' long suffering and with what they perceive as the defeatist attitude of older women who warn that the gains of early years might not be so easy to sustain later on. Higher expectations combine with the optimism of youth to produce a positive and upbeat vision of their own future. According to the author Marilyn French:

> For Northern women with some education, life today is an entirely different prospect than when I was a girl. The world closed in on us when we reached 16 or so: no matter how bright or talented we were, possibilities closed up, horizons receded. Not so today: the eager shining faces of girls and young women looking toward their future are proof of a profound moral change.[16]

Another, more cynical explanation lies behind the rapid transformation of girls' early achievements. Once girls were able and confident to compete at school and university they faced comparatively little resistance because educational achievement does not threaten the prevailing status quo. In no sense has anything been taken away from boys, despite the panicky 'boys are failing' rhetoric. Overall there are many more exam passes and qualifications being taken by *everyone*. The proportion of those achieving A level passes increased in just ten years from 19 per cent in 1985 to 34 per cent in 1995. The undergraduate population more than tripled in the twenty years from 1975. Average exam performances, at GCSE, have also improved. In each case girls have done correspondingly better than boys, but because the overall standard has risen and the total numbers have increased there is no evidence that girls' achievements have in any way damaged those of boys.

Education, especially in such an expansionist phase, is not comparable with scaling up a hierarchical pyramid (or greasy pole) because giving more prizes to one group has not meant taking away from another. The very nature of education, which deals with a constantly shifting population, means that the increasing number of girls as students is part of this overall change and is not to any other group's detriment. As an industry, higher education has successfully expanded, and girls who were previously an underutilized part of the market are benefiting. There are only very limited areas of education where the total number of men has diminished, such as the formerly male colleges at Oxford and Cambridge, which were only opened to women in the late seventies. Yet even here nothing unduly threatening happened. Julia Neuberger, one of Britain's first woman rabbis, looking back on her own time at Cambridge remarks that, when men's colleges decided to admit women, elderly male dons were easily persuaded of the charms of having pretty undergraduates around. It was only when the prospect of appointing female academics, to dine alongside them at high table, was mooted that they objected vehemently.[17]

As young women move from education into vocational training and the workplace it is unlikely that they will threaten any established order. Certainly those women who have gone into the fastest-growing areas of work – low-paid, insecure, service-sector or caring occupations – do not challenge the status quo. They can easily be accommodated, and their docile, uncomplaining attitude is one of the reasons they are often preferred over men, especially in relation to pay. Even ambitious women on the first rung of a professional occupation are unlikely to disrupt existing patterns. At this stage in most professions men's and women's needs and requirements are very similar. When they join fast-track training programmes or graduate schemes, women can usually slot in without difficulty, even if the question of sexual harassment still has to be confronted. There are advantages to organizations in taking on women rather than men. Women are still seen as more conscientious, committed, hard-working and personable. They score highly on the nineties buzzwords of complexity, adaptability, team work and communication skills. Everyone knows that working hours have risen in the last decade, but according to the British Household Panel survey it is 'professional women under 24' who work the longest hours of any category and any age group – seven hours more each week than young male professionals. Women embrace the work culture wholeheartedly.

One of the areas where young women still differ from their male contemporaries is in their estimation of how important financial reward is in their working lives. Women tend to place other criteria such as job satisfaction higher on their scale of values, whilst men are much more concerned with what they are paid and much better at bargaining for themselves.[18] This difference in attitude is sometimes cited as a reason for the enduring pay gap between the genders. Naomi Wolf urges young women to place a higher emphasis upon financial reward if they really want to achieve in the workplace.[19] However, even if money is not uppermost in the personal priorities of women under thirty, they are nevertheless being valued much more highly than ever before in relation to men. The pay gap for young women in their twenties is the narrowest of all ages. For educated young women it has virtually disappeared and, for the first time in history, amongst a strictly limited category – young, childless and educated professionals – a pay differential in men's favour no longer exists. According to very recent figures, women in this group are now earning 104 per cent of the equivalent male wage.[20]

As we approach the millennium young women have seen the world turned upside down. Expectations for those lucky enough to have the right advantages are unrecognizable to their parents' generation. As their attitudes to life have become progressively closer to those traditionally associated with men, the immediate response might be that we can now expect these substantial changes to 'work themselves through the system'. If girls and young women are now performing as well as and often better than boys then logically if we wait another twenty years, inequality between genders in the workplace will have withered away. The power structures across society that are all still comfortably occupied by men will embrace gender equality, and senior women will no longer be an isolated rarity, but instead common enough not to provoke any special notice. We will have reached critical mass. Those now at the lower levels will move onwards and upwards so that the institutions now run by men will have women in similar numbers not just at the bottom but calling the shots: in the government, the judiciary, industry, the media, the police, academia and the City. This assumption – a rather Whig-like interpretation of history, that gradually and peacefully the enlightened and progressive outcome will emerge – is widely held by schoolgirls and young women today. Just as by the 1960s women took achievements like gaining the vote entirely for granted, so a great many of today's young women have internalized the values and expectations that emerged in the second wave of feminism. The value of qualifications, the need to enter the workplace and to succeed in the public sphere are so normal for many young women that they are hardly worth comment. Twenty years ago was a foreign country. So is it true that the old battles have been won and the genderquake generation will inherit an equal working world?

2

Danger Ahead!

At first glance young women's anticipation of equal success in the workplace seems in the late 1990s to be fully justified. Equal opportunity and sex discrimination legislation passed twenty years ago changed the public face of what was acceptable in the workplace. Larger numbers of women are working than ever before, and familiar media images and extensive media coverage devoted to those few pioneering women high-fliers who have made it to the top reinforce the assumption that a radically different future is available to the rising generation of women. The rhetoric of equality is everywhere, and this combined with the high expectations of young women today strengthens their belief that 'the battles are over' and consequently that 'anything a man can do a woman can do too'. Superficially it all looks like an upward trend, so why should young women's promising achievements be disappointed later on in life?

If today's aspiring eighteen-year-old was taken forward in a time machine she would be alarmed by the discrepancies that persist behind the rhetorical belief that the position of women at work means an unbroken line of improvement. If she could see herself suddenly aged fifteen or twenty years older she might wonder about the restricted nature of change. Her aspirations and expectations would collide with the persistent difficulties of unequal pay, occupational stereotyping, and a landscape where not only do the underlying structures that operate against women remain firmly entrenched but in some cases economic change has made the barriers yet more insurmountable. Educational opportunity and career entry, where she has scored such spectacular success, pose no threat to the status quo. They involve no differences in power structures and no change in the organization of the workplace. But as she would see upon emerging from the time machine, despite many more women in paid employment, laws on the statute book and some clearly visible women high-fliers, the 'female future' is not quite what she might have expected.

A Fair Day's Pay . . .

The average woman, working full-time, still earns only three quarters as much money as the average man.[1] No matter where you look, from boardroom to shopfloor, women earn less than men. In managerial jobs like bank or building society managers women earn almost barely 60 per cent of the male wage. For general managers the figure drops to 58 per cent. In sales women earn only 57 per cent as much as men. Right across the occupational spectrum the story is repeated. According to every measurement – hourly pay, weekly pay, annual pay – across every age group and comparable educational qualification women earn less than men, with the sole very recent exception of the educated professional women under twenty-four years old who work longer hours and earn more than men. In manual occupations women's average weekly earnings are 65 per cent of those of men. And for part-time workers the position is worst of all. The average hourly wage for part-time women is currently 61 per cent of the male average wage, and it has risen only two percentage points between 1973 and 1993. The Equal Opportunities Commission calculates that according to the trends of the last twenty years it will take at least another forty-five years before women achieve equal pay with men. Yet in some areas the gap is increasing and not diminishing. According to the National Management Salary Survey, in 1996 the average woman company director earned £71,638, some £16,000 less than her male counterpart. A year later the gap had widened to £20,000 as male remuneration increased whilst women directors' pay remained much the same.[2]

Women receive less pay than men all over the world, but the differentials vary substantially from country to country. According to international comparisons Italy has one of the narrowest gaps, with women earning more than 80 per cent of the male wage; it is closely followed by Sweden, Austria and Australia. Britain lags near the bottom of the European league. In some East European countries, for example in Hungary, women are proportionately better off than in Britain; and even in the Soviet Union, under Communist rule, women's pay was 70 per cent of men's. Paradoxically the United States, with all its vociferous campaigns for equality and equal rights, has one of the worst gender pay differentials in the industrial world. The average female wage there is only 64 per cent of that earned by the average man. In 1963 the United States introduced one of the first equal pay acts, yet it made scarcely any difference. According to some figures the ratio of women's earnings to men's was 63 per cent in 1939 and shifted only one percentage point, to 64 per cent, in the next fifty years. In some of the intervening years women's earnings fell below 60 per cent of men's. In the 1980s a male high-school drop-out still earned on average more than a woman with four years of college education. And women managers in 1995 earned 68 per cent as much as their male counterparts.[3]

In any modern Western society where work and financial reward have become defining factors, what you do and how much it is worth in the marketplace are critical signals of what is considered valuable. Labour's 1997 election victory produced the unfortunate role model of Joan Ruddock, the Minister for Women, who received no junior ministerial salary because 'the ceiling on the number of ministers allowed on the Whitehall payroll had been reached by the time she was appointed'. No one considered asking a male MP promoted to the ministerial team in another department, like Defence or Agriculture, if he would mind forgoing a salary instead. A separate minister with responsibility for women's issues in Scotland was appointed at the same time. He was a former professional footballer called Henry McLeish. There appeared to be no problem in finding the money to pay Henry's salary.

Joan Ruddock was no exception. The pattern of inequality continues in the most surprising places throughout the workforce. In 1995 the hugely popular TV comedy show *Men Behaving Badly* almost came to a standstill when the two star actresses threatened to strike. Caroline Quentin and Leslie Ash were upset when they discovered that they were being paid one third less than the male stars, Martin Clunes and Neil Morrissey. The BBC was embarrassed into adjusting things. Nevertheless unequal pay for actors and actresses, as in other professions, is not at all uncommon. Two surveys by the actor's union Equity have demonstrated that women earn less overall and receive lower daily fees for the same type of role.[4] In 1997 there was further embarrassment at the BBC when it was revealed that the *Today* show, the worthy and prestigious Radio 4 current affairs programme, paid its female presenter, Sue McGregor, some twenty thousand pounds less than her male colleagues.[5]

Economists have all kinds of theories to explain the gender pay gap. The orthodox and Nobel prize-winning economist Gary Becker argued in 1985 that because of all their domestic duties women are more exhausted, which makes them less productive and therefore deserving of less pay.[6] Other economists point to the persistence of stereotypes or prejudice in the way that tasks are rewarded. Some of them highlight the historical role of unions as male bastions uninterested in promoting women's interests; these economists also point to the enduring belief that women are only working to supplement the family income and their partner's wages: women's wages are really just 'pin money' (in Morocco they call it 'lipstick money'), so women do not require the same pay as a man. And there are other explanations which demonstrate that women are more likely to work for smaller employers, where wage rates overall are lower.[7]

The psychological explanation of the pay gap argues that women do not place such a high priority on financial reward, and so they are less likely to demand more. Jack Irvine, who spent ten years as an editor and managing director in the newspaper industry, was astonished that during the entire time a woman never asked him for a pay rise. 'With the guys it was really simple . . . they just asked, in the toilet, the canteen, the pub or simply on the editorial floor'.[8] The traditional reluctance of women to pursue financial reward or to place a high financial price upon their own contribution is especially significant in a period when individual pay negotiation is becoming the norm. It is a standing joke amongst personnel managers that the best way of weeding out female applicants for a job, in the era of anti-discrimination laws, is to readvertise it at a higher salary, which discourages many women from applying at all.

For generations, different pay scales within organizations produced the man's rate and the woman's rate for the same job. Large public sector employers such as the railways continued these practices throughout the 1960s, paying men and women different amounts for performing the same task. In the 1970s this kind of blatant inequality was stopped, but unequal pay for men and women has been sustained in many indirect, even unintentional ways, at all levels of employment. A rising female management star employed by a major British energy multinational was shocked to find in her mid-thirties that she was paid much less than other graduates in the company fast-track programme, who performed similar functions. Then she realized why. Unable to take as many foreign postings as her contemporary male colleagues because of domestic constraints, she had missed out on the hardship payments, relocation bonuses and extra perks like the payment of school fees which were consolidated into her male colleagues' future salaries when they returned to the UK. So effectively this was a gender differential. She had been less mobile at key moments, and was now paid less than an equivalent man.

Similar unexpected routes to unequal pay occur in other fields. An American bank offered all its managers the perk of paying their subscription to an exclusive male club. A public company provided all its senior managers with company cars except for the one female manager whose job demanded far more travelling in the UK than most of the others who stayed at base. She felt so thrilled to have the job anyway that she said she did not want to

make a fuss and challenge this inequality. It was only the prompting of a male colleague that led her eventually to politely request
a car too. At the other end of the employment scale, in 1997 a
Tesco cashier took her employer to a tribunal because she earned
£1 below the qualifying limit for National Insurance, which
meant she failed to qualify for any state maternity benefit when
she became pregnant. As three times more women than men earn
very low levels of weekly pay, the cut-off that excludes employees
from benefits can become indirectly discriminatory towards
women.[9]

In the 1970s Barbara Castle, as Secretary of State for
Employment, was responsible for the passage of the key equality
legislation, the Equal Pay Act and the Sex Discrimination Act
(SDA). It was the culmination of nearly one hundred and fifty
years' campaigning, from the time of the original motions
demanding equal pay. The philosophy underlying the acts was
that legislation would deliver equality through the recognition of
formal rights, and the popular belief after 1975 was that as
unequal payment to men and women was now illegal, it would
cease forthwith and the gap between men's and women's wages
would be eliminated. The same assumption was made about other
forms of unequal treatment of men and women. They would no
longer exist (except in very limited areas where it was permitted
by the SDA), because the law would prevent them.

Those opposed to the Equal Pay Act made dire predictions
about the loss of jobs and the growth of unemployment that
would ensue if women were to receive the same pay as men.
Businesses would be forced to close, they warned, and jobs would
disappear. The very same arguments were deployed twenty years
later during the debates on the minimum wage. In the case of
equal pay everyone, both optimists and pessimists, got it wrong.

Jobs were not lost, and nor did the differential in men's and women's pay dissolve. In the period immediately after 1975 women's wages made some modest gains in relation to men's, but since the early eighties the gender pay gap has remained stubbornly at around 23 per cent.[10]

Part of the problem lies with the way the acts were framed. They are essentially passive legislation which depends upon brave individual women making a legal challenge. Legal aid is not available, so applicants must pay their own costs unless they can persuade a hard-pressed Equal Opportunities Commission (EOC), trade union or law centre to fund them. The legislation is most effective when dealing with a straightforward comparison between men and women doing identical jobs. Anything more complicated, like trying to make a case for different work which is of equal value, leads to all kinds of terrifying legal quagmires. In 1986 the speech therapist Dr Pam Enderby brought a claim against Frenchay Health Authority that her (predominantly female) profession should be valued as highly as that of a clinical psychologist or a pharmacist (predominantly male professions). It took eleven years, cost over a million pounds and occupied many weeks (of her paid holiday) in a succession of courts before the case was resolved, when the new Labour government agreed to settle with her. A number of linked cases by speech therapists remained unresolved – in some instances the applicants died long before the process reached its conclusion. Other similar equal value cases challenging the status quo have also become enmeshed in the same hopelessly long-drawn-out and demoralizing procedures.

The SDA was a compromise, intended to provide an educative effect on behaviour, rather than strong enforcement. It was never given real teeth because that would have led to too much disruption and possibly upset the social consensus. (In fact today the

SDA perversely acts as a brake upon programmes of positive action that are intended to help women, such as certain specially targeted training programmes or the Labour Party all-women shortlists.) Meanwhile the EOC produces worthy research papers but there has never been an onus on it to take the initiative in policing equality amongst employers and institutions in the way that health and safety at work are monitored and enforced. And so unequal pay for men and women remains a stubborn fact of life.

Who Does What?

Of course legislation – even when it is well drafted and has sufficient teeth – cannot on its own eliminate inequality. It must also be accompanied by real changes in the indirect social and institutional attitudes that devalue women's efforts.[11] Margaret Mead the anthropologist has pointed out that 'in every known human society the male's need for achievement can be recognised'.

> Men may cook or weave or dress dolls or hunt hummingbirds, but if such activities are appropriate occupations of men then the whole society, men and women alike, votes them as important. When the same occupations are performed by women they are regarded as less important.[12]

More bluntly the American writer Cynthia Fuchs Epstein asks, 'Why does it happen that, no matter what sphere of work women are hired for or select, like sediment in a wine bottle they settle to the bottom?'[13]

Whatever task is performed by a man is automatically valued more highly than when it is performed by a woman. The famous historical example is office work. In the mid-nineteenth century, clerical work was an entirely male preserve and it had a relatively high status. Over the next hundred years these functions gradually shifted to women, so that today some 98 per cent of secretaries are female. As the balance shifted so did the status of clerical work and its position within the remunerative pecking order. Or maybe the reasoning works the other way around – as the social standing and pay associated with the job diminishes so it gravitates to being a 'woman's job'.

A similar principle applies in the ranking of tasks. The more status is attached to a role, the more men will be doing it and the more likely it is to be comparatively well paid. This is equally true of the professions. The areas of the law in which women domi-nate, like family law, are less well remunerated than areas such as commercial or tax law where there are more men. In medicine the higher the status of the job the fewer women are doing it. Surgery, perhaps the most prestigious area, has one of the lowest propor-tions of female consultants. Meanwhile there are plenty of women excising verrucas or caring for the elderly.

Baroness Brenda Dean, the former head of the printworkers' union SOGAT (Society of Graphical and Allied Trades), describes a similar pattern in her industry. She discovered that some of the early-eighteenth-century printers were women, as the new machinery was seen as a novelty with little future prospect and men had little interest in it. When the economic power of printing became clear (and with the introduction of steam power), then men replaced women. The key printing trades gradually became extremely well remunerated as printers, through strong unions, were seen as part of the working-class aristocracy. When women were eventually allowed into the industry again it was only in a lowly capacity – the high-paid graphical trades remained a male preserve. Many years later when newspapers were introducing new technology, those women who had been pounding typewriters in the classified ad department before the copy was set found that they could now input straight into computers and do the setting themselves. For the operator, the job was the same; in fact computers made it easier to do corrections. Yet Brenda Dean was worried that men would now muscle in on this role and then reclassify the task as highly skilled and highly paid. She worked hard to make sure that this time round women did not lose out in the transformation of the industry.[14]

According to one study, 90 per cent of men work in a predominantly male environment and 70 per cent of women work in a predominantly female workplace. Meanwhile the Labour Force Survey shows that over half of all women in employment were clustered within only four occupational groups – clerical, secretarial, sales and personal services.[15] Only 16 per cent of employed men worked in these areas. There is some evidence that after the implementation of the Equal Pay Act employers encouraged further segregation as a means of evading equal pay provisions. It can often be quite arbitrary whether a task is considered a male or a female one. Yet the iron law always holds that when the task is performed by a man it is more valuable than when it is done by a woman. One study contrasted the production of paper boxes and cartons. The actual processes are very similar, but one is less automated and is officially defined as less skilled, so therefore is less well paid – and employs a predominantly female workforce, whilst the higher paid task has a male workforce.[16] Across cultures a similar task might be performed variously by one gender rather than the other. Chicken plucking, for example: in those countries where it is a male task it is given a higher status and relatively higher rewards. In Russia (as in the former Soviet Union), where more women work in medicine, the status and pay of doctors have always been comparatively lower than in the West. Cause and effect are difficult to disentangle. The tasks a society considers to be low-status tend to attract women. Equally the predominance of women ensures the task will be viewed as low status and rewarded with low pay.

If these occupational stereotypes are to be overcome women must be employed in what have traditionally been seen as male jobs, and vice versa. Men are resistant to entering female-domi-nated areas of work precisely because they are seen as of lower status and are usually less well paid. It is only where men take over a previously female area *en masse*, then redefine it as male and move it up the hierarchy, as in printing, that they willingly cross gender boundaries. Spinning, obstetrics and nursing management are other diverse instances where men have successfully taken over a previously female occupation and colonized it for them-selves, ensuring higher status and better pay.[17]

When women enter a male area, men are more inclined to leave it in favour of other pastures, like the male secretaries and clerical workers of the nineteenth century. And when men start to leave, it is a sign that status and power will slowly drain away. Nowadays, in a period when status is more fluid than it once was, the same patterns can still be discerned. Women start to come in just as occupational status (and relative pay) are slowly slipping away (although the argument is equally convincing that women are only able to enter a new field because men are no longer so attracted to it). There is an interesting manifestation of this is in Scandinavian public life. In recent years female parliamentary representation in Sweden and Norway has risen to nearly 50 per cent. At face value this looks like a significant advance for women, attributable to a culture that promotes progressive views on equal-ity. Yet the achievement is somewhat illusory, masking another form of segregation. Women are entering parliament while men are deserting the public sector. In an era of global corporations, when the real power resides in the private sector (with companies that might control far more than the GNP of a single country), ambitious men no longer seek advancement through the legislature of a small country. Membership of the European Union has also downgraded the role of a Swedish MP, whereas the power of international commerce is undiminished. Scandinavian men have turned instead to the well-remunerated private sector, where women are still very poorly represented at the highest levels. Meanwhile women are left worrying about parochial social issues.

It is quite possible that Britain may follow this pattern. No sooner had women reached Westminster in reasonable numbers at the 1997 general election than it became clear that there were really too many MPs without enough serious work. The leadership anxiously looked for ways to keep their surplus troops busy so that they would not make trouble for the government. Britain has 659 MPs for 50 million people. The US has 435 congressmen for 250 million. Back-bench MPs spend a large part of their time as glorified social workers dealing with constituents' problems: ideal work for caring women. Women MPs have traditionally received much larger mailbags than their male colleagues[18] because constituents seeking help with their problems see them as more approachable. Power meanwhile continues to flow to the executive, and Westminster becomes more of a backwater. Diane Coyle of the *Independent* remarked soon after the election that 'the woman's place is in the House of Commons; at the heart of the Government, in the Treasury and No. 10 (for example the policy unit) the jobs belong to the boys'. As one insider remarked, 'You knew for sure it was a New Lad administration when there were reminders to bring your football strip to the policy away days.' Meanwhile in the commercial heartlands – just as in Scandinavia – the senior echelons of ICI, BP and the City remain firmly in male hands and the remuneration is far more substantial than that of a mere legislator.

The argument about Westminster as a woman's domain received a further twist in July 1998 when all the senior parliamentary jobs were filled by women. There was concern that women had gone from running big spending departments to 'housekeeping' tasks. The post of Chief Whip, hitherto one of enormous power (address: 12 Downing Street), when occupied for the first time ever by a woman transmuted into an 'organizing' 'glorified Nanny' role.

Female Dwarves

The workforce is being feminized and women now outnumber men at work. In the nineteenth century it was almost exclusively women from the working classes who participated in the paid workforce. For them, employment in factories or domestic service was a necessary economic evil, and wherever possible they aspired to be like their middle-class sisters and leave working to men. The growth of stronger trade unions and the notion of the bread-winning 'family wage' meant that more working women achieved the status of being able to stay at home. It was only after 1914 that the possibility of mainstream professional employment for middle-class women arose and became an issue for contemporary feminism. Even then, gaining entry to wider job opportunities was only considered appropriate, or legal, for single women who had no marital or family responsibilities. With the exception of wartime emergencies this remained firmly the case until the end of the 1950s. Since then, there has been a well-documented explosion in the female workforce. During the 1990s the number of women in employment steadily approached 50 per cent. In some parts of the UK they started to outnumber men, and in the third quarter of 1996, according to the Office for National Statistics, women in paid employment outnumbered men by 12,000, something that had never happened in peacetime before. Men still comfortably outnumber women in self-employment, although here too women are steadily increasing their presence. But the raw figures tell only of female workforce participation, and size certainly is not everything. Whatever gains may have been made by women entering higher-status jobs are overshadowed by the multitudes who head for the 'pink-collar' ghettos. Until recent years there was little research on female wage inequality because it was not considered much of an issue. Comparatively few women worked, and very few indeed received high pay. Today the research shows that there is a widening gap between those highly educated, usually full-time women who have entered well-paid, secure employment and the majority, over 90 per cent, who occupy lowly, insecure and badly paid jobs.[19] Fewer than 5 per cent of employed women earn enough to pay higher-rate tax.[20] And of all the higher-rate tax payers women are a mere 15 per cent, which means that increasing top rates of tax has a disproportionate effect upon men, whereas increasing benefit rates for the poorest helps far more women than men.

The other way of understanding this is to look at the proportions of women amongst the lowest-paid. In 1995, 31 per cent of women earned less than £4 per hour and three quarters of all those earning below £4 were women. As the national indices of wage inequality have steadily widened, women fall further to the bottom of the scale, which partly explains the persistence of the gender earnings gap. Whatever progress is made in combating discrimination and providing more equal opportunity is counter-balanced by the fact that wages in the era of flexible labour markets are overall becoming rapidly more unequal. This effect is neatly described by some economists as 'swimming upstream'.[21] The gap between top and bottom earners has steadily widened, so if there are mostly men at the top end, where wages have increased so substantially, then the male/female earnings ratio will be affected by overall wage inequality no matter what anti-discrimination or equal opportunity measures are introduced at the same time. This is why the gender pay gap is still especially wide in the United States despite all the equality rhetoric: wage rates there are historically extremely unequal – top chief executives earn 212 times the wage of the average worker in their company, compared with a ratio of seven times more for chief executives in Japan.[22]

In the UK the bottom 10 per cent of wage earners still receive the same pay as twenty years ago. However the top 10 per cent, a predominantly male group, have seen their income grow by 50 per cent in real terms, and they now control the same amount of income as the whole of the poorer half of the population.[23] Whoever is at the bottom will end up relatively worse off, and most frequently that happens to be women.

Economists have a handy way of presenting income inequality. They have invented an imaginary procession in which the entire working population of Britain marches by in an hour and income is ranked according to height (this is known as the Pen parade).[24] First they describe all the midgets coming past and how it takes thirty-seven minutes before a person of average height (and income) can be seen. By the last quarter of an hour the figures grow to seven feet tall and in the final minute huge giants, hundreds of times bigger than a normal person, are striding by. The parade would probably finish with someone like Bernie Ecclestone, appropriately enough the boss of Formula One motor racing, speeding out in front with his annual salary estimated in 1996 at £54 million. What economists do not bother to mention in telling this tale is that an overwhelming number of the dwarves are female. Once average human height is exceeded there are fewer and fewer women to be seen. A mere 17 per cent of working women earn over £15,000.[25] By the time the serious giants stride along, only the Queen and a couple of others with the right family connections are left to march past. (Observers estimate that after the Formula One share flotation Mrs Ecclestone, who owns most of the shares in the company, could forge ahead of the Queen.)

Globally the situation is even worse. According to the sociologist Anthony Giddens, women own less than 1 per cent of the world's wealth, they earn around 10 per cent of the world's income, and they perform two thirds of the world's labour, and 'there are no societies in which men do not in some aspects of social life have more wealth, status and influence than women'.[26]

Flying High

Yet despite the realities of work for most women – unequal pay, job segregation and discrimination – the official media message is still an upbeat one. It certainly does nothing to alert young women to unchanging attitudes and structures in the workplace. Instead the media loves to dwell on successful achieving women in prestigious positions, like the annual Woman of the Year lunch at the Savoy or the Veuve Cliquot award for the business woman of the year. Newspapers and magazines regularly publish lists and profiles about women who are reaching new heights, along with all the accompanying domestic detail. Everyone knows that Barbara Mills, the first female Director of Public Prosecutions, was a mother of four. No one remarked that her (male) predecessor also had four children. Seen in isolation these accounts make comforting reading. They tell of busy, single-minded women who have overcome obstacles to reach prestigious positions in a variety of walks of life.

On closer inspection the lists are not all that they seem. In spring 1997 the *Guardian*, in a three-part series on the fifty most powerful women, was delighted to report that 'for the first time in British history you can assemble fifty women who wield real power – that does not rely on inheritance, sex appeal or manipulative guile'. Yet in order to make up the numbers, the criteria were stretched to include both the Spice Girls pop group and Princess Diana. But the real test comes when these surveys are put alongside all those other mainstream lists like 'Who Is Really Who in Modern Britain' the *Sunday Times* 'Richest 500' or the '300 Most Powerful People'. Suddenly the balance looks quite different. In nearly every general list of successful movers and shakers the representation of women is minute. It becomes obvious that the list of wonderful women is a highly selective one. *Euromoney*'s 1997 list of the top fifty women in finance[27] sounds impressive when read on its own, yet only one of those fifty women, Carol Galley, who was the vice-chairman of Mercury Asset Management, appeared in the *Punch* list of the most influential figures in the City published a few weeks later.[28] Every one of the other twenty-six City achievers in the *Punch* list is a man. *Euromoney* admits that it was tough going to find fifty top women in finance and 'investment banking was especially difficult'. On closer inspection the *Euromoney* list omits many of the biggest institutions and necessarily includes random positions well down the City pecking order. Confirmation of this lack of high-flying women came in November 1997, when Lazards bank hosted a grand City lunch in honour of the prime minister. Eighty guests were invited to the lunch: Carol Galley was the only woman.

The same is true in nearly every other sector. The *Punch* list of influential media figures names only two women of power and influence; one of them is Elisabeth Murdoch, who at twenty-nine years old might well not have been there had she had a different surname. Women in Computing proudly promotes the growing achievements of women in this field and seen in isolation it looks impressive, but when *Vanity Fair* published a list of 'Fifty Leaders of the Information Age' only two women rated a mention, appearing at numbers 40 and 48 respectively.

In academic life the story is similar. The 1997 *Guardian* list of fifty high-achieving women includes an upbeat account of some women professors; subliminally the message is that women are making terrific strides in the universities. But when this list is read alongside the 1997 *Times Higher Educational Supplement* survey on who has made it to become a professor in modern Britain the perspective changes – a mere 8 per cent are women. It is almost an optical illusion. There are far fewer women, but the nature of the coverage makes them more visible and you scarcely notice that it is the same few popping up and being quoted, so that it seems that there are many more women in powerful positions than in fact there really are.

A handful of exceptional women have reached senior positions in some fields, but this should not, despite the media coverage they receive, distort the picture. There is certainly no steady upward march of women's involvement. In fact, rather than there being more women in higher positions, sometimes it is the exact opposite. Between the mid-seventies and the mid-eighties the proportion of women in senior management dropped by 3.5 per cent, although more women reached middle and lower management.[29] In 1965, 23.7 per cent of all secondary school head teachers in England and Wales were women. Eighteen years later the figure had dropped to only 16 per cent. By 1995 the number of women heads had risen to 21.7 per cent, but that is still less than the proportion who were head teachers thirty years ago.[30]

In primary schools the picture is different, but equally unbalanced. Amongst head teachers the genders are equally represented at around 10,500 each, but lower down the scale, in the classroom, there is a wide disparity with nearly 150,000 female teachers and only 33,000 men. As the hierarchical pyramid narrows in any organization, the proportion of women automatically declines. Banks and financial institutions employ around one million women, yet women occupy less than 5 per cent of senior management posts.[31] According to an equal opportunity survey at NatWest, where an enlightened chairman has made real efforts in this area, women still make up two thirds of the workforce but only a quarter of managers are women. Of the one third of the workforce who are men, two thirds reach management. Other reports by the Society of Telecom Executives, the Institute of Management and the Policy Studies Institute all identify the same patterns, as does a study of senior managers in local government.[32] In retailing, which is overwhelmingly 'women's business' since women are the ones who do the shopping, there is the same pattern of women's employment: thousands of Indians and very few chiefs. At Marks and Spencer, for example, the workforce is 85 per cent female, but only 24 per cent of senior management are women. Even amongst the ranks of non-executives in big retailing companies, women are a rarity, and yet it seems logical that they might be far better placed to understand what the customer really wants.[33] The International Labour Organization (ILO) produced a report at the end of 1997 confirming that the same pattern is replicated across the world, with tiny numbers of women reaching the higher levels of management.[34] In the top grades of the *Fortune 500* companies women make up 1.9 per cent of the highest-paid officers and directors. Interestingly the ILO study confirmed other evidence that women in developing countries such as Colombia, the Philippines and Venezuela do comparatively better than women in the richest countries. Higher proportions of women reach the top of professional and managerial hierarchies. The economist Amartya Sen has pointed out that there are more tenured women professors at Delhi University than at Harvard and more women in the Indian parliament than in the US Congress.[35] So there is no necessary link between economic progress and women's advance in the workplace, just as the Whig view that eventually, as more educated women come into the workforce, the proportion of women at the top will become equal is not supported by the evidence.

To test this latter theory, in 1993 the economists Paul Gregg and Stephen Machin studied the progress of 20,000 managers in 400 British companies.[36] They concluded that women were simply not proceeding through the organizations at the same pace as men. Even when more women enter an organization at the bottom, they face a steeper climb than their male equivalents. Gregg and Machin used a series of independent measures of competence, qualifications and track record to identify the rate of promotion and progress through the ranks. Tracking the promotions and remuneration from 1989 to 1992 they found that women were overall less likely than men to be promoted. And the few women to rise up the hierarchy had to wait longer to be recognized.

In 1990 the Report of the Hansard Society Commission,

Women at the Top, revealed that there were still very few women in senior positions throughout the public and private sector.[37] This report led to the establishment of the Business in the Community initiative, Opportunity 2000, which was supposed to achieve a 'better balance of men and women at work'. It proclaimed itself to be 'business-led' and 'business-driven', but behind the fine words, a long list of blue-chip-company members and prime ministerial approval, Opportunity 2000 had no real power at all to promote equal opportunities – beyond gentle exhortation. According to one observer it was like using a toy spade to dig the Channel Tunnel.[38] In December 1996 Opportunity 2000 had to face the rather embarrassing fact that the number of women board members of its member companies – which include many large PLCs – had actually dropped by one third in the previous year. But as the chairwoman, Lady Howe, pointed out, the numbers of women board members are so small that even a couple of departures makes a big difference to the percentage. Peter Davis, the group chief of the Prudential, which is one of the Opportunity 2000 participants, said that the low number of women was 'counterintuitive' as far as his experience was concerned. What he probably meant was that as successful women are so much more noticeable there always appear to be more of them than really exist.

A follow-up Report to the Hansard Society Commission on *Women at the Top* looked at the overall progress that women had made a few years later, and concluded that it 'was not spectacular'.[39] The most disappointing area that this second report identified was in corporate management. Between the first and second surveys the Society conducted in 1990 and 1995, women had increased their representation as executive directors on main boards of Britain's top companies from 0.5 to 1 per cent. Half the companies surveyed still had no women on their boards, even as non-executives. At this rate of increase it would take five hundred years for women to be represented in equal proportions.

According to the Hansard Society Report, the proportion of women senior managers in the companies they surveyed had risen from 7 to 8 per cent between 1990 and 1995. Even though at lower levels things had improved, somehow the higher proportions of junior and middle managers did not seem to be coming up through the ranks at the expected rate. The Hansard Society concluded in its measured way, 'Generational change does not appear to have done the trick and the evidence suggests that waiting for it to do so may well take a long time.'

Although conditions in the public sector are different, at the very top the problems are the same. The Treasury is considered the elite department of the civil service. Jill Rutter, who was once a senior Treasury official, noted that in 1997 there were exactly the same number of women at under-secretary level (three) as there had been when she first joined in 1979, illustrating how in her view the Treasury's position as a long-standing member of Opportunity 2000 was simply window-dressing: nothing had changed, and the top-level jobs were no more accessible to women than they had been twenty years earlier.

The disappointing numbers of senior women in academic life reflects the same pattern. Even in Sweden, a country with the very best support systems for women, and where 44 per cent of bio-medical PhDs are awarded to women, they hold a mere 25 per cent of postdoctoral positions in the bio-medical field and only 7 per cent of professorial positions. Substantial numbers of Swedish women have been entering academia since the 1970s yet they have simply not succeeded in 'working their way through the system' as conventional wisdom holds. In May 1997 the scientific journal *Nature* reported on a Swedish research project investigating why so many women scientists had apparently dropped out of academic careers.[40] The researchers came up with strong evidence of basic gender discrimination in the appointment and preferment of male scientists for jobs and funding. Using independent criteria such as overall research productivity and the number of published papers, they showed that a woman had to achieve far higher results than a man to be judged equally competent in the all-important peer review system. When gender-blind assessments of candidates were made, women did far better. And interestingly 'both women and men rate the quality of men's work higher than that of women when they are aware of the sex of the person to be evaluated, but not when the same person's gender is unknown'. The conclusions of the project seem to uphold the adage that 'in order to succeed, a woman has to be far better than a man'.

The Leaky Pipeline

The optimistic opinion that as more well-qualified younger women pass into the system then things will gradually even out, already looks rather shaky. But why is it that women still find it hard to progress up through the system? Some are simply overlooked for promotion in favour of male appointments, as the Gregg and Machin research demonstrated, but women also drop out at a far higher rate than men. It is clear that the small numbers of women who are at the top today in the public and private sectors are themselves only the remnants of much larger entry groups. Today women's entry levels in some fields exceed 50 per cent, but even in the seventies a reasonable number of women were leaving university and had aspirations to advance within a career; however, they dropped out somewhere along the way. This pattern of women being unable to sustain their position, leaving their chosen careers and maybe later returning to work in jobs for which they are overqualified is a very familiar one. Paul Gregg describes 'the underachievement of educated women . . . and the subsequent loss of valuable human capital resources'. He cites figures showing that whilst 60 per cent of male graduates are in managerial or professional jobs, the same proportion of women graduates are in clerical or administrative jobs, with even higher proportions in those roles when part-time jobs are included.[41] A US study of women leaving scientific careers describes the problem of the leaky pipeline: the tendency of women who make a promising start to fade away later on.[42]

The drop-out amongst professionals follows similar patterns. The Association of Women Solicitors is concerned that one in three women who qualify as solicitors eventually leave the profession. If women continue to leave in the same proportions as they have always done, the optimistic assertions of the think-tanks and the 'genderquake' arguments about the enduring shift in women's perceptions and the inevitability of equal achievements will never be fulfilled. All the trends of androgyny and merging values between the genders describe women under the age of thirty-five, after which age things may well come to an abrupt halt. The evidence does not extend beyond there, and it is much more likely that traditional models reassert themselves. Pat Dade, who has done much of the research which supports the genderquake conclusions about the changes in women's values and growing self-esteem, concedes that 'business is always behind cultural change' and that we may see a period of transition before the new values of younger women can be identified on a large scale amongst older women too. He attributes this lag to the fact that 'The structural policies are not yet in place.'[43] Until there is a change in the crucial structures surrounding women at work, he believes, the pipeline will continue to leak.

The experiences of corporate woman are sometimes described in terms of an immigrant arriving in a new country: she may strive to learn the language, observe the customs and fit in with the locals. Yet, however hard she tries to integrate, there is always 'culture shock' on both sides, and ultimately the new arrival is always regarded as a 'foreigner' and never really accepted by the natives.

> On good days I feel like a tourist who has learnt enough to pass as a native if only temporarily and for specialised moments. On bad days I feel like an outcast among beings whose ways and aims I haven't a chance of understanding . . . mostly I feel as though I am trudging solo through a half-mapped jungle occasionally being ambushed and reacting like some sort of guerrilla fighter in a brief affray . . .[44]

Kay Graham, the famous and influential boss of the *Washington Post*, has described how even in the Washington of the 1960s, she would spend the day running the paper, but then to her annoyance when she attended dinner parties she was always expected to retire with the ladies and leave the men to their serious discussion over port and cigars.[45] Whatever her achievements and abilities she was still not considered one of the boys.

Even when families and children are not an issue, there are still many ways in which women face obstacles and exclusion at work, as immigrants to the culture. The cliché of the glass ceiling is an inadequate image to describe the experience of women in many working hierarchies. It inaccurately implies that there is one single barrier to shatter and that once the glass is broken, success and the

woman's goals will be achieved. The reality is much more complicated. Many women in fact experience a range of barriers, from
restrictions in the workplace to covert prejudice. The Institute of
Management 1992 report, *The Key to the Men's Club*, surveyed
two and a half thousand female managers and discovered that it
was the attitudinal barriers, prejudice and 'existence of a men's
club network' that women found the most difficult problems to
overcome in achieving seniority in the workplace.[46] The report
highlighted large numbers of women, without families, who experienced isolation and antipathy from male colleagues, superiors
and subordinates; this indicates that it is not even concrete benefits like childcare provision that are hurdles in the workplace.
Lady Howe, chair of the Hansard Commission, quotes what she
calls Hansard's Law: 'The clubbier the culture, the less likely
women are to make the top.'

The survey responses in the two reports of the Hansard Society
Commission on *Women at the Top* reveal a range of intangible
attitudes and prejudices which were highlighted as the biggest
hurdles. Frequently the responses (from both men and women)
indicated that a woman 'had to be better'. There was a tendency
not to want to take a risk with women, not to want to give them a
big challenge, so the problem was more of a glass wall whereby
women were constrained from moving sideways to gain crucial
complementary experience, which is frequently a forerunner of
moving upwards. A leading headhunter who has puzzled over the
problem of why there is a continuing dearth of senior women,
despite all the rhetoric, believes this barrier in general management at a key stage is critical:

Even though they might be starting to succeed in specialist
functions like personnel, marketing or even finance, it is the

crucial transfer into wider responsibility somewhere in the early thirties that is so often lacking and prevents women from reaching the top.[47]

A survey by Dr Judi Marshall, *Women Managers: Travellers in a Male World*, reveals how women feel perpetual outsiders and on trial. A reflection of this is the way they are frequently given the job of 'acting' this or 'acting' that, or the role without the pay rise. In 1995 Marshall[48] produced a further survey entitled *Women Managers Moving On*, analysing the high number of women who left what they perceive as a hostile environment, where they felt alienated. In the majority of cases, it was not the family question that precipitated their decisions to leave. And one of the other studies on the slow progress of women into higher management had the memorable but appropriate title of 'Waiting for Fish to Grow Feet! Removing the organisational barriers to women's entry into leadership positions'.[49]

These reports and other observations point to a range of well-aired difficulties which women experience in achieving a senior level of employment in many institutions. There is an inevitable preference to recruit in one's own image, so men will naturally prefer male versions of themselves. The mentoring and informal networking amongst men is much more highly developed than that among women. A 1995 study of male and female MBA students found that men were able to make far bigger career strides, achieve better promotions and higher pay rises after gaining the MBA. Many of the women had no children, but even those that did were well able to organize satisfactory child care. The difficulty was that women were less adept at the kind of networking that takes place at the cricket match or the golf club, or lacked the confidence or desire to play the male political game. There was a prevailing attitude that 'if I work hard and do my job well then recognition will follow'. Sandi Mann, an occupational psychologist who has studied this issue, calls this the 'deputy director syndrome' – the tendency of women to reach the number two position, taking on the burden of the boss's workload, conscientious and efficient, while the director has the profile and takes the credit. Women continue to believe that working life is just like school where talent, application, efficiency and a helpful nature are sufficient, and promotion will come naturally to those who deserve it.[50]

A major US survey of the progress of nearly a thousand female graduates of Harvard's law, medical and business schools reaches the same depressing conclusions. It documents the very high drop-out rate of women MBAs in particular. Some 25 per cent of those surveyed had eventually left the workplace, frequently because they felt forced out once they had children. In addition to the more blatant obstacles, it describes the 'micro-inequalities' that occur daily in the lives of these professional women. 'By themselves they seem inconsequential, but over time they may severely constrain a woman's career progress and blur her perception of her own competence. Often they are hidden in the informal channels of communication within an organisation.'[51] Oxford professor Susan Greenfield makes the same observation:

> . . . one of the problems is prejudice of a sinister type. I have never been aware that I have been denied a job because of my gender but I have made remarks on university committees and been ignored as though I were invisible. Women are not seen as being as competent as men. We are going to have to think about how women deal minute-by-minute, day-by-day with snide remarks and put-downs.[52]

Dr Moira Hamlin, a senior clinical psychologist, said that for ten to fifteen years she never thought that being a woman held her back. 'Yet now at a senior level, it's harder to have credibility – there are so few women at a high level in this field. You have to be extra good to get in at the same level.' She described a meeting of the Clinical Audit (at which doctors assess themselves with the input of outside bodies):

> The meeting was chaired by a medic and full of arrogant male consultants sitting there, flicking through magazines of classic Jags. There were four women who were totally ignored and because I was sitting next to the chair and am a woman, I was asked if I would be taking the notes.

It is not uncommon for those who do achieve high-placed positions to feel that it is not breaking through which is the problem, but sustaining the success once they arrive. Gail Rebuck, managing director of Random House, quips that breaching the glass ceiling does not mean arriving in a sunny penthouse: 'It is just as likely to be a cold attic full of creepy crawlies who wish that you were not there'. Many women are aware not only of the much higher profile they automatically have but also of the sense that they are always on trial as an outsider. When Ruth MacKenzie was appointed chief executive of the Nottingham Playhouse she faced a hostile appointment board and got the job by just one vote. Afterwards one of the board members told her that he had voted against her 'because they had had a woman once before and it hadn't worked out'. This kind of prejudice and blatant stereotyping, so far from the vision of political correctness of official and reported life, is still alive and well in many institutions. Beverley Stone is a corporate psychologist who specializes in consultancy work for big companies in transition. She recalls entering the room of the chief executive officer of a multinational, who picked up the phone and asked for the human resources director. Beverley's androgynous first name had caused confusion. She heard the CEO say, 'I expected a consultant and you have sent me a woman.'[53]

Another psychologist, Belinda Brooks-Gordon, made a study of the five categories into which men working in the macho trading environment of the International Petroleum Exchange classify women:[54] babes (young, attractive but little professional credibility), mums (unattractive and ignored by male traders), lesbians (feminists), dragons (old, unattractive and the most rudely treated) and, finally, 'one of the boys' (women who behaved like men – the only category that progressed within the company). The observations of Anna, who works as a dealer in another City trading room, provide further evidence for such attitudes: 'The City is hellishly sexist, you have to take the crude jokes (the men put a joke, often sexist, on the computer network every morning) and animal behaviour in your stride and learn to bite back.' She is frequently manhandled by a director who likes to comes up behind her and fondle her.

> The argument within the job is that it is very stressful and people don't have time to be polite and also that they have to release their aggression – so you wouldn't get sacked for throwing a telephone across the room and the net result is that the men seem to think that they have to behave in this way to maintain their macho credibility.

All these attitudes are light years away from the world of the carefully framed equal opportunity policy. Yet paradoxically sometimes the well-meaning intention can make things even worse. 'The company has an equal opportunity policy so how can there be unfair treatment?' it is asked – even if the policy is no more than a few bland sentences about not discriminating against any applicant. One of the few women partners in a top five City law firm has experienced this sentiment.

> The firm believes that they have done what they were asked, the policy is in place and there are still not enough women coming through, so 'it is not our fault' . . . they fail to understand that the career expectations which are projected are still very much male models.

Indeed she believes that in recent years since the policy was drafted, hostility to women has increased; she observes the rise of what she calls 'the young male fascists' – men whose wives do not work, men who are resentful of women who do and loath to make any concessions, but who instead delight in making things tough.

The study of Harvard women graduates mentioned above concludes that it is ultimately 'the work culture, not the courts, which determines how people are treated on a daily basis . . . and the professional work ethic is derived from a social structure created by men whose wives did not work outside the home'. Many of the ex-Harvard respondents commented on the 'distant reality between the policies on paper and what is allowed in practice for women who want to keep their careers on track'.[55] In extreme cases this meant having a baby on Saturday and returning to work on Monday. Professor Lotte Bailyn at MIT's Sloan School of Management endorses these conclusions.

> The family friendly policies introduced by some companies with much fanfare often don't hold up in practice. They are

wonderful, but under-utilised. Men hardly ask for them and
if they do they're seen as wimps. If women take them, they're
put on the mommy track.[56]

Of course this is in the much tougher employment environment in the United States – the only industrialized country with
no statutory maternity provision, and where any maternity benefit is seen as a special concession. Yet the same divergence between
what is said and what is done happens in the UK. Liz Forgan was
once the most senior female manager in the BBC, holding the
post of Managing Director of Radio before her very abrupt departure. She observed:

> On paper the BBC looks like the perfect equal opportunity
> employer – with extremely well-thought-out and
> comprehensive policies to attack discrimination in the
> workplace – BUT the reality is quite different. When the
> pressure on budgets came it led to unrealistic demands upon
> all staff and all possible scope for balance in many areas
> simply disappeared. Furthermore when the BBC has one of
> its periodic earthquakes or returns to year zero it throws out
> all good employment practices, for most jobs there was no
> advertisement, simply the same old boy arrangements as
> before . . . so it tried hard in theory but not in practice.[57]

The same well-formulated policies in the civil service can also
look quite different on the ground: theory and practice may
diverge. Yolande, a senior official in a major public arts organization, asked, after nine years in her job, if, for domestic reasons, she
might work four days a week, for correspondingly less pay and
fund two days of a researcher with the money. She was told that

although the plan sounded reasonable, it could not possibly be allowed because it might encourage too many other people to try the same thing. Candidates with all kinds of 'caring responsibilities' for elderly or handicapped parents might want to work less hours. But the biggest *cause célèbre* in the civil service was the departure in 1996 of Dame Pauline Neville-Jones, the Foreign Office high-flier who seemed to fall at the final hurdle. After a lifetime of distinguished service as Britain's most senior female diplomat – chairman of the Joint Intelligence Committee, leader of the British team at the Bosnian peace talks – she was expected, like most other officials who had reached her level, to finish her career with a plum ambassadorial post. But instead she was thwarted: there was a whispering campaign insinuating that she was 'difficult' or 'abrasive', with 'not quite a top-drawer brain', and the ambassadorship went instead to a younger man with a wife.

Dame Pauline says that over the years she had never faced much discrimination – although she might have moved up the system faster as a man – just attitudinal problems.

> Lower down the system you can just walk away fast . . . the issue is being at the top and wanting to be treated equally, not being treated as somebody who has been granted a privilege . . . that's the barrier . . . and it's not susceptible to equal opportunities legislation, it has to do with deeply subtle human things.[58]

In the end she departed for NatWest, and the Foreign Office was left protesting that it was not unfair to women. Eighteen months later the Labour government appointed the formidable erstwhile trade union leader Lady Symons as a Foreign Office minister with

a brief that encompassed the introduction of more equal opportunities. She is said to have enjoyed 'spirited exchanges' with some
of the old guard who found even the most basic of her proposals
for including more women on job shortlists 'heartbreaking'.

The argument that equality is no longer an issue because there
are policies to address it means that women paradoxically have
greater difficulty in speaking out about discrimination. Frequently
women regard it as a purely individual problem, a personal failing
and a private problem which reflects their own situation. This is
then exacerbated by the isolation many women face at work especially in senior jobs, which can often lower self-esteem so that
'most men cannot even comprehend the mechanisms of how
women feel excluded'.[59]

When one woman finally left her management job in BP,
having been put on a fast-track programme, she concluded that
'there was not so much a glass ceiling as one of reinforced concrete – if it was glass then the glass is six foot thick'.

> With all the equal opportunities and attempts to change,
> basically they (the middle-aged grey men) can see no other
> way of being that is not being like them. . . . Forget the
> culture change and all that . . . what I remember are the awful
> 'nights out with the boys' management wanting to form team
> spirit, ending up drinking in hotels miles from anywhere,
> being presented with souvenirs like Bavarian beer mugs, being
> always the only women, having to sit up late, maintain a
> strong liver and judge the time at which to go, not too early
> not too late . . . I had to disappear before they got randy and
> always make sure that my hotel room number was a secret.

Dawn Airey (now director of programmes at Channel 5) became

the Controller of Planning for Central TV at the age of twenty-six. She had to attend the regular ITV network planning meetings, a traditionally macho set-up where the companies haggle over the future schedules. At her second meeting a very senior planner from one of the other companies called her a 'fucking cunt' because she disagreed with something he had proposed. She was not shocked by the use of language[60] 'but shocked that in a meeting of senior people from our respective companies he believed that the way to progress an argument is to call someone a "fucking cunt"'. Doubtless his company's equal opportunity officer would never have believed it. Dawn Airey's own reputation for toughness meant that although taken aback she could shrug off such an incident, but many other women find that such attitudes, especially when encountered on a regular basis, severely undermine their confidence in their own abilities. The sense of isolation is very common amongst those who start to climb a corporate ladder and brings on all the problems of self-doubt that have traditionally plagued women. It is one of the reasons that women give for dropping out, especially from mainstream corporate life. Many of the growing band of women entrepreneurs setting up their own small businesses have done so as a result of disenchantment with corporate life and the culture they find inside many large organizations.

It is a catch-22 situation: only when more women have reached the top will the culture and the system be conducive for women to advance smoothly. Yet so long as the culture is hostile many women will feel disinclined to stay, and those who survive will often find that the best individual strategy is to go native, as far as possible – just like the women who held their own as 'one of the boys' in the Petroleum Exchange. The crucial arguments always turn upon achieving a critical mass (whatever proportion that may be) rather than upon the outstanding individual who has battled against the odds. In the meantime the gatekeepers are wary of who is allowed in. This is the opposite of what has happened in education where during a period of expansion, everyone is invited to join and nothing is being taken away. Lady Symons recalls that when she was a civil service trade unionist pressing for more equal opportunity, a colleague once said to her, 'I don't mind if there are more promotions for women as long as there aren't any less for men.' Even the most minor adjustments such as 'attempts to formalize employment practices' are often regarded with incomprehension or unwillingness, and accompanied by defensive assertions that 'no one is discriminated against here'. Equal opportunities are intensely political and not a once-only 'breakthrough'. If the policies are successful they disrupt the status quo, which then engenders hostility.[61]

Women have taken to heart the feminist message that work is the most important thing in life. Yet the workplace in admitting women did not change its fundamental structures or attitudes to make things more accommodating for them. On the contrary, work has simultaneously been driven by other changes – quite independent of the transformation of women's expectations. And the point at which women have embraced work in such large numbers and with such high expectations has coincided with a period – not dissimilar from the Industrial Revolution – when work is reinventing itself and the demands of the labour market are becoming tougher than ever. Under those circumstances, to confront the structures and attitudes that hamper equality in the workplace will become an even greater challenge in the future.

3

What Is Happening to Work?

Deckchairs on the *Titanic*

Women's changing public role has been called the biggest social revolution of the twentieth century. Not since men left their homes on the land and disappeared into cities and factories in the late eighteenth century have we seen such a transformation. Yet women's entry into the public domain has coincided with another shift. The jobs that men left home for are becoming an endangered species. For two hundred years the job market has waxed and waned according to the economic cycle. This time it is in danger of shrinking forever.

Work has always been with us. By comparison the social construct of 'the job' is a modern invention. The sociologist Anthony Giddens points out that most pre-modern societies did not even have a word that meant 'work'. It was just something that went on according to seasons and needs with everyone participating as necessary, mostly in and around the home. 'Working wasn't readily distinguishable from other activities . . . in so far as it was recognised as a distinctive type of activity, work, it was not something which defined a specifically male role.'[1] This is the pattern that had existed for thousands of years and still persists in much of the developing world, where families depend upon agriculture or small-scale home-based craft activity, and everyone – adults and children – plays a role, alongside general domestic life.

The Industrial Revolution changed all that. Men went off to work in jobs. In fact the habit of seeing the family as a single employment unit continued for a while after industrialization so that women and children were sometimes jointly employed in an enterprise. But the practice soon disappeared and women were left to preside over the domestic sphere, even though many poorer women still had to earn an income. A woman was not meant to work and have a job, her place was in the home and that is what she was expected to aspire to. At home she did not have a job and so was no longer officially working. The 1881 census officially designated housework as unproductive and so the category 'housewife' became a non-occupation. Whatever a woman was doing in the house, it was not work.

Real work was inextricably associated with having a job – which was something that men did all day, in the years after full-time education and before retirement. At the same time, the concept of having a job became fused with moral meaning and personal identity. Its converse – not having a job – left the unemployed male without any social value. Job losses and job creation have become crucial economic measures, that historically always trailed the boom and bust of the economy. But in the last recovery, during the early 1990s, the stable, permanent, 'real' jobs did not return at anything like their previous level – and the evidence is that many of them are lost forever. William Bridges, in his book *Jobshift*, says our constant preoccupation with playing 'musical jobs', as we chase after an ever-declining number of them is now hopelessly misguided: 'to our counterparts at the end of the 21st century today's struggles over jobs will seem like a fight over deckchairs on the *Titanic*'. The 'job for life' has disappeared. And as in the eighteenth century when jobs for men were invented as an artificial device, a way of packaging work, the two concepts are unravelling – 'work' and 'job' are no longer synonymous. There is still plenty of work to be done but 'the future is going to be very different from what we grew up to expect . . . and most of us are no more ready for it than 18th century villagers were for jobs in 19th century factories'.[2]

Today's model is the world of the temporary contract and the service provider, where each individual is encouraged to perform as a 'Me & Co.', selling themselves into the marketplace. In the interminable jargon of 'downsizing', 'delayering', 'outsourcing', and 'outplacing', jobs have disappeared and been replaced by functions. Organizations have become like a series of concentric circles. The inner circle has shrunk back to contain only an irreducible core of staff who perform the key roles. In the next circle are the freelancers, contract providers who perform the functions, sometimes highly skilled, that have been contracted out. At the outer edge are the interchangeable casual, freelance, temporary workers who are taken on as and when they are needed. Furious, unceasing change and technological innovation are simply a way of life. As 'organisations today operate in such a turbulent environment that no arrangement serves them for very long . . . so individuals . . . need the ability to bend and not break, bounce back quickly from disappointment, to live with high levels of uncertainty and find security from within rather than from outside'.[3] Developing a career used to have the same certainty as filling in a painting-by-numbers kit, but today it is like applying paint to an empty white canvas.

If this is the brave new world of work that women have entered, how are they placed for the future? Most of the modern management gurus are optimistic, pronouncing that women display just the 'adaptability', 'flexibility', 'juggling abilities', 'parallel thinking' and all the other management buzzwords that are needed in this changed work environment. What the fashionable commentators sometimes fail to see is that beyond the slogans there is a serious mismatch between women and what is happening to the workplace. Certainly women are associated with flexible, temporary, part-time work, but historically this has been because they will accept low pay, low prospects and low status. As for permanent jobs, the workers left at the core operation – the stayers rather than leavers – the diminishing numbers left in full-time permanent employment will now have to conform to a much more demanding workplace where the pressures, and sometimes the rewards, will be ever greater. Then there is the emerging world of the portfolio worker and service provider, who balances a range of interests and works for different clients, but this way of life has hidden drawbacks for women, that a management guru may not always appreciate.

When Work Never Stops

In the seventies the future of work seemed quite different. At that time theorists such as Alvin Toffler and André Gorz produced an optimistic vision of the leisured future that was just around the corner. Technological advance, efficiency, increases in productivity seemed to have an obvious and rational outcome.

The theorists confidently predicted that by the end of the century we would all be working less and enjoying more leisure, and thereby work would become less central to self-definition and personal identity. It seemed logical, after all, that the steady, century-long decline in full-time working hours would continue, leaving everyone with more leisure. But during the eighties the opposite happened. Gradually the working hours of the shrinking proportion of full-time workers began to increase, especially in Britain and the US. Instead of spreading out the diminishing numbers of jobs amongst more people, so that everyone would have a sensible balance of work and leisure, fewer people were now doing more work, whilst the role of work in defining social status became more important than ever.

The popular management guru Charles Handy describes how the ideal became to employ half as many people, pay them twice as much and increase output by three times as much ($\frac{1}{2} \times 2 \times 3$).[4] He demonstrates that the 100,000 hours of the traditional forty-five-year working life is now being squeezed into thirty years – a period in which there is precious little time for anything else but work. Far from the predicted thirty-hour week for everyone, by the start of the twenty-first century it is more likely that half the workforce will be putting in sixty hours and a great many of the rest will have no work at all. A pattern of longer weekly hours over a shorter working life, which starts later and ends sooner, is not good news for women.

In the United States the increase in working hours has been even more extreme than in Britain. In a bestseller entitled *The Overworked American: The Unexpected Decline of Leisure*, Juliet Schor, a Professor of the Economics of Leisure, showed that instead of the much-proclaimed increase in leisure, the average American is working the equivalent of an extra month every year compared to a full-time worker in 1948.[5] According to this trend, in twenty years' time the average US working week will extend to sixty hours. Professor Schor urges her readers to revive the public discussion on hours of work in order to break what she calls the work and spend cycle. She wants to put an end to the cultural pattern in which time is sacrificed for money and a system that equates longer hours at work with greater personal status so that the longer you spend in paid work, the more important you are. According to Schor, given all the advances in productivity that have been made, if we could be satisfied with the prosperity and living standards of 1948, then by now a full-time working day would be a mere four hours long. Alas, in the acquisitive society, leisure became the casualty of prosperity. And time has become a commodity that we seek to exploit more effectively. It is impossible to acquire extra time, so since we refuse to limit our consumption, we have to use more of what is available. The incentive structures of capitalism tend inexorably towards longer hours, in order to fund the ever-growing consumer possibilities and choices. Shopping has become capitalism's ultimate leisure activity. If happiness is the fulfilment of perceived needs and desires, it is well known that capitalism's role is to create infinitely more consumer 'needs'. And so work never stops.

It is interesting that men and women have always felt differently about working time and financial reward.[6] Men have tended to be more inclined to sacrifice time for additional money – even those who earn more than they can possibly need and have no time to spend it. And the one-track attitude towards pay and financial reward has dominated the male trade union agenda. The shorter working week for men has never been at the expense of sacrifices in pay. Women have been more inclined to seek a trade-off, to give them more time, because they were not so fixated upon monetary reward. Large-scale surveys of women working full-time regularly find that over 40 per cent would like to work fewer hours if they were able to.[7] And taking a specific example of hard-working women, in 1997 one third of full-time female accountants said that they would like to work fewer hours and receive a lower salary, if the working culture permitted. It is unlikely that one third of male accountants would say the same thing.[8] But women, in joining up to the male working culture, are obliged to rank money before time. And for many men, working time itself is a status symbol: the more time spent at work and away from the home, the more significant is the job and the more important is the individual.

Britain is top of the European league when it comes to measurable working hours.[9] The average male working week is now forty-five hours, seven hours more than in Belgium and five and a half hours more than in stereotypically hard-working Germany. When the EU Working Time directive was applied to Britain in 1998, stipulating a maximum of forty-eight hours a week in certain occupations, it was estimated that four and a half million Britons were exceeding that, a rise of nearly 600,000 since 1992. A 1995 survey by the agency Austin Knight questioned 2,400 people working for 22 high-profile employers and found that one quarter worked more than fifty hours a week. The *National Child Development Study* (questioning everyone born during one week in 1958, rather like an academic version of the TV documentary, *7 Up*) reported in 1997 that fathers of children under eleven years old average forty-eight hours at work each week, one in four works over fifty hours, while one in ten works over sixty hours, and many would expect to work during evenings or weekends.[10]

In semi-skilled and manual activities, regular long spells of overtime have increased working hours. The steady emergence of a twenty-four-hour society means more antisocial and disruptive

working hours, which are often linked with increased stress and
health problems. Many workers, such as long-distance lorry driv-
ers, may have to keep to a gruelling schedule; in some cases, like
the 1988 Clapham rail crash in which thirty-nine people died,
excessive hours can end in tragedy. At the inquiry into the crash it
emerged that the engineer responsible for the faulty wiring, the
father of a young child, was working a sixty-hour week and had
not had a day off for the previous 13 weeks. But it is the professional middle classes in particular who have become the modern
'work-rich, time-poor'. Head teachers, doctors, lawyers, bankers,
consultants are all affected by a long-hours culture, and all worry
about the social cost. Occupational psychologists highlight the
coincidence that Britain has both the longest average working
hours and the highest divorce rate in Europe. When Margaret
Cook, a consultant haematologist, wrote movingly about the collapse of her marriage to the Foreign Secretary Robin Cook in
August 1997, she referred both to the increasing demands arising
from her work in the 'free market' National Health Service and to
the endless hours kept by ambitious politicians like her husband.
In a landmark legal judgment in 1994 John Walker, a social
worker in Northumberland, described how he had suffered two
nervous breakdowns which were directly due to overwork. The
court found in his favour and he received substantial damages
against his employer.

Technology, instead of liberating employees, has in many ways
reinforced the pressures of work. In 1934 the historian Lewis
Mumford produced a classic, *Technics and Civilisation*, which
described the divorce between home and workplace that began with
the Industrial Revolution. Today the reverse is happening. Work in
many fields now has no precise location: it attaches itself to the
person and with the fax, mobile phone, laptop and pager can follow

them everywhere. For many workers frequent and disruptive travel is a way of life. It is vital to communicate with the other side of the world from the Far East to the West Coast of the USA, never mind the time difference. Multinational companies such as Glaxo have employees in areas such as research who are known as 'hoppers' – constantly criss-crossing the Atlantic, with a home on two continents. Taking a fax machine or laptop on holiday, keeping in regular touch on the mobile phone are standard practice. Some companies require that voice mail and e-mail should be checked every few hours, including during holidays and weekends. One senior British television executive was spotted wearing his pager during his wedding ceremony.

It is often companies with a substantial US or Japanese influence that are most prone to these notions of constant availability. Being there for the client at any moment is what matters above all in this culture of twenty-four-hour service. This is the antithesis of the traditions of continental Europe with its sacred weekends, unassailable lunch hours, long summer holidays, and regulated working hours. In the US, with its long-standing habit of twenty-four-hour retailing, even the regular annual holiday entitlement of two weeks can be seen as excessive. In some Wall Street firms, employees are discouraged from taking both weeks together, and junior lawyers who submit leave forms have recounted how they received a quiet call from a senior colleague asking whether they had fully considered how their clients might feel if they were to go away on vacation. The way to get on is through total commitment. A similar ethos has entered the British labour market at every level, from the all-night petrol station and supermarket to the ever-available professional advisor. Lazards – the bank that organized the lunch for the prime minister, Tony Blair, inviting seventy-nine men and one woman – held a graduate recruiting session at the London Business School in 1997. A casual enquiry about company policy on paternity leave and expected working hours received an extremely frosty response from the platform. After the meeting there were angry rebukes and the questions were labelled 'offensive and irrelevant'.[11] An investment banker with another company neatly summed up his way of life when he said, 'I am working so hard but this way I'll have time to get to know my grandchildren.'

In a survey of two thousand parents, undertaken by Parents at Work, on the question of pressure of work, 64 per cent reported that they regularly worked longer hours than they were contractually bound to do, due to pressure of workload and the culture of long hours. They made the familiar observation that even when there is no concrete work to be done, the way to show commitment is to stay late. Nobody dares to be the first to leave. And on top of this, when work is finished there is the all-important requirement of extra-curricular socializing, entertaining clients, attending dinners, or just going to the pub. The psychiatrist Anthony Clare has observed the detrimental effect this degree of commitment has upon those unlucky enough to be pushed out of corporate life. 'There is no point in telling these executives who have lost their jobs to cultivate wider interests. Late twentieth century capitalism demands that people give their all to the company.'[12]

The Insiders

For the survivors of downsizing, those who remain fully employed as the essential inner core of corporate life, the pressures are exacerbated. In many cases the total workload does not reduce as the numbers of staff decline – and there is the additional, tricky problem of motivating the insecure and demoralized workforce left behind, anxiously looking around and worrying about who will go next.

There is furious disagreement about how insecure work has really become. Many of the figures on job tenure are very misleading because they conveniently exclude those under twenty-five and over fifty (one third of the labour force). But even if objectively job tenure has not declined as much as we think, there is undoubtedly a widespread perception of and anxiety about possible job insecurity and erosion of employment rights – especially when instability and fears of job losses reached the middle classes. And those who are still left when the music stops find themselves working harder and feeling more uncertain about their own future. This anxiety about *potential* redundancies arising from change and restructuring was a crucial part of the last Conservative government's inability to capture the elusive feel-good factor. And although, as a wide selection of politicians and pundits like to remind us, job movement and redundancy have always been there, the consequences now for those who are involved are invariably much more severe and unpleasant – so that unemployment in early middle age may be catastrophic.

The good news is that whilst the demands and pressures upon those staying in full-time work have become greater, so have the rewards. For some who are willing to accept the relentless pace, the constant availability and disrupted private life, the financial rewards can be awesome. In the economist's jargon, it has become a winner-takes-all system. There is much ogling and vicarious fascination about the sharp rise in remuneration at the upper end of the salary scale: the City bonuses that resemble telephone numbers, the golden egg of share options, and hourly rates of pay for professionals that are beyond comprehension. These are the forces leading to the inexorable trend of ever-widening inequality, where the bottom remains consistently low but salaries and income at the top have gone out of control.

If the dramatic rise in salaries at the top is a result of market forces, as economists like to think, then one of the reasons must be that professionals with the right qualities are in short supply. Management consultants – whose activity is commonly associated with both high pay and long hours – complain that it is sometimes difficult to recruit exactly the staff they require for the highest and most demanding positions. Headhunters find that only a very small pool of candidates both have the right skills and are willing to make the grinding commitment that is now required at the uppermost levels.

Such commitment provides the extreme end of the work-rich/time-poor equation. Money is used to buy time in every possible service. There are dentists available to come to the workplace to replace a lost crown, just as masseurs are on call to ease back pains, or shoe cleaners are available to polish whilst the client remains seated at the desk. In the United States some companies will organize valet birthday parties for their busy employees' children; there are services that can arrange your family photo album, and agencies called 'Grandma Please' enable children to phone for an adult with time to listen or help with homework.[13] Greeting cards are on sale with messages like 'Sorry I can't be there to tuck you in.' Every imaginable service is available for the busy well-paid executive. And this trend of personal service is spreading to Britain. In 1997 a Mintel survey claimed that the size of the UK domestic service sector was at least £4 billion, a fourfold growth in ten years. This sector represents the work-rich buying other people's time for themselves.

But of course the catch is that this area of the labour market –

the full-time staff positions where the hours have increased and the demands have multiplied in return for ever-greater rewards – requires a degree of dedication and single-minded application that only certain individuals can deliver. Will Hutton has described the increasingly polarized 40:30:30 society, divided into the secure and comfortable 40 per cent, the 30 per cent facing chronic insecurity at work, and the marginalized 30 per cent either unemployed or drifting in and out of temporary work. According to this template it is clear that the comfortable 40 per cent includes the group who hold the permanent jobs with the fringe benefits, attractive bonus schemes, pensions, training opportunities and who have seen such a steady rise in their real income. Yet if those all-or-nothing jobs are requiring more from their incumbents, the effect is to squeeze out anyone who is not able to deliver more because they may have constraints on their availability and other responsibilities to think about. Women with anything else on their minds had better not apply.

As everywhere else in the workforce, the buzzword is 'flexible'. Once upon a time this was a word associated with flexitime and flexible hours which enabled workers to suit the job to themselves. Now the idea is reversed: the word has switched its meaning to describe the individual who is required to accommodate the demands of the workplace. So whereas jobs used to be flexible, now it is people – the workforce – who must be flexible. For those at the upper end of the labour market in full-time jobs, flexibility means constant presence and availability. Being a genuinely flexible employee is difficult to reconcile with other commitments. The absorbing demands of work can become like the routine of a medieval monk. There are interesting parallels in the lifestyle. Just as the monks rose before dawn and spent over twelve to fifteen hours in single-minded devotion, so in many professions, total commitment and unquestioning long hours are absolute requirements. The rest of life is pushed to the messy edges and seems untidy compared to the purity and dedication of the working cause.

The long-hours culture is often cited by women who leave corporate life. The trend of women leaving full-time employment in order to start their own enterprise has shown a big increase in recent years, and many of these women voice frustration with the patterns of business organization as well as the expectation that employees will put in long hours, whether or not they are productive. Noelle Walsh was sacked as editor of *Good Housekeeping* when her second baby was two weeks old. She has set up a successful company, the Good Deal Directory, and marvels at the contrast between corporate life and running her own enterprise. She realized when she was employed by National Magazines that she was not a political animal and could not bear the meetings that are the lifeblood of big organizations.

> I used to be there at nine and leave at eight . . . and between ten and six I'd be in meetings, more than half of which had nothing to do with editorial directly. They were marketing meetings, budgeting meetings or personnel meetings, redundancy meetings . . . and they weren't those sharp meetings where you go in and discuss it, make a decision and leave. They were meandering around the subject for two hours and always more people than needed to be there and the men there would all feel they had to say something and you would sit and listen and think, What are they saying? What was the conclusion of that sentence, that fifteen-minute diatribe? And I would be sitting there thinking, What can I do to get out of this meeting? I wish these people would hurry

up and make a decision. But we never did; we'd have meetings for two years and never make a decision.

This attitude of women towards the rules and patterns of corporate life is not unusual, even if not all women who follow the increasingly common path to self-employment are as successful at creating their own enterprise as Noelle Walsh. The psychologist Professor Andrew Samuels describes[14] how women have been far less inclined to subscribe wholeheartedly to the politics that success in the traditional corporate environment demands. They are much more likely to maintain an ironic detachment from the institution, principally because their whole identity does not become associated with the company. Jane, another exile from corporate life, describes the meetings 'that began with an hour of male ego parade before the proper business began, and the continual requirement of the workplace for longer and longer hours. Even if the real work was over there were the semi-social events after working hours. It became impossible to maintain any kind of outside life.' Catherine Goodison, who was a corporate finance lawyer, found herself in an aggressively competitive male working culture which was client-driven and meant working all hours. 'No one was ever thanked and there was no sense of personal responsibility, I just felt like a cog in the huge wheel of a deal.' She left to set up her own millinery business which has provided her with far more satisfaction, though less income.

John Viney, a leading headhunter, believes that one of the reasons women fail to reach the top of corporate life is that they are unwilling to make the 'Faustian pact that will give up all else, balance, family life, other interests . . . sublimate them to work, and accept the need to move, along with a partner who will happily participate . . . few women would even consider this way of life.'

In fact he admits that many men would think twice about the crazy demands that are now required in some very senior posts.

> These days a typical CEO candidate may be forty-eight, but with a mental age of barely twenty-eight . . . inevitably they will be two sticks short of a bundle such are the crazy demands and the need for total support at home and work . . . historically women simply lack that degree of singlemindedness and selfishness of a Da Vinci or a Mozart . . . required to reach the top . . . it means giving up so much, and most women by their mid thirties are more balanced and less likely to enter this typically male contract.

Whilst women's expectations and aspirations may have changed, the rules of work have also changed, making it inhospitable to them in new ways.

An unintended consequence of the way that the workplace has been restructured has been to stack the odds against women's chances of promotion. Several studies have shown that the emergence of more flexible and 'flatter' organizations – fewer people and a less hierarchical structure – is often to women's disadvantage.[15] The erosion, for example, of the traditional secretarial role looks as if it means an improvement for women when the job is recategorized as that of 'administrator', but there is rarely an accompanying change in pay or conditions. In some sectors like hotel and catering or personal finance, women have been given more management titles but these roles are usually of lower status, less secure, and with lower pay than the equivalent jobs held before, mainly by men. Leaner organizations in many fields have tended to devolve responsibility, often to women, but without giving them increased authority or a role in decision making. This new, downgraded layer of management is more likely to be expertise- than power-based, which is the typical pattern of women's employment, and it also frequently lacks any secretarial or administrative support. Many of the low-paid management jobs in the restructured flatter companies have neither the status nor the pay that had previously been associated with the title 'manager'.[16] And this kind of delayering makes the chasm between the new downgraded levels and top management wider than ever and correspondingly more difficult for women to bridge. There are fewer opportunities for promotion and the competition for top jobs is intensified.

Part-time Equals Second-class

If the big shifts in full-time work are not such good news for women, what about the other big change in working practice – the rise and rise in the part-time workforce? Historically part-time work was considered to be something that suited women with children. Nowadays it also suits employers. Britain has the largest part-time female workforce in Europe. One of the common explanations is that the lack of public childcare obliged women to find part-time work that could be fitted in with looking after children. The flexibility of working fewer than the typical male forty hours a week came at a high price in pay and conditions. These jobs were typically a twilight factory, cleaning or supermarket shift, which could be accommodated with family childcare available for 'free' in the evenings.

According to some analyses of the labour market, employers offer part-time, but low-wage jobs under the pretended guise of equal opportunities. Yet there is nothing inherently emancipatory about the increased female employment when women make up the bulk of the new peripheral workforce.[17] Part-time jobs in Britain have a lower status than in other Western countries.[18] They were traditionally poorly paid and with few benefits attached. All that has changed in the contemporary workforce is the increasing numbers of men as well as women now experiencing these conditions. Indeed some might say that the lowly status of part-time work only started to become a cause of concern because it spread to affect men too.

According to the official definition, part-time workers are those working fewer than thirty hours a week. On present trends nearly one third of the workforce will soon be employed part-time, compared with only 5 per cent in 1951 and 15 per cent in 1971. By 1996, 45 per cent of working women were part-time and 8 per cent of men. The enormous growth in women's employment was until the mid-eighties predominantly in part-time work. (Since then, full-time female employment has also been increasing, in particular amongst the more qualified.) Part-time male employment doubled in the last decade to reach 889,000, including a growing proportion of men in the prime age group, 25–49. The biggest trend in male employment is the decline in the number of men in full-time jobs. The overwhelming number of the 'new jobs' that have arisen out of new technology and the demand for services are 'typically degraded, highly automated in a tightly policed environment, part-time and lowly paid'.[19] Part-time workers remain overwhelmingly at the bottom of the pile: as Barbara Castle remarked in 1974, 'Part-time workers are second-class citizens entitled to third-class benefits.'

There has been substantial academic debate about the nature of female part-time employment. The conventional wisdom was that women were satisfied with part-time work because they wanted to accommodate other commitments and they had a low attachment to work. However there has been great tension between the lowly nature of most part-time work and this apparent satisfaction. On closer analysis it appears that women often say they are satisfied only because there are no available alternatives. Instead of being an opportunity, part-time work is 'a trap from which it is difficult to escape'.[20] The extent to which many women are overqualified for their part-time employment indicates that it is the nature of the job rather than the characteristics of its occupant that makes women appear uncommitted to their work. If the job requires little initiative, responsibility or skill, it is unsurprising that women are not greatly attached to the employment. The evidence is that women would like to have jobs with shorter hours, which is an option readily available in France, Sweden or Denmark, and not to retreat into the Cinderella world of part-time work. In Britain there have been isolated legal cases on this point, in which women sought reduced hours after maternity leave. Some individuals have succeeded, against employers such as the Home Office and British Telecom, but any progress is piecemeal, and under the current legislation there is no prospect of wider change.[21] Sometimes a woman who goes to court because she is refused part-time work or a job share is awarded an out-of-court settlement, as happened in a case against Zurich Insurance in 1997. The press reported it as a triumph when Janet Schofield was offered £20,000 instead of being allowed to share her £40,000 a year job. Yet paying someone to go away hardly represents a victory in the transformation of the structures of the workplace.[22]

At the upper end there is a small pocket (7 per cent) of well-paid part-timers in the professions who are women.[23] This group in turn accounts for around 10 per cent of all part-time women. Beyond this the picture is bleak. Wages for part-timers are sometimes squeezed beneath the threshold at which employers have to pay employees' National Insurance contributions, cutting employers' overheads and the workers' entitlement to state benefits, such as sick or maternity pay. (This is what prompted the sex discrimination case against Tesco for maternity benefit discussed on page 32.) An increase in the number of women paid just below the National Insurance level has been one of the incidental effects of compulsory competitive tendering, in which services are bought in from outside organizations. Some employers will advertise several jobs at less than the £64 threshold instead of employing one full-timer.[24] But even for those above this limit, the hourly rate of pay is usually well below that for full-timers, and in the majority of cases there are not the same (pro-rata) fringe benefits. The biggest concentration of the low-paid is amongst part-time women, 48 per cent of whom earn less than £4 an hour. On all the standard measures of inequality it is part-time workers who are worst off. For example the gender pay gap for men and women is around 76 per cent, but the hourly wages for part-time women when compared with men are only 62 per cent. And since the seventies a growing difference has opened up between part-time women and full-time women. Economists have demonstrated that the big gap between mothers and non-mothers – the so called 'family gap' – is the result not of having children but of entering (badly paid) part-time work.[25] Mothers who take a short maternity leave and remain in full-time employment may find that their prospects are diminished, but the disparity with their childless colleagues is not nearly as wide as for part-timers.

Low pay and the second-class status of part-timers is a sensitive political issue. Part-timers (more often than not women) used to have to work five years before they were entitled to the same protection against unfair dismissal that full-timers (more often men) had after two years. A landmark decision of the House of Lords in 1994 obliged British employers, on the grounds of sex discrimination, to even out the protection, so that part-time workers now no longer need to have been employed for five years to qualify. But other benefits still do not apply – even though the House of Lords judgment (interpreting two European Directives) warned that 'non-standard is not sub-standard'. Part-timers typically lose out on holiday pay, pensions and training. In the *Road to the Manifesto* which the Labour Party published in 1996, reference was made to the European decisions which were welcomed 'as we recognise the value of part-time workers and *the need for equity with full-time workers*'. The anticipation was that there would be further measures to bridge the gap between full- and part-time conditions. By the time the Labour election manifesto was published in April 1997, the only reference was to welcoming the court judgments; the intention to harmonize conditions for full- and part-timers had disappeared from the agenda. Meanwhile in Holland in 1996 a bill was passed that forbade discrimination against part-timers, saying that all workers should have the same rights and obligations (pro rata), even those part-timers working very few hours a week.

One reason that the demands for equal treatment for part-timers have achieved so little success in the UK is a continuing ambivalence about the nature of part-time work. Economists such as Paul Gregg and Jonathan Wadsworth, who are close to New Labour, have argued over a number of years that part-time jobs are overwhelmingly taken by women with employed husbands. Such is the logic of the current tax and benefit system that women with unemployed partners, that is, those in the greatest need, cannot afford to take up part-time jobs (except in the black economy) because the family could lose some of its benefit entitlements and end up worse off. The result is that part-time jobs go mainly to families where someone is already in work, and this results in greater income inequality between households – polarized into those who have two jobs and those who have none. This leads Gregg and Wadsworth to the overall conclusion that the 'rise in women's employment has led to a more unequal society'.[26]

The implications drawn from this analysis are not always encouraging. The impression is that women who work part-time are already comfortably off and do not need the money. Indeed, Wadsworth went so far as to describe part-time work as 'the preserve of the rich'. Matilda Quiney, of the trade union GMB, has pointed out in response that such an argument can be easily misused to demonstrate that women should 'get out of the labour market and leave men to reclaim their full-time jobs'[27] and also to support the idea that higher wages do not really matter for part-timers ('female part-timers are taking jobs from needy men because of a selfish desire to buy pins'). Quiney is clear that household inequality should not override gender inequality. In any case, for many households the first wage is not a family wage and the second part-time wage is critical in lifting the household out of poverty.[28] And this undermining of part-time work fails to take into account what is happening in the labour market, where part-time employment grew by 77 per cent between 1971 and 1993. John Prescott, the deputy prime minister, remarked in 1994, 'If I want to create employment, should I target full-time men who are on the dole and may never get a job or should I encourage low paid part-time employment for mostly middle-class women?'[29] He could have mentioned a third alternative, given the inexorable growth in 'atypical' employment, which is to improve the pay and status of part-time jobs for everyone – to bring part-timers in out of the cold. For Prescott or anyone else the option of returning to a world of proper jobs for full-time men may just not exist.

Working five days a week from nine to five is a minority activity. According to a government survey, by 1997 the proportion of families containing a full-time employee declined from two thirds in 1979 to just under a half.[30] Yet there is a stubborn persistence in the attitude that anything less than the traditional male forty-hour week is inferior. The same attitude persists at the upper end of the labour market. A partner in a London law firm asked, after nine years, if she could work a four-day week. The firm agreed but said that she should be paid three fifths instead of four fifths of the full-time rate 'because if she was not around on Friday she would not take home work over the weekend'. Yvonne, a consultant in a London teaching hospital, wanted to drop one of her nine weekly sessions, again after many years, but was warned that she would not be taken seriously if she was 'just part-time'. In a survey of female Harvard graduates,[31] respondents said that 'to go part-time is to kill your career'. 'If you work part-time you must have half a brain' was the reaction in another survey on working women.[32] Part-time invariably means accepting lower status, even when there is no demonstrable reason for this, simply because of ingrained prejudice.

Alisa works for a multinational as a corporate lawyer specializing in property. Her contract is part-time but she nearly always works more than her official hours. She says it would be impossible not to. Colleagues tell her to go full-time because at least then she would be paid for the extra effort, but she knows this is not feasible.

Over the past decade the expectations of full-time working hours have become so enormous that I could never undertake a full-time job. It would mean being available at all times including weekends. It is impossible to compete with men who are able to offer this total flexibility. And being considered part-time means that it takes many years to build up credibility and to develop a reputation for being reliable and responsible.

Of course in an increasingly fluid working environment there are many different interpretations of part-time. To an investment banker putting in a macho eighty-hour week, even forty hours is a mere part-time commitment. But, as is often pointed out, the non-executive director or quango chairman on a highly paid part-time contract of a few days per month never suffers from the stigma of being considered uncommitted and a mere part-timer.

An Ideal World? Portfolio Woman

As the workplace has polarized into the tight inner circle of the full-timers and the outer circle of the casual part-timers, an intermediate circle has also emerged which is in many ways the most distinctive outcome of all the recent upheavals. The transfer of staff positions onto shorter, fixed contracts for service has happened across the workplace, not just in cleaning and catering but also in areas like the media or academia. It represents the move from lifetime jobs in organizations to workers who are told to think of themselves as offering services. Of course some try to have it both ways. John Birt, the director-general of the BBC, occupying the supreme insider corporation position, sought the tax advantages of offering his services as John Birt & Co, until it became embarrassingly public.

The freelance service provider, moving between short-term

contracts, is supposed to be an ideal model for women. The management guru William Bridges points out that it is the East Europeans, cushioned by years of permanent full employment and guaranteed jobs for all (even if there was no work to do), who are in the worst position to adapt, whereas educated and ambitious workers in the developing world might be in the best psychological shape to prosper in the 'dejobbed' economy because they never had an Industrial Revolution and the habit of mass jobs in the first place. Unfortunately the reality for many women is not so straightforward. The apparently happy coincidence of women as the perfect portfolio workers, based at home, moving between assignments and balancing other demands, has substantial drawbacks.

At the most straightforward level, developing a selection of skills and services to offer to the market takes time. In all but the most basic cases, training and experience are vital before a freelancer can provide anything useful. This is part of the reason why 'proper' working life is starting later. Today many graduates seeking a job in their early twenties are in a hopeless position. There are fewer jobs and more graduates competing for them. Research by the Institute for Employment Studies in 1996 revealed that only one in four graduates moved straight into permanent posts after graduating, and the breakdown of traditional career paths means that most will take at least four years before they find themselves in the job they really want. A new graduate who does not get a job will not gain the skills to be a proper portfolio worker. The best way to start working life is to gain experience inside organizations in order to develop the future portfolio skills, but this means facing the conundrum of 'no one without experience need apply'. As a result the trend has been for many graduates to tread water in menial work, performing badly paid so-called Mcjobs, whilst seeking more training and the magic 'experience'.

In the summer of 1997 Reed Graduate Services estimated that only four in ten people who had graduated the previous summer had found proper jobs in their chosen career. That leaves a large number waiting on tables or working for free. In some areas work experience or, seen in another way, the exploitation of free labour has become standard practice. Graduates say that on average a period of eighteen months is common before attaining a job in the most sought-after areas, such as the media. Relying on free graduate effort has become accepted practice especially in highly competitive areas like television, journalism or publishing. Politics depends upon it too. Many MPs, including some who are now in the government, have relied upon the hard graft of unpaid researchers who survived on benefit whilst waiting, sometimes years, for a real job. Valuable work experience sits uneasily with the idea of a meritocratic workplace. It is invariably easier to find for someone with the right family connections, sound finances and no rent to pay.

The one career that has always operated along these lines has been the Bar. For centuries aspiring barristers had to do at least a year in pupillage or unpaid work experience. After the period of pupillage the lucky ones would find a place as a self-employed barrister. Unsurprisingly barristers were nearly all upper-middle-class white men. A few years ago the Bar Council woke up to the fact that this system discriminated badly against anyone without financial means and family connections. They enforced a rigorous system of equal opportunities in the selection of pupils and insisted that henceforth there must be proper remuneration so that poorer candidates should not be excluded. There is an odd paradox in this arrangement: at the same time as the Bar was beginning to change its ways, other occupations were evolving a totally informal pupillage arrangement of their own – long-term unpaid work experience for those who got in on the right connections. And just like for those starting out at the Bar, the paid work at the end of the work experience is likely to be the hand-to-mouth uncertainty of self-employed, freelance existence, moving from contract to contract.

Highly developed societies tend to prolong the period of dependency of the young. The lengthening process of acquiring skills, training and experience in order to enter the workforce is a clear example of this. Its consequences for women who may eventually want to have children are especially disadvantageous. If it takes so much longer to become established in a career, such women must either delay childbearing or opt for children before having built up a strong track record, both of which entail different kinds of risks.

Age barriers at the other end of working life, early retirement and the tendency for careers to finish sooner, all discriminate against women with children, but the same principle can operate at the start of working life. This may be one of the reasons behind the much more focused attitude that careers teachers are now perceiving in girls, as described in Chapter 1. There is an awareness amongst young women that they might have a limited time in which to achieve results.

Once the Me & Co existence is established it can be very fulfilling. Moving between short-terms contracts and freelance opportunities, although insecure, can mean a life full of variety and new challenges. But for many women the world of the contract, when it is combined with the routines of domestic life, is not ideal. Even William Bridges, who sings the praises of the new de-jobbed world, admits that the stress of constantly marketing oneself, which is what the new order is about, can take a big toll on home and family life. He describes the need for 'vendor mindedness' and the self-managed career in a world of non-stop change, where everyone must adapt to living with the tension of doing different things for different clients at the same time. Although he says vaguely that women who have not done that well in the existing economic order are better suited to the new one, there are still big hurdles.

The pattern of working increased hours is not only a problem of those who hold full-time staff jobs. Working hours can so easily expand for atypical and temporary contract workers who are 'selling their services'. The publication *Health and Safety at Work* describes how short-term contracts frequently lead to longer working hours. There is a limited time to perform a function and the pressure is on to fulfil the task no matter how long that may take: the next assignment could depend upon how well the current one is fulfilled. So the contract worker has no choice but to finish the job within the deadline, and that often means irregular and demanding hours. The Low Pay Unit has produced research to show that flexible work can be detrimental to family life. Home workers in the clothing manufacture trade, for example, are subject to sudden deadlines where they must drop everything and work at a moment's notice.[33]

Different contracts for different clients can mean hugely varied working patterns and hours. Reconciling this with regular child-care and children's routines can be difficult. It is self-evident that if small children are involved there is a requirement for stability and regular routines, yet the freelance life means there can be periods of intense work and then no work. Only the most exceptional childcare arrangements can be easily harmonized with this kind of unpredictability. Organizations including Parents at Work or the Family Policy Studies Centre have posed the awkward question, how is it possible to satisfy children's needs for security whilst the working world is undergoing such a radical transformation? The term 'labour market flexibility' has become an economic cliché and a political mantra. This official language conveniently disguises the wider social costs of the slogan and avoids discussion of what is involved at home for parents who have to present an appearance of total flexibility and availability to the world of work.

The Temporary Life

By 1995 there were one and a half million workers in temporary jobs, a figure that had increased 10 per cent over the previous year and by 50 per cent in the previous ten years. It seems that the recent growth in temporary contracts has been affected by the increased protection against unfair dismissal given to part-time staff by the House of Lords in 1994 (see page 83). As a result of this it became advantageous to employers to use more temporary workers rather than employ part-time staff.

One of the biggest increases has been in the use of agency temps across a whole range of skilled and unskilled functions. Reed Personnel Services produces a regular index of the growth in the use of contracted temporary staff, and this shows that in the past few years business has boomed. It grew by 13 per cent in the first three months of 1996 alone. The year-on-year growth was 23 per cent. The agency Manpower is now the biggest employer in the United States, supplying the just-in-time workforce to the employers that have been through downsizing and outsourcing. In these circumstances all the carefully crafted employment policies – built upon a loyalty compact between company and employee – fringe benefits, training and equal opportunities no longer apply. The workforce is simply a resource, and the responsibility of an outside supplier.

In the television industry the short-term contract is now standard practice. As soon as a producer or researcher starts one six-week or three-month contract they need to begin looking for the next source of work. It can take up to ten working days even to gain a password for the system, which represents a substantial chunk of a short-term contract. In addition the contract will usually refer to work on a particular programme or even a particular programme item rather than with a particular company 'so there is no incentive for the employing company to map out any career pattern for such employees, to consider their needs or even allow for personal commitments'.[34] The individual is employed to deliver a particular function, and it is in the employer's interest to squeeze as much as possible from the employee while the contract lasts. Just like full-time permanent workers, temporaries may need to work long and antisocial hours; unlike members of staff, though, once their temporary contracts finish they will be out of work unless they have lined up another.

All the certainties of the staff position vanish in a world of short-term contracts. There is very often no provision for payment during sickness or holidays, and no occupational pension scheme. Sometimes the employer will even insist on specific waiver clauses renouncing rights to compensation for redundancy or unfair dismissal. The advertising agency FCB conducted research on how people on short-term contracts feel about their jobs. A large number replied that they were unable to take out a mortgage because of their perpetual hand-to-mouth existence and the uncertainty of their future salary. And because their income was so insecure, many felt unsure about ever being able to marry and have children. Other reports have highlighted temporary work's combination of poorer pay and conditions with contemporary patterns of atypical and non-standard ways of working, reflecting what the Equal Opportunities Commission calls the 'inflexibility of flexible working'.[35] The EOC accepts that flexible working is widespread and here to stay, but believes that the challenge is to tackle the inequalities in the way flexible working can operate to the disadvantage of women because the insecure conditions arising from temporary employment are more likely to apply to them. Although women are over 48 per cent of the workforce, they hold 55 per cent of temporary contracts. Not only are they the majority of part-time and temporary workers, but three quarters of a million women hold two or more part-time jobs – one third more than men. And the number balancing two jobs increased by 68 per cent in the decade up to 1995.

Trade unions such as the Manufacturing Science Federation (MSF) say that they often face worried enquiries from women concerned about how to build a stable working life on a succession of insecure short-term contracts that contain no provision for training or continuity of benefits. In 1995–6 over 40 per cent of the teaching, academic and research staff in British universities were on fixed-term contracts. The tendency in the academic world for women to be employed on fixed-term contracts and for men to occupy more staff positions has become the subject of a legal case. A female lecturer is arguing indirect discrimination, on the basis that if women are given fixed-term contracts more often than men, they are more likely to face the disadvantages of insecure employment. A union campaign against the increasing casualization of higher education (both amongst the professional and support staff) highlighted, in addition to all the usual problems of job insecurity, the inferior training and development opportunities faced by temporary staff as well as the way that fixed-term staff were often not properly integrated into university life and were therefore unable to take a broad view of the quality of the university experience received by students.[36]

Discontinuous short-term contracts and freelance work mean no provision for maternity leave or benefits. This suits employers but is clearly detrimental if a woman is thinking of starting a family. When the supply of labour is transferred outside to contract providers, any requirement to ensure equal opportunity and fairness is also diluted, if not removed altogether. The whole concept of equal opportunity policies and ensuring fair play can only apply to a stable and relatively secure workforce. As the workforce polarizes into those on the flexible outside and the full-time insiders, fewer women than ever will in future be in the type of employment where traditional equal opportunity policies are relevant.[37]

This is the real meaning of the flexible workforce: the individual rather than the company has to adjust to the changing patterns and demands of the labour market and to absorb the insecurities that were previously contained within institutions. Before the full-time workforce was downsized, it was the company, not the individual, who had to adjust to periods of slack when the labour force was comparatively idle. Now that slack is transferred in many cases directly to the individual, who must adapt to periods of unpaid inactivity. As soon as the service is not required the individual is excused to find other work. The extreme form of this transfer is the zero hours contract, under whose terms the worker is on standby with no guaranteed income, only the promise of pay when they are needed to work – when there is a hamburger to fry or a bed to make.

When it used to be jobs rather than people that were seen as flexible, the employee would be prepared to accept lower pay and conditions in return for the convenience of flexible work. Now the position has reversed so that it is the workforce that is supposed to be flexible and accommodating, but instead of being rewarded for their trouble, flexible workers have found that the pay and conditions for atypical working have remained poor by comparison with those for full-time/staff jobs. And this is the experience of most women in the labour market. They work in ways that are regarded as non-standard and different from the typical full-time male working week and thereby the terms and conditions of employment are usually inferior to the norm. The small group of women who are comparatively highly paid are in secure, usually full-time, employment which has the benefits of pension, share options and maternity pay. But employment in these conditions is at a premium and there are often other sacrifices involved for undertaking this type of job. Charles Handy points out in *The Empty Raincoat* that many women who opted for the insecure portfolio life would really have preferred to stay at the core, but it had become too inhospitable – given the other constraints in their lives.

Women in large numbers have joined the workforce and entered the public domain at a time of huge change, and almost permanent revolution. Jack Welch Jnr, the chairman of General Electric and a champion of downsizing, warned at the beginning of the nineties, 'The events we see rushing toward us make the rough tumultuous eighties look like a decade at the beach.' He told his shareholders, 'Ahead of us are Darwinian shake outs in every major market place, with no consolation prizes for the losing companies and nations.' Welcome to the contemporary workplace which feels like a roller-coaster ride, compared with the stable conditions of the past. And the gurus of work say the only certainty is that total change is now a permanent way of life – which is not good news for women. For whilst work has been subject to constant upheaval, other areas of social and domestic life have hardly altered. It is like comparing the ceaseless convulsions of a volcano with the incremental pace of a glacier. Women may have altered their perceptions and gone out to work, but at home nothing has changed at all.

4

No Change at Home

Gender identity is hard-wired into the psyche. It informs
everything. We cannot process information about a baby or
an adult without first knowing their sex. The cross-dressing
females in Shakespeare's *Twelfth Night* or *As You Like It* encapsu-
late perfectly all the assumptions built into gender identification.
Centuries after Shakespeare the writer Jan Morris vividly highlighted the assumptions based on gender by describing her daily
experiences after a sex change – as one of the few people over five
years old who has ever visited both a gents' and a ladies' toilet.

> Having in the second half of the twentieth century
> experienced life in both roles there seems to me no aspect of
> existence, no moment of the day, no contact, no arrangement,
> no response which is not different for men and for
> women . . .[1]

When the actor Dustin Hoffman was preparing to play a woman
in the film *Tootsie* he used to put on his costume, high heels, wig,

and false bosoms and walk the streets of Manhattan. He described how this experience made him gradually aware of all the myriad of non-verbal differences in the way that women are perceived and interact – the glances, the looks, the secret codes – which he had never before realized.

The construct of gender and differences we ascribe to masculine and feminine vary according to place, but they evolve only slowly across time. This is why all the tired stereotypes of the 'aggressive' woman boss or the 'too emotional' female response are so stubbornly resistant to change. Anthropologists have shown, however, that the characteristics ascribed to each gender may be radically different depending upon the society. There are parts of New Guinea, for instance, in which men are prudish and flirtatious, preoccupied with cosmetics and their appearance, while women take the initiative in courtship.[2] Meanwhile the nature/nurture debate continues to rumble over the question of how gender-specific behaviour is determined. On one side of the argument is the view that women are not born but made and that all gender-appropriate behaviour is entirely a matter of cultural expectations; so that as the social barriers lifted this pre-empted the radical changes in women's achievements and public participation. On the other side of the debate is the assertion, currently in the ascendancy again, that many gender differences are biological, imprinted into the genes, so that there is significant variation not just between male and female sexual characteristics but between male and female brains; for example, according to some scientists there is now an identifiable gene that is responsible for feminine intuition and women's highly developed social skills. (Of course the corollary to this would be that men are socially inept through their biological make-up and are therefore quite helpless to do anything about it.)

Despite disagreements over the origins of gender identity there is no doubt that expectations of gender at the end of the twentieth century have changed for girls, but not for boys. A ten-year-old girl playing with engines or planes is a novelty that causes mild interest. A ten-year-old boy playing with dolls causes most parents anxiety. A girl or a woman can wear anything from tomboy jeans to frilly skirt, in any colour she likes. Appropriate clothes for a boy cover a much narrower range. The same is true of appropriate behaviour for boys. And similarly, at least in the West, whilst men are much the same, women's potential roles have expanded. No longer is a woman 'only a wife or mother'. Yet there is a sense in which all the other roles, be she airline pilot, stockbroker or engineer, are somehow contingent upon the enduring traditional view of her gender. She is not a real woman unless she also fulfils the traditional expectations of her sex. And the idea of what it means to be a 'good mother' has remained stuck in the same narrow groove for the last fifty years. The reverse is true for men. Whilst the role of men has hardly changed and still remains a narrow one, there is remarkably wide latitude over what is officially considered as a 'good father'. Fathering is seen as an optional extra role. Most of the recent writing about so-called 'new fatherhood', (in which trendy fortyish men gush about the wonders of babyhood) has the same flavour. Being a father is an extra leisure option, a part-time hobby for the hip. So a man who rarely saw his children from Monday to Friday except for an occasional bedtime kiss would not necessarily be seen as a bad father. He would just be performing his role in one of a whole range of possible but acceptable ways. A woman who did the same would inevitably court disapproval, however, because an immutable perception of 'gold standard' mothering, dating from over forty years ago, still remains the norm.

The unspoken assumption is always that a good mother is first
of all a full-time mother, just as a good job remains a full-time
job. And the good mother is one who is there for her children.
Like so many other myths this is in fact a fairly recent concept; it
is not how mothering has always been. Historically childcare took
place around the home and the locality. Mothers did not explicitly
'stay at home for the children'. Their lives and tasks revolved
around the home, where the children were also taken care of. This
pattern continued in the nineteenth century for poorer families.
As for wealthy Victorians, they certainly did not see that childcare
required much more than the nightly parental nursery visit.
According to the childcare expert Penelope Leach, full-time
childcare first emerged as a distinct domestic activity for mothers
in Nazi Germany. Under Hitler, 'Kinder, Küche, Kirche' and
breeding babies for the Fatherland were explicitly defined as
women's entire destiny. Mothering was now a complete definition
of womanhood and a lifetime activity, for which medals were
awarded.

According to Leach, in the period after the Second World War
full-time motherhood became idealized by the countries of the
Western Alliance as a convenient means of removing women from
the jobs they had worked in during the war, of shutting nurseries, and of giving jobs back to demobbed soldiers. The 'milk and
biscuits image of motherhood was a maladaptation to a post-war
world run by men'.[3] Somehow the patterns of the fifties became
frozen in time. There is a perception that the type of idealized
family depicted in the Kellogg's or Hovis adverts is the way it has
always been. The myth of the good mother, like any other myth,
falls apart under scrutiny but its hold is persistent: it continues to
retain a grip on the popular imagination far beyond the tabloid
press. By the early nineties barely one fifth of families lived in this

way, and the proportion had almost halved over the previous decade.[4] Forget the Hovis wife who finds her ultimate fulfilment in her whiter whites or her sparkling floors: either she was encouraged to get a good degree and is out with her briefcase, or she is a single parent with no husband to wave off or she is out doing several jobs to support her family. But the common perception of what 'proper' family life consists of stubbornly refuses to go away. Institutions, officialdom and parts of the media continue to function as if this arrangement was still one against which everyone must be judged – even though it is now confined to a diminishing minority of families.

Official figures on childcare use a classification of the different childcare options that assumes any arrangement other than the mother as primary carer is an exception. The list of possible alternatives – including playgroups, school, childminders – also offers the father as another possible choice of 'other arrangements'. The assumption is always that it is the mother who is available for a child's dental, optical, and any other appointments – just as she is presumed to be on hand to wait all morning for the electrician or delivery man. And less tangibly she is also there to provide all the invisible social glue that makes households and families work – remembering the birthdays, keeping in touch with the relatives, and generally acting as a service station for the family's needs; as the therapist Susie Orbach puts it, women function as 'the family's emotional sewage system'.[5]

The majority of schools operate on the assumption that there is a mother at home able to contribute her time when necessary to collect a child found with head lice, or a sore tummy. Rarely indeed is a father expected to do voluntary reading practice, accompany the school trip or run the PTA. Even in the most politically correct environments the same habits persist. One senior female politician was asked by her child's school for her contact numbers in case of emergency. She asked why they did not want her partner's numbers as he was more easily available, but was told that was not the school practice. Another woman recalls being summoned to the phone to speak to the school about her sick child in the middle of giving an important lecture. She later found that the school had made no attempt to ring her husband, who was quietly doing paperwork in his office. Despite all the changes of the past twenty years these assumptions and habits are deeply ingrained. Anyone transgressing them causes suspicion.

Sue Douglas was for nine months in 1996 a much-profiled and highly controversial editor of the *Sunday Express*. Her work meant that she spent four nights a week at a London flat away from her young children. This information more than any judgement about her journalistic skills polarized opinion about her. 'Every mother in the land read about that with a shudder . . . and it was a shudder unrelieved by her pointing out that men have done the same thing for ever,' wrote the columnist Carol Sarler. It was not just the feature writers who were so amazed. Such are our expectations that it is culturally difficult to take on board such a breach of accepted behaviour. Of course Sue Douglas is correct that thousands of fathers have left and do leave their families for the working week or far longer. They live apart in all kinds of circumstances, from jobbing builders to musicians to sailors, but no one calls them bad fathers. In fact no one remarks on it at all.

One of the biggest American media trials in recent memory was the 1997 case of Louise Woodward, the British au pair in Boston accused of killing the baby in her care. It had prime-time coverage and made the front page for weeks. But in a bizarre twist halfway through, the American public seemed to turn its attention away from the au pair's actions to focus on the behaviour of the mother, who happened to work part-time, three days a week, as an eye specialist. On the phone-in programmes, callers yelled that the baby's death was her own fault, indeed she 'deserved for him to die' because she should have been at home instead of selfishly pursuing her medical career. She received hate mail accusing her of leaving her child for the sake of her lifestyle, and one newspaper described her as 'a public symbol of maternal neglect and yuppie greed'.[6] Whether or not the baby should have been in the care of an untrained, discontented eighteen-year-old is another question, but as usual the role and expectations of the father in this saga were totally invisible. He also was a doctor, but the radio chat shows and the thousands of letters passed no comment on him at all.

Again and again the stereotypes and expectations recur. When the climber Alison Hargreaves died on K2 in the Himalayas in August 1995, leaving behind two small children, there was a torrent of comment in the UK press (800 paragraphs and 64 photos) on her dereliction of maternal duty and her irresponsibility in undertaking such a dangerous sport. But when in the same month another climber, Geoff Tier, died on another mountain there was only commiseration (twenty paragraphs, no photos) for his family and assessments of his fine record on the peaks.[7] At no time was his career perceived to have made him a bad or inadequate parent to his six-year-old daughter. The same is true when a father sails round the world or takes to the skies in a hot-air balloon. Mutterings about poor paternal performance are deemed irrelevant.

When a baby is born to a mother over fifty there is widespread revulsion at her selfish irresponsibility. If a man becomes a father at that age there is general backslapping and congratulation. The argument 'he'll never be around when they are grown up' does not seem to matter. When a woman leaves her husband for a man some twenty years younger (like the actress Francesca Annis who left her husband and children for the filmstar Ralph Fiennes) the public reaction verges on hysterical horror. Of course there are older men who seek solace with far younger lovers every day and merit no attention. The same old stereotypes about acceptable and gender-appropriate behaviour will not go away. Take the cult success of *Bridget Jones's Diary*. It divulges the outpourings of a nervy single modern woman, her slothful habits, body image and other neuroses. She is supposed to be the ultimate nineties woman, with her own flat, career and independence, yet underlying all her agonizing, nothing has changed. Like a Jane Austen heroine, there is really only one big question for Bridget, how is she going to get her man, her Mr Darcy, and live happily ever after?[8]

While achieving professional women are given much media coverage, the suspicions about them, especially those with political husbands, have not changed at all. The public had to be loudly informed in the case of both Hillary Clinton and Cherie Blair that they were marvellous home-makers. Cherie edited an edition of the women's magazine *Prima*, to which she contributed her own knitting patterns and recipes. Her capabilities were closely measured against Norma Major's cooking and domestic achievements. For the image makers, the fact that Cherie Blair was a QC was irrelevant and if anything an electoral hindrance. Hillary Clinton famously argued with Barbara Bush, the wife of President Bush, during the 1992 election campaign about the best cookie recipes. No one ever suggested that Denis Thatcher (or any equivalent male spouse) had to demonstrate his DIY, car maintenance or gardening skills to prove himself as a real man. The subtext in the case of both Cherie and Hillary clearly was 'she may be a good lawyer but don't worry, she is a proper woman too'.

Even if nowadays roles have widened and broad new horizons are open to women, the same stereotypes about mothering, home-making and what it takes to be a real woman endure. Reams have been written about stereotyping, but while there is more public awareness about sexist remarks some of the deepest social assumptions and habits have not really changed. New roles for women have simply been grafted onto the old ones. Meanwhile men's roles have stayed almost exactly the same. Sheila Rowbotham concluded in her thoughtful and weighty *A Century of Women* that 'Twenty years of agitation and an employment structure which had turned inside out had modified notion of gender but left some parts untouched. Slippage seemed to produce an exaggerated reworking of earlier idioms of masculinity and femininity.'[9]

Many of the assumptions about gender stereotype and the sexual division of labour are still a direct hangover from the Stone Age. The patterns of who does what were established amongst tribes of hunter-gatherers where frequent pregnancies and long periods of breast-feeding led to a strict sexual division of labour. Today physical strength has disappeared as a requirement for most work, and the average time a woman spends in her life preg-nant and breast feeding has drastically reduced over several millennia, but many of the same assumptions about sexual stereo-typing remain.[10] Joan Smith has eloquently illustrated how in many ways the differences between the sexes are exaggerated, while the anthropologist Margaret Mead pointed out in 1949 that 'In every known society mankind has elaborated the biological division of labour into forms often very remotely related to the original biological differences that provided the original clues.'[11]

Who's Doing What?

In 1973 a widely read sociology text called *The Symmetrical Family* analysed the likely changes in family roles.[12] The authors, Michael Young and Peter Willmott, argued that it was logical to suppose that women's emergence into the workplace would be complemented by men's parallel involvement in the home. They observed the change from women working in the home and men working outside towards a pattern where women were taking on two demanding jobs – one outside and one inside the home – whereas men still had only one job, outside. They predicted that men would eventually take up the slack; the symmetry would be complete when both partners had a job inside and outside the home, so instead of the original two jobs there would be four. Young and Willmott predicted that this development would lead to additional strain and inevitably increasing marital collapse. They were right about the divorce, although they underestimated the extent of the rise in family breakdown, but the symmetry never came.

Much domestic work is routine, repetitive and boring. Maybe men feel they are better off without it. They are probably right; it takes up a huge amount of time but is socially trivialized, and men feel happier when they are doing less of it. According to the most recent survey by the *National Child Development Study*, published in 1996, the women who felt happiest in their marriage (or cohabitation) were the ones with partners who were most prepared to help out at home.[13] The unhappiest men, however, those who expressed the least satisfaction in marriage, were the ones doing most of the helping out. Another paradox is the apparently unequal view of the benefits of marriage and partnership. Nearly all the evidence, quantitative and qualitative, shows that men are better off when they are married or in stable cohabitation: they earn more, inflict less harm upon themselves and upon society, and are in better psychological health. But the reverse is true for women. Single women overall show less incidence of depression, express more satisfaction with their lives and are likely to have achieved more at work. According to research conducted by One Plus One (the charity that researches into relationships), when asked what they thought might have happened to them if they had not married, women saw marriage as limiting ('I'd be a theatre sister by now'), and men saw it as redeeming ('I'd be drowning in whisky by now').[14] Obviously there are much wider issues about emotional satisfaction, but the persistently unequal division of domestic labour is a significant factor in the unequally perceived benefits of marriage. One study found that every year of marriage increases a man's earnings by 0.9 per cent so that after ten years a married man earns up to one fifth more than a comparable single man; the study concluded quite simply that 'married men are more likely to have a woman taking care of their domestic needs, leaving them with more free time and less hassle'.[15]

The impetus behind much early feminist writing was to argue that housework was dreary and soul-destroying and women should not be lumbered with having to do it all. This was hardly an enticement for men to take up their share. Ann Oakley, in her pioneering 1974 study *Housewife*, described women's domesticity 'as a circle of learnt deprivation and induced subjugation'.[16] She argued for a 'revolution in the concepts of gender identity'. But despite a mountain of subsequent analysis of the domestic role and the politics of housework, roles and responsibilities have hardly changed since 1974.

In 1989 the American sociologist Arlie Hochschild coined the phrase 'the second shift' to describe the daily arrangement of work and domestic labour coinciding with women's mass entry into the labour market.[17] She produced a landmark study of American families, tracking in detail the double burden upon women who worked both inside and outside the home. It was a grim picture of chronically exhausted women, in a wide range of occupations, who shouldered the domestic burden to 'keep the marital peace' and who felt lucky and grateful when their partner occasionally 'helped out'. There is no doubt that since 1963 – and the publication of Betty Friedan's *The Feminine Mystique* – the world has been transformed; the trouble was that when Friedan told women to 'Get a life' she was rather less emphatic on the subject of what needed simultaneously to happen at home. Today it seems obvious that if women are out at work this will create a vacuum in the home – but men have not rushed in to fill it. Just as women adapted to the male working culture in order that they could assimilate quickly, they simultaneously did nothing to disrupt the status quo at home.

Since Hochschild, numerous surveys have looked at the division of domestic labour. These studies have been carried out by market research companies, advertising agencies, BBC audience research, academics and government departments, and every one comes up with some version of the same unsurprising conclusion: no matter what household chore is studied – washing, cooking, shopping, cleaning, childcare – the vast majority of women do more than their partner, and that includes women in full-time employment outside the home. One major study released in 1997 showed that women working full-time on average perform nine hours a week more housework than the men they live with.[18] Women do more when they are working and their partner is unemployed, they do more (about six hours more) when they are working longer hours than their partner and they do more when both work full-time. In every permutation women do more work in the home.

Exactly how much more it is that women do of each task depends upon which survey you read, as does the rate of change. Certainly men are participating a little more than previously, according to most (but not all) surveys – yet over three decades they have increased their contribution by only a few minutes a day.[19] According to the British Social Attitudes survey and some other studies, both sexes, but especially women, aspire to a more equal division of tasks than actually exists ('I believe that things *ought* to be more equally divided').[20] In other studies, however, men admit that they are pretty happy with the status quo and not inclined to desire any change.[21] And in those surveys where self-reporting is used, men always *think* they are doing more than they are. The amount of time and effort they estimate to have spent on a particular chore always outstrips what their partner estimates they have done. This often ties in with a sense among men of limited responsibility for domestic activity. Whilst a woman's effort is taken entirely for granted, frequently when men contribute this is perceived as a 'help', an 'extra', in the sense that men do not own these tasks. Their effort is more likely to be regarded as a bonus, optional contribution, in the sense that 'I have done this for you.' There are echoes of the old joke, 'How many men does it take to change a lightbulb? Answer: Two. One to change the bulb and another to collect the reward.' Recent evidence shows that even male sea horses, traditionally cited as wonderfully devoted fathers who carry around their brood, do much less in practice than has generally been assumed. Female sea horses are far from being the uncaring mothers we always thought, because they actually provide all the nutrients that sustain the eggs. Seahorse dads were just very good at claiming all the credit.

When the type of tasks that men contribute are analysed they are more likely to be discretionary, non-urgent, occasional jobs like washing the car, painting or gardening. Women are far more likely to carry out time-sensitive and regular daily tasks like making the children's tea or doing the washing. Interestingly in one study, the only ungendered and equally shared activity was window-cleaning, representing the threshold between inside and outside work.[22]

The precise division of domestic tasks obviously varies widely, and many men argue that as they work more hours outside the home, naturally they are excused from contributing much inside the home. But there is another way to look at this, by asking how much leisure time is left after adding up the effort expended inside and outside the home. On this measure men are always ahead. One Australian study estimates that men have over eight hours a week more leisure time than women. The Henley Centre calculates that men have over fourteen hours more free time, so the 'leisure deficit' for women is nearly two working days a week.[23] Even using the UK government's most recent official figures, the time that women spend on domestic and paid work combined adds up to a total weekly figure of six and a half hours more than for men.[24] The same survey shows that men spend more time on sport, self-education and self-improvement. The participation of men in sport and leisure is hardly a surprise. Perhaps the reason why the ten top-earning sports stars are all men is because the members of the public who have the most leisure time and money to train and to spend watching sport or buying sponsored merchandise are men.

The attitudes of both sexes towards the home are also revealing in their approach to domestic labour. There is evidence to show that the traditional attitude towards the home as a refuge of peace and relaxation, 'an oasis far from the maddening throng', is far more common amongst men than women. Stress hormone levels in men and in childless working women reduce when they reach home in the evening, presumably because home represents a haven of rest. According to one psychological study, however, stress levels in mothers who work outside the home remain as high as ever when they return home.[25] Following her ground-breaking book *The Second Shift*, Arlie Hochschild produced a study called *The Time Bind*, which looked at the competing stresses of home and work.[26] It was based on detailed observation of employees at an unnamed US corporation. The conclusions demonstrated that women prefer being at work, because they feel more stress and demands upon them in their domestic life than they do in the relatively orderly world of work. Hochschild reached the surprising conclusion that *some* women were even turning down offers to work less and spend more time at home, because being at home only led to more stress. In a sense she was just confirming what many mothers have long felt – that they go to work for a rest. Work is the only place where they are sure of being able to visit the lavatory alone and in peace, to finish a sentence or to read more than a paragraph without interruption. The same disjunction between men's and women's views on home life appears in other ways. The advertising agency J. Walter Thompson conducted a survey in October 1997 into how people thought of Christmas. Whilst nearly 80 per cent of fathers saw it as a relaxing holiday break, only 35 per cent of mothers had the same view. Most of the remaining mothers (the overwhelming majority) associated Christmas with very hard work.[27]

In 1939 Margery Spring-Rice published a vivid account of housewives' lives which later became a classic. In most cases the descriptions are of unremitting hard physical effort:

About half the women get up at 6.30 or a little before and go
to bed at 10.30 or 11. Half the women say that they are twelve
hours or more a day on their feet. The majority say they have
two hours' 'leisure' in the day – but this is spent in shopping,
taking the baby out, mending, sewing and doing household
jobs of an irregular kind which cannot be fitted into working
hours, such as tidying cupboards, re-papering a room,
gardening etc.[28]

It is an unusual concept of 'leisure pursuits' by today's standards.
According to the journalist Rebecca Abrams, the problem with
women today is that they need to learn how to play more.[29] They
spend too much time either at work or in the service of others.
Men and children make play a part of their lives, she argues, and
women ought to do the same. For many women in the prime of
life this is a hollow joke.

Margery Spring-Rice made a number of recommendations at
the end of her investigation into housewives, such as better housing subsidies and improved leisure facilities for women. Nowhere
does she even hint at the then inconceivable idea that men might
do more in the home. Sixty years later, naturally the conditions of
housework have changed. Equipment that would have seemed an
unimaginable luxury to women in the thirties is now commonplace. However, as Kate Millett, one of the first to comment on
the emerging double burden, pointed out in 1977, 'the invention
of labour saving devices has had no appreciable effect upon
drudgery even if it has affected the quality of that drudgery'.[30]
Contemporary accounts of time use by women employed outside
the home confirm this pattern: some of these women do their
housework at 7 a.m. and at 10 p.m. Some tasks are done much
more efficiently than fifty years ago but others, like shopping,

take far longer than they used to.[31] So whilst the work may be different, for some women the hours involved are comparable with those Spring-Rice observed in the thirties.

Even in a household where both partners work full-time, women spend over three times as much time as men on domestic chores and over twice as much time on childcare – and these, unsurprisingly, are the households where the burden is most equally shared.[32] The real losers appear to be women working part-time. The domestic division of labour between these women and their partners barely differs from those households where the woman does no work at all outside the home. It appears that men feel moved to make a contribution – albeit a modest one – if they live with a partner working full-time. When she works part-time they can behave as if she did not work outside the home at all.

There are further paradoxes. According to Jonathan Gershuny, one of the foremost authorities on time use data, when women take on paid work their domestic contribution does not reduce anywhere near proportionately. For every extra hour of paid work their domestic work reduces by only half an hour. Hence the second shift. Gershuny's data do not record the same pattern for men. Men who have no paid employment actually spend less time on childcare than they did in the sixties, and their time spent on domestic work has barely altered.[33] Indeed the most recent *National Child Development Study* data (which confirm the usual pattern of women doing much more than men, even in dual earner households), give an interesting twist on those households where the woman is the sole breadwinner. Only 39 per cent of men in such households with pre-school children were classed as 'sole carers', and just over 50 per cent were in families with children over five.[34] So if a man is not in the labour market it is likely that he will not be undertaking significant childcare either, which begs the question of who is looking after the children and what the man is up to? With the possible exception of the idle rich, the reverse is unthinkable for women. If a woman is not in the labour market she is automatically assumed to be on duty at home.

Men Who Care

The proportion of families where men undertake full-time child-care and domestic responsibility is tiny. And tracking down househusbands is a difficult business. When they do emerge it is self-evident that the situation for many of them is involuntary. Most are unemployed and there by default: if something better came along, like a job that paid more than childcare costs, they would be off. (When the new childcare subsidy for the low-paid is introduced at the end of 1999, it is feasible that men like this will no longer stay at home to care.) Only a tiny proportion of male primary carers say that they are there by choice and are doing this for the foreseeable future in preference to anything else. There are a few international studies on men whose full-time task is domestic caring, but the sample sizes are inevitably small. Most of them conclude that there is no evidence to show that men cannot parent as effectively as women, even if differently.[35] And those accounts that question men's caring abilities, asserting that men are less responsive as primary carers and that this arrangement of responsibilities can lead to less overall marital satisfaction, do not take into account the enormous social stigma that is still attached to men as primary carers.

Kevin is the father of a toddler who is staying at home as care-giver and 'trailing spouse' while his wife undertakes a demanding foreign posting. He feels the full blast of societal disapproval.

As soon as I thought I had made the adjustment, I would go through another bout of internal turmoil about the role I had taken on. As 'liberated' as my wife believes me to be there was still a conflict within that I was not doing what a man 'should' be doing. Men go to work and provide – that's the aboriginal paradigm. And those able-bodied men who don't work are bums plain and simple. Never mind that child rearing is often a Herculean task in and of itself; it's outside the boundary of man's work. The Archetypal Man is making things happen not hanging around the campfire or mixing up infant formula.[36]

Other insights into the lives of men who have taken this route are fascinating. One man described how he does the hoovering on his knees so the neighbours cannot see him through the windows. There are frequent stories of strong disapproval by parents and in-laws. 'They were always giving me grief saying I had such a cushy life.' Another man described how he was always the only father at the mother/toddler group. One day he picked up a crying toddler who had fallen over – the child's mother was at the far end of the hall. The mother came screaming over and told him that he was a pervert who must never touch her daughter again. For six months no one at the group spoke to him. Another man, even without any such transgression, said he spent years collecting children at the school gate before anyone spoke to him. And a father who was proud of having won custody of his two young children described women's suspicious attitudes towards him and his constant desire to excel and prove himself as a primary parent. Like women who enter a male workplace, a man who takes on the role of primary parent sees himself as a foreign traveller seeking acceptance in an alien culture.

Officialdom is clear that being a man, until retirement, must mean either a paid job or unemployment. There is no other alternative. Denise is a senior nurse and her husband Neil used to be a builder. They decided jointly that he should stop work to look after their two children, now aged six and two. They tried to put Neil down as a 'househusband' on various official forms, like the second child's birth registration but were told that this was unacceptable and they must put 'unemployed' instead. In the end the compromise was that he should put down 'builder' even though this description was no longer true. With the car insurance, too, the authorities preferred the entry to be inaccurate rather than accept the category 'househusband'. The official reaction simply confirms the social response that Neil finds to his role in the small village where he lives. 'Folk look at you like you're from another planet. All the blokes round here go out to work, expect the tea on the table when they get home and then go down the pub. At the weekend it's the same but with more pub.' Denise says, 'People think he's a bit simple. Why isn't he in a proper job? I have to defend him.'

Other men who try to reinvent their role report the incredulous and shocked reaction they receive at every encounter ranging from milkman to playgroup, pub to dinner party. James Leith wrote a hilarious account of being a 'houseworm' to his wife Penny Junor, four children and assorted pets. *Ironing John* (whose title is a parody of the American men's movement tract *Iron John*) recalls hair-raising domestic disasters and amusing tales about folding underpants. It reports the shocked silence at a very grand dinner party when Leith was asked what he did for a living and replied that he was the primary carer.

These people had no way of reacting to this information. I might as well have told them I suffered from an unfortunate bowel condition. Not even a chilly 'how interesting' could cope with a breach of etiquette of this magnitude, but all of them had children, kitchen tables and dirty socks to deal with.[37]

Yet beneath all the jokes the book has a serious message. Leith says he was moved to write it as an alternative to studying psychology 'to try to understand the incomprehensible reactions and attitudes of my fellow men and women to my new occupation'. Perhaps it was Leith's former career as an actor that enabled him so successfully to reinvent himself as a househusband.

In 1973 the BBC *Man Alive* series transmitted a programme entitled 'My Wife Wears the Trousers' which featured a suburban middle-class family in which the father was the primary carer and the mother worked as a lecturer. The reaction to their lifestyle both in the film and the ensuing heated studio discussion suggested that this couple, by acting outside their expected gender roles, represented some kind of bizarre freak show. Nearly twenty-five years later there was another BBC documentary featuring househusbands and the reactions were very similar. The concept of rearranging the sexual division of labour is such a simple one yet whenever it is discussed in public it takes on the guise of an apocalyptic revolution.

A father who was left to deal with the home when his wife had an extended stay in hospital described how he managed to cope.

[Yet] for demonstrating this humble expertise, I was treated by female friends as a kind of secular saint. That was bad enough – how easy it is for a man to be equitable in a woman's eyes, how low standards are. What was worse was the blank incomprehension of my male friends. Either they didn't ask how I was arranging things at all – assuming I suppose that grandma had materialised to make everything right – or, if the subject came up they just looked fuddled. Where were the kids kept, they seemed to wonder? On Mars? Who cooked the meals, who tended the hearth? It was uncannily like the reaction of the Cavaliers in the 1640s or Louis XVI and Marie Antoinette in 1789 faced with other worlds turned upside down.[38]

And there are indeed parallels between men and a privileged group that clings on to an established position because change will bring little benefit. In any social revolution some will have more to lose than others – from the Kulaks in the Soviet Union to the Whites in South Africa – and for the group losing a privilege it feels like discrimination and hardship. The view of the male trade unionist who said he had no problem with equal opportunities and the prospect of more promotions for women – provided there were no less promotions for men – extends into the private sphere. Men do not mind if women do any less domestic work so long as they do not have to do more. In some, more privileged homes this is how the problem is tackled. Child rearing and domestic tasks are largely subcontracted to another (poorer and possibly foreign) woman so the remaining burden to be split is substantially reduced. In a well-off dual career couple the man still does less, but the overall burden is reduced, giving an illusion of greater equality.

If so much domestic work is repetitive and soul-destroying, just as Ann Oakley and others have painstakingly described, it is hardly surprising that men have been satisfied with the status quo, even when women are employed outside the home. It has been manifestly in their interests to perpetrate the myth that 'men are really not suited to domestic effort'. So even if a man is perfectly able to understand all kinds of complicated machinery it is quite acceptable for him to remain ignorant and incompetent about the controls on a washing machine or to be unable to follow the simplest recipe. The occasional turn with a lawnmower or electric drill of course poses no such hurdles. It is the daily indoor domestic tasks and machinery that are so unconquerable – interestingly research has shown that the microwave is one of the few domestic machines used indoors that men have successfully come to terms with.[39] Somehow this was seen as a sufficiently gender-neutral machine enabling most men to suspend their normal helplessness. The myth of men's domestic incapacity is a convenient and carefully cultivated one. It is reminiscent of all the negative myths about what women could not do, whether it was that they were not competent to vote, obtain university degrees or read the television news.

The Nappy Trap

This picture of unchanging domestic stereotypes does deserve some modification. A survey in 1998 came up with the exciting news of a rise in the overall proportion of men who did the weekly food shop – but then it revealed that the increase consisted entirely of high-earning men under twenty-four years old. What appears to have happened is that the division of labour amongst the young and childless, especially amongst well-educated professionals, has begun to shift to more equal proportions, which is a change from previous generations. Rabbi Julia Neuberger recalls that when she was at Cambridge in the sixties the tough-minded head of her female college lectured the undergraduates that she did not care who or how many men they slept with, but on no account must they end up

doing their menfolk's washing. When Julia Neuberger later wan-
dered down into the college drying rooms she saw rows of damp
Y-fronts and realized that the warning had gone largely unheeded.

Thirty years later the message seems to have been understood.
Young women say that they have no intention of doing any more
than 50 per cent of household chores with their partner. And
there is evidence that for many of them words translate into
action. The most enlightened men are those who have spent time
living alone. The laziest still move from mother to live-in girlfriend or wife and 'never learn that loo paper doesn't grow on
little wooden branches sticking out of the bathroom wall'.
Paradoxically, for many decades the men with the greatest domestic potential used to be those who had done National Service and
had been forced to learn a degree of self-sufficiency. However, the
gender map they discovered when they left army life encouraged
them to forget it all very quickly.

Contemporary soap operas portray a much more egalitarian
division of tasks amongst young people, and the point is reinforced in the Demos research about trends towards androgyny in
the under-35s. For many members of Generation X domestic
tasks are fairly interchangeable. But it is meaningless simply to
project these attitudes into the future. It is true that survey
responses and the Demos genderquake research indicates that a
substantial number of women believe that tasks should be shared
when children arrive, but the evidence still shows that they are
not. Nora Ephron's observation in her novel *Heartburn* that
'having a baby is like throwing a grenade into a marriage' remains
an accurate and grim warning.

Domestic responsibilities before and after children are clearly of
a totally different order. This is why it is impossible to believe
optimistic statements that 'When we have children my partner

and I will share the burden equally.' The estimated time required to look after a pre-school child averages seven hours a day (seven days a week), more for under-twos and less for over-fours.[40] This is time required over and above household tasks not directly attributable to the child. And it is self-evident that many of these childcare-associated tasks are also more awkward because they are highly time-sensitive. The food or clean nappy is always required immediately. Sharing responsibility for the odd visit to the laundrette or an optional supermarket trip bears no relation to life with children. And so far there are no labour-saving devices to reduce the time and effort of childcare – notwithstanding disposable nappies and commercial babyfood.

If a child means an extra forty-nine hours a week of domestic effort, you would logically expect both the father's and the mother's contribution to increase. But according to several surveys fathers actually do a smaller share of the work than men without children.[41] Egalitarian good intentions are thrown out and men tend to revert to a more traditional division of labour. The Nobel prizewinning economist Gary Becker has written about this in terms of 'efficient specialization'. He argued in a series of contributions from the 1960s onwards that it made economic sense for members of the household to 'specialize' in their tasks.[42] As in the mythical fifties-style family, Father should carry on his (higher-paying) job, Mother should give up work and stay at home undertaking all domestic activity for the foreseeable future, freeing up the father to earn the maximum return from the paid labour market, to the benefit of the whole family.

While since the fifties everything else has changed – wage structures, labour market stability, security in marriage – the familiar pattern where children altered forever the sexual division of labour still remains fixed. Even if a woman stops work for a few months and then resumes a full-time or part-time occupation, the evidence shows that the balance of domestic labour will have shifted for ever. A Birmingham University study looked at married couples before and after childbirth and found that even amongst those who had initially shared housework and breadwinning equally, and who always intended to continue doing so, there was a reversion to traditional roles after parenthood.[43] Gill Cappuccini, a psychologist involved in the study, reported that many respondents found the arrival of a baby an unexpected shock: 'They tried to make sense of a very new situation and find themselves adopting the old traditional roles.' Research by One Plus One confirms the same pattern.

The attitude of Penelope Leach to this issue, as Britain's foremost childcare guru, is a fascinating one. In her 1979 book *Who Cares?* she was firmly of the belief that only a mother could care and mothers *must* be there to care. Any substitute childcare, including by the father, was merely a necessary evil. She spoke disparagingly of a 'male substitute mother'.[44] It was still a matter of 'he had his job and you have yours, which is to care' – there was even a startling analogy with an architect who might have routine or boring tasks to do within his professional life but who would never contemplate asking his sexual partner to fill in and help out, just as a mother should not try to offload her caring on to her partner. In 1983, when she discussed attachment in her book *Babyhood*,[45] Leach made no mention of mothers who had paid employment outside the home. Yet ten years later she had transformed her view of fathers' abilities: 'Of course a man can take full daily care of his child. Any suggestion that he cannot is as insultingly absurd as the suggestion that his partner cannot run a corporation.'

Leach[46] was now clear that a father was quite able to provide the care a child needs. Her picture of the process within the home as a new baby arrived showed how, in spite of all previous resolutions, imperceptibly the responsibility and control shifts to the mother:

> . . . objectively these skills can be learnt by anyone over 10 but crucial familiarity and practice means a gap which steadily widens. . . . week by week there is a collapse of duties that she takes over from the previously egalitarian set-up and things are never the same again.

Leach describes how the mother might change the first few nappies, so by the time the father tries she is already better at it and able to tell him what to do. Gradually a competence gap develops which was not there to start with, when both parents were equally clumsy and uncertain. The mother becomes just a little more attuned to the baby's crying and moods than the father because of those early hours and days in hospital. At this stage he is certainly in a position to catch up, but usually he never does. And this is the root of so much stereotyping of identity: the tiny shifts in behaviour and attitude that on their own mean very little become magnified so that they drastically transform a whole way of life. Whatever the biological tendencies and instincts that may exist, alone these would be relatively insignificant were they not constantly reinforced by social forces and supplemented by cultural influences.

Nina is a hospital consultant married to another consultant. She recalls how in the dazed early weeks of motherhood she was overwhelmed by the baby's all-encompassing demands.

> . . . sometimes he would take the baby and pace around for a

while, but at the first signs of crankiness he always returned,
saying, 'I am sure she needs feeding.' When I replied that the
baby had been fed barely an hour ago he used to say
indignantly, 'But I have looked after her for an hour for you,
can't you take her back now.' It was the idea that in holding
and carrying the baby he was doing me a personal favour,
because this was my duty and my responsibility that he had
assisted with. I reminded him that he was in fact the baby's
father.

But this pattern is all too common. The father comes to be less
familiar and the mother gains increasing control and ownership of
these issues, which she never gives up. The trouble is that it is not
just baby care that gradually tilts in one direction. While she is at
home anyway all day (even if it is only for a few months' maternity leave) she might as well do his washing along with all the rest
of the laundry, and cook him supper and generally organize things
in the home. Once a new pattern of tasks is established it becomes
ever more difficult to go back to the equality of the past.

Paternity leave has been hailed as the solution to getting fathers
involved and overcoming the strict sexual division of labour. The
prospect of European directives on paternity leave sent the last
Conservative government, notably Michael Portillo (in his role as
Secretary of State for Employment), into a state of apoplexy. The
paternity leave issue became for Conservatives an example of how
the perfidious European Social Chapter would damage Britain's
economic future. How could businesses survive if men were given
a few days off? But in fact even a week at home sharing care is
unlikely to bring revolutionary change in roles and responsibilities. Mother is still likely to be left doing it all, or just as
important, taking control. In families where there has been an

effort to rearrange these gender stereotypes the most significant shift of all is when control and responsibility over the domestic sphere no longer belong to the mother. In *Ironing John* James Leith is refreshingly honest about the issue of men's reluctance to take control and women's unwillingness to relinquish it.

> I tried 'helping out' but my every instinct told me that I should do NOTHING on my own initiative. I always asked. I could make pastry when I was 10 years old but at 30 I knew it was (officially) HER department and I should (loudly) interrupt her work to find out the proportion of fat to flour. . . . I might occasionally force myself to act without instruction but a wife and mother no matter how engrossed . . . can hear the click of the lid of the nappy bucket from the other side of the house, can remember to the minute when the sterilising solution went in and can yell 'don't rinse yet' without stopping typing.[47]

It is not fair simply to accuse men of putting their heads in the sand. The difficulty in altering perceptions is far wider than that. There is a whole literature on the 'reproduction of mothering' (the title of a classic work by Nancy Chodorow).[48] Boys from the start are rarely presented with caring role models of adult males either in the home or in any other forms of childcare or schooling. Indeed the problem is so severe that a male childcare worker or nursery nurse is frequently assumed to be a potential abuser. Then there are the wider social assumptions, like those of elderly male judges who in the vast majority of cases still cannot conceive of male custody of children following divorce. But most intangible and difficult to pinpoint are the attitudes of women, who are often their own worst enemies when they complain about 'doing it all'.

So long as women subliminally expect to 'marry up' to a man who at least on one level will 'take care of her' and are resistant to finding a partner who is younger, less ambitious, less educated or earns less, in other words a man who would be ideally suited as a primary carer, then the traditional underpinning of the existing sexual division of labour will remain. Women's aspirations in other areas may have transformed, but often their expectations from a partner or spouse have altered much more slowly.[49]

Many years ago it was unimaginable that a woman would actively desire a partner who did not conform to the accepted pattern. So while the male doctor might date or marry a nurse, the female doctor could not do the equivalent. She would expect to marry either another doctor or someone of equivalent or higher status and earning potential. Yet very slowly there have been changes, which extend beyond the extreme cases of a total role reversal, where father is the primary carer. It is now socially acceptable for a woman to have a younger partner – although not too young – and in one out of five couples women earn more than their partners.[50] This is a huge increase – and the proportion has nearly trebled in the last twenty years – but it is still treated as an aberration and a departure from the accepted norm. The only way to overcome the Stone Age model is for both men and women to change their historical assumptions and take a more flexible view of gender identity. Women need to 'train up, marry down and give men lots of solo time with their babies'.[51] Not until there are sufficient women who are psychologically prepared to take on primary breadwinning and to redefine motherhood will there be a real possibility of inventing a new set of patterns.

Traditionalists of all types shudder at this idea, warning that it will lead to a bleak, genderless future. The difficulty is that the debate is so often framed hysterically as an all-or-nothing issue –

'men are being chained to the kitchen sink, they are emasculated by a caring role' – with the stark alternative of total role reversal and the ridiculous vision of the emasculated man in a pinny. What about the much more complicated scenario of a gradual shift towards sharing responsibilities for breadwinning and unpaid domestic labour, which challenges the rigid stereotypes? It need not even be a simultaneous process. In a long-term partnership there is scope for a different distribution of roles across the years. There is evidence to show that this kind of arrangement, of greater longitudinal equality, although uncommon can yield a high degree of mutual satisfaction. Charles Handy gives an interesting account of how such patterns can work.[52] He describes the 'portfolio marriage' where, instead of the serial monogamy that is so common in the West, the partners gradually evolve new roles so that the marriage changes to their mutual satisfaction without either having to change partners. The trouble is that the all or nothing of the contemporary labour market does not favour such solutions.

Invisible Work

The status and meaning associated with paid work have risen for both men and women. As work has come to mean having a job, the counterpart to work is seen as leisure. Everything else is invisible. So a time chart that reads 'rise at 6 to feed a baby, spend a day full of cleaning the house, cooking, attending to the needs of elderly relatives, shopping, washing, childcare and finishing with a night-time feed' would not officially count as work. It is the same in a labour ward: the midwife, anaesthetist, tea lady, doctor, nurse and cleaner are all working, because they are paid. The woman

who is *in labour* producing a future member of the human race is
not considered to be doing any productive work, because her effort
is not recorded in the Gross National Product.

Work is only work when money changes hands. And every
first-year economics student knows that 'when a man marries his
housekeeper, the GNP will drop'. The woman may be performing
identical tasks as an unpaid wife but they will no longer count as
work. Now that women, especially married women and mothers,
have increasingly come to participate in the visible world of paid
work, this has thrown up awkward questions about priorities. The
assumption behind the traditional sexual division of labour is that
men's paid work relies upon a shadow economy of unpaid
women's work. If women are now also in the formal paid workforce then what is the status of what had always been a 'labour of
love'? One solution is to argue that the concept and values of the
market must extend to incorporate what had always been considered non-work. According to some interpretations, the traditional
'free' labour of women should be seen as a form of taxation
whereby society benefits from their input, just as if they were
paying directly to the state.[53]

In some ways the official invisibility of domestic effort is a
continuation of the attitudes of the wider labour market. Roles
and work associated with women command less status and less
money. Just as Joan Ruddock as the Minister for Women was
unpaid, domestic work is overwhelmingly associated with women,
has low status and is unremunerated. Until recently the idea of
paying for domestic labour and campaigns like Wages for
Housework were treated as a joke. But gradually the discovery of
'unpaid work' has emerged from feminist theory and entered the
mainstream. The insurance company Legal and General recently
produced a survey entitled 'The Value of a Mum' which stated

authoritatively that mums work an average of sixty-two hours a week and that the value of this work was £313 in March 1997.[54] From an insurance point of view, if mum is not around this is what it would cost to replace her efforts.

This idea that the invisible 'love labour' should have a monetary value is a new concept and has only become seriously recognized since mothers started going to work and employing someone else to undertake domestic activity, which then suddenly became real, paid work. Yet in official parlance there is still little understanding, and huge discrepancies prevail. As far as Britain's 20,000 widowed fathers are concerned their deceased partner's effort is considered to have had no value, but a widow will receive generous tax allowances, lump sum and continuing state benefit payments in recognition of the missing father's financial contribution. A man in the same position receives no payment, presumably on the basis that his wife's death represents no future financial loss. Two widowed fathers are travelling the tortuous legal route to the European Court in an effort to challenge this inequity. They had reduced their paid work so that they could properly care for their families, and they suffered severe financial hardship as a result. (Widowers left with dependent children provide an interesting insight into the whole caring debate. Unlike fathers who fight for custody, widowers have not actively chosen to become primary carers and yet the great majority – including the most unlikely cases – become extraordinarily competent in every way, easily refuting the 'men aren't very good at it' arguments.)

Housekeeping and the care of young children are not the only roles that have no official recognition as 'real work'. At the other end of the life cycle, the growing number of carers who undertake responsibilities for the elderly also throws into relief the substitution value of such effort. An estimated 6 million people have some form of caring responsibility for the old and the sick, and one third of them have a full-time job as well. Even amongst women in their twenties it appears that 16 per cent now put in between twenty and thirty-five hours a week as carers – a proportion which has doubled in the last few years. The potential savings in residential care and nursing are enormous, because it is all done for free – or at least any caring allowance covers only a tiny fraction of the equivalent institutional cost. The numbers in need of care are steadily increasing so there is growing awareness of the paradox of this officially invisible effort. In fact elder care might become pivotal in the association of women with unpaid domestic labour. All the arguments about 'maternal instinct' and the task of breast-feeding which link women with caring for young children disappear. After all, there is unlikely to be a biological reason why a woman is better than her spouse at emptying her mother- or father-in-law's bedpan.

Many industrial countries have decided that the time has come to acknowledge the 'informal economy' alongside the official calculation of the Gross National Product, which measures only the financial transactions in the economy. Cheryl Gillam, the energetic (salary-earning) Women's Minister in the last Conservative government returned from the Fourth World Conference on Women in Beijing in 1995 determined that Britain should follow suit. She persuaded fellow ministers, and in particular the Treasury, to accept the principle of producing what are called Household Satellite Accounts which attempt to compute the value of domestic labour. So the Office for National Statistics, formerly an offshoot of the Treasury, decided that from October 1997, for the first time since housework became a non-occupation in 1881, they were going to start putting a value on it.

According to economists who specialize in this area, if we were to put unpaid work in the UK measured in the Household Satellite Accounts alongside the official GNP, it would amount to between 56 per cent and 122 per cent of the entire economy, depending upon the rates of pay.[55] No mainstream voice is yet suggesting that housework should be paid for – after all, where would the money come from? The objective is simply to demonstrate how much effort and value resides in this sector. Some cynics argue that it was only because men have started to perform a small proportion of these tasks that the idea that they have any value has suddenly arisen, in the same way that worries about the low status of part-time work became more urgent when men experienced the consequences.

But assigning commercial worth to domestic labour can also be seen as a retrograde step, symptomatic of a society in which anything free is treated as valueless. Radical economists have argued that market values were always absent from the private sphere which depended upon other merits such as love, interdependence, loyalty.[56] Putting a financial price upon this effort simply converts everything into a purely commercial transaction and makes it part of the accountancy culture. But it seems inevitable that the only way that domestic effort can be assigned any social status is through financial value, because that is what a market-driven society dictates.

It is not only domestic work that has raised these paradoxes, but the whole sector of voluntary work and caring which has been associated with women. From meals on wheels to charity sales or helping out in schools – in almost every community there is a traditional shadow economy of voluntary good works which acts as a pillar of social support. According to very rough estimates, this kind of voluntary work is worth £11 billion (in potential wages) and its welfare role is a substantial one, from helping in hospitals to visiting the elderly.[57] The trouble is that as women have changed their relationship to the labour market, so their availability for voluntary work has become severely restricted. Citizens' Advice Bureaux (CABs) report that the profile of their voluntary advice workers has gradually changed. Instead of the traditional middle-aged woman who trains after the children grow up and remains an advice worker for many years, her modern equivalent is off working in the labour market. A typical advice worker now, certainly in urban areas, is a young graduate busy looking for transferable skills, who will use the experience gained through CAB work as a springboard into the job market.

Voluntary effort is no longer sought by women as an alternative career structure in the way that it used to be. Many women cannot afford to be a volunteer, and the better-off may feel that voluntary unpaid work, just like domestic work, does not have the kudos of paid employment. Sue was once a City solicitor, but after having children she returned to work as a part-time law centre volunteer. She is annoyed at the enormous disparity in status between the two roles, even though in both cases she is using her professional legal training. It becomes hard to imagine many of today's educated twenty-somethings as charity volunteers in their forties and fifties. Even organizations such as the National Childbirth Trust find it more difficult to sustain their culture of volunteers and mutual support as new mothers take less time off from paid work.

In the vast majority of cases, voluntary effort, like motherhood and apple pie, is an unquestioning force for good. Yet despite all the rhetoric about community and giving, the prevailing culture of work undermines the status of voluntary contribution. The alternative is to take a step backwards to question the relationship between work and other parts of life and to try to devise a harmonious way that working and caring can be best shared. And crucially this depends upon the relative status of paid and unpaid work. There has to be a mechanism where status is not dependent upon paid work and where non-paid activity, either at home or in the community, is genuinely accorded esteem and value. That is the only way that anyone, male or female, will want to do it.

Yet instead of this, the reverse is happening. The paid labour market is seen as the salvation for everyone. The commercial ethic is what matters, and the rhetoric of giving and caring sits uneasily alongside this imperative. For the young and childless this translates simply into the task of finding valuable work. It is later on that the contradictions emerge. As the gender stereotypes remain so resistant, either women have to do it all or they have to sub-contract some of the caring duties onto other, less well-paid women. The symmetrical family where everyone participates in paid and unpaid labour and contributes voluntary effort is a mirage. And for obvious reasons this kind of rearrangement can only take place when everyone moves together. The successful combination of paid and unpaid work is difficult enough. But if it is only women who are seeking this balancing between domestic labour, caring, voluntary effort and maintaining a position in the labour market in a world that values principally paid work, then the challenge becomes impossible in the long term. And so the question remains, why have men and the expectations of the male role hardly changed at all?

5

Men Holding the Line

Simone de Beauvoir was not the first or the last to observe that men are the norm. In her seminal work *The Second Sex*, published in 1949, she outlines the position of women as the 'other'.[1] Men are the central characters who are there to do, whilst women's function is to keep things (including the human race) going. And to misquote the Greek philosopher Protagoras it is still men, as in the male sex, that are 'the measure of all things'. This is the way our language and cultural assumptions have always worked, so that we have developed the strange habit of regarding all other groups, including that which makes up the majority (52 per cent) of the population, as 'other' to the mainstream. 'Being a woman is not yet a way of being a human being,' according to the philosopher Martha Nussbaum. When Michael Jackson went to run Channel 4 and (belatedly) criticized the BBC output as too masculine, a commentator observed that what he really meant was 'not that there are never any programmes about women . . . it was the fact that the way they are dealt with is as if they are a departure from the normal male world'.

The same is true of many other institutions. If a Martian landed on Earth and was given a tour of all the dominant centres of power she would return to her spacecraft with the view that the overwhelming majority of the population consisted of men in suits with a sprinkling here and there of skirts. If she started her British tour by visiting the law lords or the bishops, or the top echelons of the City, she would infer that the population was entirely male. (Howard Davies tells a story that in eighteen months as deputy-governor of the Bank of England he had to receive nearly 250 delegations of visiting bankers, and not a single one of them ever included a woman.) If Miss Martian looked in the newspaper obituary pages she would infer that far more men had lived (and were dying) than women. Hearing the Radio 3 compilation of the '100 most culturally influential individuals of the twentieth century' she might deduce that 10 per cent of the population were women – and most equivalent lists of notable achievers would give a broadly similar impression. Were she to take a tour of major company boardrooms she would assume the proportions to be roughly 98:2. When she reached Westminster this would reduce to 82:18. She would have to descend very many rungs down the institutional stepladder before she could correctly deduce that the inhabitants on Earth consisted of slightly more females than males.

It was this observation, that the male view was the standard by which women were perceived as a minority, which inspired the growth of the Women's Studies industry over the past three decades. Down the centuries there had always been occasional voices pointing out that men were in fact only half the picture, like those of Aphra Behn, Mary Wollstonecraft or the suffragettes. In 1869 J. S. Mill wrote in *The Subjection of Women* that 'the generality of the male sex cannot yet tolerate the idea of living with an equal. Were it not for that, I think that almost everyone would admit the injustice of excluding half the human race from the greater number of lucrative occupations.' In 1897 the American feminist Charlotte Perkins Gilman published *Herland*, a Utopian novel about what the world would be like if there were equal opportunities and participation for women. And in 1913 the first leader of the Labour Party, Keir Hardie, described 'the ferment among women' as 'far and away the most important event in the history of the world'.

During the 1970s Women's Studies emerged to tackle the imbalance. Academic courses, journals, publishing houses and university departments began placing women centre stage. Some of them took the view that women had made substantial contributions in many spheres – as scientists, artists, composers, managers – but their story had never been told. Others concluded that we were brainwashed into hearing the wrong story. History was not just about kings fighting wars. There was a whole parallel domestic world (herstory) which was equally significant. Women's Studies went on to explore new territories, such as feminist psychology and psychoanalysis. No longer would all academic study feature only the achievements of 'dead white males'.

As the Women's Studies industry developed, a paradox arose. If there were whole departments, university courses and publishing imprints devoted to analysing the position of women, where did that leave men? Men had hitherto been the accepted mainstream against which everything else, from feminist history to feminist economics was judged. So, gradually out of Women's Studies emerged Gender Studies. (In Ann Oakley's opinion 'women's studies' had to become 'gender studies' because the only real study is the study of men!) More forests were devoured to look at the crisis of masculinity. Robert Bly in the United States started the ball rolling in his book *Iron John*, which asserted that 'every modern male has lying at the bottom of his psyche a large primitive being covered with hair down to his feet'.[2] Then there was the much more appealing (and profitable) work of Nick Hornby, agonizing about what it means to be a 'bloke' in the 1990s. In between was a growing shelf of books with titles like *But What about Men?* or *What Next for Men?* And in the United States several colleges set up men's courses and workshops in 'How To Be a Man', designed to 'explore men's experience as gendered beings'.

In a sense Bly and the others were trying to secure their own place for men as contemporary victims. There had been a continuing emphasis upon the culture of victimhood since around the late sixties. Much of the early feminist theory depicted women as victims and this theme continues in the work of writers like Andrea Dworkin. Racial minorities and persecuted religious groups could of course claim to have their own status as victims. And now men in the form of Iron John and all his followers wanted to join in. Men as we have always known them are now an endangered, threatened species they argued, because the rules of the game are changing.

The Jungian analyst Andrew Samuels believes that what is happening to men is that after centuries the 'male deal' is starting to falter.

> In the male deal the little boy at around four or five years old strikes a bargain with the social world in which he lives. If he will turn away from soft things, feminine things, maternal things . . . and become the trad men we all know, then the world will reward him by giving him all the goodies in its

possession. In return for the gift of power he promises to be a good provider and keep unruly and subversive women and children in their places.[3]

A man is a full-time, lifetime worker, without deviation. This is written deep into the psyche, that a man *is* his job; from brain surgeon to plumber. Conversely a man without a job is not really a man at all. When a large US steel company began closing plants in the early 1980s, it offered to train the displaced steelworkers for new jobs.

> But the training never 'took'; the workers drifted into unemployment and odd jobs instead. Psychologists came in to find out why, and found the steelworkers suffering from acute identity crises. How could I do anything else? asked the workers 'I AM a lathe operator.'[4]

Since the concept of a 'job' was first invented for men during the Industrial Revolution, the paramount status associated with having one has become ever more important. The Marx Brothers joke would no longer sound so funny when they quipped that 'If work was so good why didn't the rich do it?' They do. And frequently they work very long hours indeed. The occupation of gentleman has disappeared, and today we talk about the 'work-rich' as opposed to the 'work-poor'. Even the Queen's youngest son has to work, of course not for financial reasons but because he has to be seen to have a job, to *be* a television producer. And asking any man what he is or does will bring the response, I am a . . . Job. Rare indeed is the fellow who will answer, I am a father, or a husband. It is more likely to be, I am unemployed.

The Redundant Male

It is difficult to overestimate the devastation that unemployment causes for the majority of men who experience it. Many report that their entire sense of self falls apart when they lose their job. A research project in west Yorkshire in 1983 revealed that a decline in sexual potency was a not uncommon result of unemployment; in the interviews some women responded, 'A man's not a man without a job.' The 80 per cent rise in male suicide over the past ten years is partly attributed to unemployment. Male suicides outnumber female by four to one. In recent years more men than women have been calling the Samaritans, and the Royal College of Psychiatrists issued a special factsheet in 1996 which targeted men, and in particular young men, to help them handle depression.

In 1997 the low-budget but highly popular film *The Full Monty* captured the despair of a group of unemployed Sheffield steel workers who eventually turned themselves into a male strip show. The most vivid and disturbing character of all was the displaced foreman desperately clinging on to his petit bourgeois habits and status, symbolized by his garden full of gnomes. But most pathetic of all was that for six months after he was made redundant he could not bring himself to tell his wife that he no longer had a job. He went through the charade of dressing and leaving for work each morning, as she ran up frightening sums on the credit cards. The motivation behind his elaborate pretence was totally convincing. And the symbolism of the film was perfect. For a man like him not to have a job was the equivalent of appearing naked in public.

A great deal is heard about the rising insecurity of the middle classes. Yet the phenomenon of white-collar and middle-management unemployment is comparatively recent. It is blue-collar men from the heavy manufacturing sector, predominantly in the North, who have suffered most. The decline and disappearance of these industries over the past twenty years has been a catastrophe for millions of unskilled and semi-skilled men who have been thrown on the unemployment scrap heap. As the coal mines, steel mills and shipyards closed down, men in their thirties and forties were sent home never to find regular work again. Today their sons leave school with no prospect of entering the lifetime jobs that their grandfathers and fathers had taken for granted. The statistics of male unemployment are grim. In some households there are teenage boys who are the third generation unemployed. Average male unemployment on some council estates is 50 per cent.[5]

Yet the world beyond the official statistics is even more depressing. In the 1980s the civil service elevated rewriting and redefining the unemployment figures into a highly creative art form. Frank Field, the former Minister for Social Security, once counted thirty different revisions to the way the totals were calculated, twenty-nine of which meant that officially recognized unemployment became ever lower.[6] The eventual outcome was that an estimated 2 million unemployed men were no longer counted as looking for work, and dropped out of the system. Today only one person in five of working age, who is not working, is classified as unemployed.[7] The critical measure now is not 'unemployed' but also covers many of the 'economically inactive', a term that is conveniently opaque,[8] including for example discouraged workers who have given up looking for work or those drawing incapacity and ill-health benefits. This latter category has increased inexorably, despite there being no evidence that overall health of the working population is declining. In 1997 the government highlighted the relentless growth in ill-health benefits as part of its campaign on welfare reform. It pointed to the uncanny correlation of high rates of invalidity and sick pay with areas of high unemployment. In the Welsh former mining town of Merthyr Tydfil – the sickness capital of Britain – a staggering rate of 24 per cent of the working population claim sickness and invalidity benefit.[9] The implication was that officialdom had colluded in this as a convenient way of trimming the unemployment figures. Between 1977 and 1991 official male unemployment (defined as those claiming benefit and looking for work) rose from 5.1 per cent to 9.4 per cent. But the percentage of working-age men without jobs rose from 9 per cent to 18 per cent. Estimates of real unemployment put the figure at closer to 4 million. According to some economists, by 1992 one third of low-skill men were not in employment.[10] And there are stubborn structural patterns to the distribution of unemployment, even during a period of economic boom, so that in 1997 for young black men leaving school with no qualifications the jobless figure was 80 per cent.[11] The Labour government has poured billions of pounds into its New Deal to offer training and work to the under twenty-fives who are prepared to accept them, but there are still millions of older men who face a future without steady employment. And the emphasis of Labour's ambitious New Deal programme is upon smoothing the path for the excluded to enter work. The question of the kinds of jobs available to them when they work remains unanswered. There is no magic wand on offer to recreate a labour market of stable, secure jobs with attractive pay, conditions and prospects.

The social consequences of men not having work are immense. Imagine a neighbourhood in which most women of working age are not in paid jobs. This might conjure up a picture of tidy homes, children playing, laundry drying, and women chattering over the garden fence. But what if most of the young men are not working? The picture now is a more sinister one – of crime, disorder and decay. Non-working men are feckless and trouble. Non-working women are mothers. There is no doubt that the availability of motherhood as a significant, indeed central, identity generally makes redundancy much less devastating for women than for men.[12]

For the men in some communities there are parallels with the Luddites who raged against the new industrial order two hundred years ago. Only this time the file servers and robots are well secured or production has disappeared abroad, so that rage and violence are frequently turned upon their own community. Appropriately it is in many of the areas of the original Industrial Revolution that the disarray and dislocation are felt most acutely.

Crime has typically been a young man's game. Confidential surveys funded by the Home Office reveal that up to one third of young men when guaranteed anonymity will admit that they have committed a crime (other than drug use and motoring offences). Historically, with better employment prospects, the crime rate dropped sharply when young men reached their early twenties and were settling down. Now that no longer happens. According to the Home Office research, the proportion of men involved in property theft now *increases* in the mid-twenties, pointing to the rising number of 'career criminals'.[13] The same report concludes that the lack of the prospect of a stable job makes it difficult for many young men to become responsible adults. For girls the picture is different. Although the rate of property theft amongst teenage girls is almost as high as for boys, by the age of twenty-two it has sharply declined, with only a tiny number of young women still committing such crimes.

The conservative right frets loudly about the decline of the family and the rise in the numbers of single mothers. But when theoreticians like Charles Murray or politicians like John Redwood (in his incarnation as a former Welsh Secretary) complain about unmarried mothers, they fail to observe what is happening to potential fathers. The distinguished American sociologist William Julius Wilson has studied mass male joblessness in inner-city Chicago and looked at the correlation of work and marriage. He devised a 'marriageability index' to describe whether a man is an attractive economic prospect and worth marrying. The ratio of marriageable young black men to women has dropped dramatically, to the extent that the marriageable young black male is a threatened species.[14] The number of babies born to young black women in their late teens and early twenties has not changed much over three decades. What has changed is the likelihood that they will be married to the father.

It is the US inner city that has seen the sharpest rise in the fatherless society. There are nearly two hundred areas in the national census in the US in which more than 90 per cent of the homes with children lack a father. Aside from deprivation, the social consequences of absentee fathering can be devastating. In his book *No Matter How Loud I Shout*, Edward Humes describes a year in the life of the Central Juvenile Court in Los Angeles.[15] It is a grim account from the very front line of delinquency and youth crime. In this community fathers are hardly in evidence. A clear link emerges between the lack of resident fathers and the increasingly violent, sometimes psychopathic, juvenile crime wave in the USA.

It has become very fashionable to talk about fathers and their significance. Yet for every man who glories in the new discovery of fatherhood – busy changing nappies the way his father never did – there are many others who have almost no involvement with their offspring. Steve Biddulph, the best-selling Australian family therapist, sometimes described as the present-day heir to Dr Spock, urges fathers to become more involved for the sake of their sons.[16] He argues that the contemporary malady, attention deficit disorder, may indeed be more accurately described as 'dad deficit disorder'. The trouble is that fathering cannot have it both ways. If paternal attention is valuable and significant then it cannot be an optional, contingent ingredient – nice when you can get it but not vitally necessary. Adrienne Burgess, who has become a guru of fatherhood, is deeply concerned about paternal neglect and the key role that a father's presence can have in the prevention of delinquency – especially amongst young boys.[17] According to Burgess fatherhood has had a bad press and we tend to overlook the fact that in nearly all circumstances, rich and poor, the continuing presence of a father has a positive and beneficial effect. She goes on to report the startling observation that even where a father himself has a criminal record, his sons are less likely to get into trouble if he is at home and plays a regular role in their upbringing.

In Britain a similar pattern to that in the US is emerging. Young uneducated men who are likely to be unemployed are most commonly the fathers of the teenage mother's children, but if they cannot be a provider, what is the point of marriage? On one occasion when Peter Lilley, as Social Security Secretary, was fulminating about single mothers his civil servants produced two national maps: one depicting the highest incidences of single mothers and the other illustrating male unemployment. The correlation was remarkable. Men who cannot support a family do not form one; nor are women eager to marry them. This is hardly surprising when study after study shows that when men are asked to define their role, being a good provider remains top of the list. Perversely, according to the British Social Attitudes Survey, it is those men with the least education who are the most likely to agree with the proposition that 'a husband's job is to earn the

money; a wife's job is to look after home and family'.[18] For these
are the men who are least likely to be able to earn enough to support a family. So fatherhood ends at conception.

Of course many women have historically been left to bring up
children alone, typically in wartime. Even in peacetime the armed
forces' employment of poorly educated men left many thousands
of women at home alone, holding the baby, but this was seen as a
respectable route for family life. The absent father with his pay
packet from the state, remained the provider, and the arrangement had communal support. Today the army has followed heavy
industry and has little call for the uneducated, low-skilled man
any more. So another route to stable family life is shut off.

Charles Murray and others insist that for 'young male barbar-
ians', marriage is an 'indispensable civilising force' whilst
simultaneously offering an alternative to 'welfare motherhood'.
But this completely misses the point. For many of these unskilled
young men, the lack of secure employment is not a temporary blip
which will disappear when the economy picks up. It is a permanent way of life which is the result of fundamental economic
restructuring. So they can offer no prospect to the (single) mother
of acting as provider or breadwinner. Economically marriage will
make no difference to the single mother and frequently the benefit system means she could be worse off. Emotionally these men
have had no chance to advance beyond adolescence because the
central rite of passage of becoming a worker has never taken place.
The anthropologist Margaret Mead observed that 'in every known
human society everywhere in the world the young male learns
that when he grows up one of the things which he must do in
order to be a full member of society is to provide food for some
female and her young . . . every known human society rests firmly
on the learned nurturing behaviour of men'.[19] So if a man can no

longer provide, the age-old process whereby men are civilized within marriage can no longer take place. They remain mired in a Peter Pan netherworld of casual sex and crime.

For many conservatives like the former Tory MP Derek Coombs, 'the absence of responsible adult men in many poor neighbourhoods is one of the great social disasters of our times. The flight from fatherhood has arisen because the link between sex and commitment has been broken.'[20] They lament the consequences of this collapse of commitment for children born into a fly-by-night society , with no model of stability and self-esteem. Conservative US theorists like Francis Fukuyama talk about the 'great disruption' which includes the sharp deterioration in the social status of unskilled and uneducated men. They observe the growing 'moral irresponsibility' of men towards the women whose children they father.

> A kind of moral vicious circle emerges. . . . as women become
> more economically independent, men become less morally
> obligated to them and their children; as men become less
> reliable as economic providers, women in self-defence begin
> to acquire better education and skills so as to be financially
> self-sufficient, reinforcing in turn the diminishing male sense
> of responsibility toward them.[21]

Characterizing these changes in terms of moral decay does not help. It is the critical absence of the means of becoming a grown-up that is at the heart of the problem, and for a man this has always been synonymous with acquiring a full-time job. Yet there are different patterns of caring behaviour and responsibility towards others that could equally well be considered, if only we could widen the concept of what is accepted male behaviour, and if only a man without a lifelong full-time job were not a social outcast.

The inability to grow up is something that Robert Bly is very concerned about in his most recent book, *The Sibling Society,* where he makes some powerful points about a society where adults remain childish and children never become adults.

> . . . the unprecedented failure of fathering in our time will have effects to the sixth and seventh generations . . . the increasing dislike of human beings by human beings concentrates itself in the current neglect of children. Perhaps this is the first time in human history that children, en masse, have picked up the idea that they are not wanted, not needed.[22]

The point about children is well made in a culture which paradoxically views them both as objects of abuse and alternatively as new consumers and designer objects. But the whole question about failing to grow up is critically relevant to that section of the community that has so tragically become excluded from the mainstream – predominantly the uneducated, unemployed young man. This is the fallacy of the so-called men's movement: it takes a dilemma that confronts a specific group of men and tries to apply that to society as a whole. Blue-collar men are in trouble at work and at home, but from that we are supposed to conclude that *all* men in our society are under threat.

Some of the literature of the men's movement is like reading *Alice* [or *Albert*] *in Wonderland*. Not only are all men threatened, but women are to blame. According to *The Myth of Male Power* by the American men's movement advocate Warren Farrell, modern man is 'a slave by any other name'.[23] He is forced into studying boring and unpleasant subjects like science and engineering because these will yield a higher-paid job. Women can study fun things, like literature and languages, because they are not under such pressure to earn a decent living. Boys at school have to repress interests in art, history or languages because they will not pay enough to support their family. In their spare time as adolescents boys are 'forced to choose lawn mowing rather than babysitting' because they need money to take a girl out and presumably grass-cutting is more lucrative. It did not seem to occur to Warren Farrell, who refers to himself as a 'feminist', that the gender of the worker might determine the pay and status of the job in the first place. His assertions become increasingly bizarre as signs of men's slavery are spotted everywhere. Men, according to Farrell, have been forced into putting more effort into creating safe homes and gardens for their wives than into making safe coal mines and construction sites for themselves. And it is blatantly unfair that more men are in prison and suffer capital punishment.

The contemporary British version of men's liberation tells a similar story of hardship. It reveals, for example, that women are more likely to carry out domestic violence than men. Men cannot reasonably take on more domestic tasks because they do more work outside the home. In the media, it says, men are denigrated as a result of thirty years of psychological, social and political brainwashing. Men have been made to suffer by the 'feminist victimology' industry which includes bodies as diverse as the National Lottery Charities Board in the way it awards grants and of course the Equal Opportunities Commission. In January 1997 words became deeds when the national UK Men's Movement was launched at the Pike and Eel pub near Cambridge with the slogan 'For evil to triumph it is only necessary for good men to do nothing.' This was men's answer, twenty-seven years later, to the 1970

Ruskin College conference that launched the women's liberation movement in Britain.

A strange assortment of men joined forces at the Pike and Eel to complain loudly about the 'greatest social evil of our time' – feminism.[24] Some of them made quite well-substantiated points about the lack of equity in custody arrangements, and about uneven pension provision, but most of the outrage against women's apparently superior position and the yearning for 'a restoration of patriarchy' was not quite so grounded in reason. Take Edward Crabtree and Clive Potter, who were active at the Pike and Eel and who style themselves the Equality Squad of Leicester. These men, both unemployed graduates, have devoted their full-time energies to taking the local authority through complicated legal procedures over library opening hours. Leicester has a large Asian population and initiated a women's-only session at a local library so that Muslim women could use the facilities. The Equality Squad pursued a 'crusade', taking Leicestershire County Council to court to stop the weekly session. They persuaded the Equal Opportunities Commission to agree that such a session is potentially discriminatory, but they were angry that the EOC would not fund the legal costs of the challenge.

The EOC and all it is supposed to represent is a key target of the men's movement. Ironically the EOC and the way it is constituted have been criticized by women for lacking the critical legal and political muscle needed to enforce equal rights effectively. (The stubbornly wide pay gap between men and women discussed in Chapter 2 is a continuing reminder of the slow rate of progress.) However, the nascent men's movement takes a different view. Their stated intention is to undermine the Commission and bring about its abolition, partly by overwhelming the system with complaints from men. In 1996, for the first time, the number of

complaints from men (820) about unfair practice in job recruit-
ment outnumbered those from women (803). It is not clear
whether this outnumbering resulted from deliberate sabotage by
grumpy men, or whether men are just much better at complain-
ing. As Woody Allen famously said, 'If women get a headache,
then men get a tumour.' Or more commonly, when women get a
cold, men get the flu.

The tendency of men to overreact is everywhere. In 1997 when
three adverts appeared that reversed gender stereotypes and poked
fun at men there was a collective gasp of horror in the tabloids and
on the chat shows. A Lee Jeans ad showed a women's stiletto-
heel boot resting on the buttock of a naked man with the slogan
'Put the boot in'; a Nissan ad had a man clutching his crotch with
the line 'Ask before you borrow', and the 'Dress to Kill' campaign for Wallis stores had men in danger of being killed because
distracted by beautiful women. The Advertising Standards
Authority received nearly a hundred complaints deploring what
was seen as tasteless, inappropriate material. The authority did not
uphold the complaints, but it warned agencies to think twice about
using such 'girl power' imagery. What was conveniently overlooked was that for thirty years much of the ad industry's output –
from washing powder to car advertisements – had consisted of
material that was patronizing, humiliating and offensive to
women. It has never caused a murmur of concern that ad men
devised a whole genre of adverts known as the 'two cunts in a
kitchen' scenario.

When a report identifying a growing trend of female violence
was published in November 1996 and used as the basis for a BBC
Panorama programme, it caused a huge media stir. The headlines
said that in thousands of households women were attacking their
husbands. Men beating women is not a story, it is simply part of

life's rich tapestry. Women beating men (no matter how few are involved) is not only a story but a cause for pandemonium. As soon as men are subjected to a fraction of what women have had to put up with for centuries the world needs not only to hear about it but to take action. The whole well-publicized phenomenon of women acting violently and the rise of the so-called girl gangs bring widespread media revulsion and shock, but we are not told that the numbers are still, by comparison with male violence, very small indeed.

The growth in female crime is also a myth. A sober look at the facts shows that what has really grown is not the crime rate but the female prison population, as a result of a far harsher sentencing climate. The tendency of judges to operate a double standard and deal more harshly with female crime has not abated. In five years the female prison population rose by an extraordinary 76 per cent, over twice the rate of increase for men. There is general panic alleging the existence of more women criminals, yet the National Association of Probation Officers has shown that there has been no perceptible rise in serious crime by women, and convictions for serious offences have declined in five years.[25]

The panic about boys under-performing at secondary school follow a similar pattern of hysterical disregard for the facts which show that over the long term both boys and girls have improved results – but boys have not improved as fast as girls. Commissions of inquiry are set up to investigate why boys are now falling behind girls, after centuries of being ahead. The topic was even designated an official theme of Britain's EU presidency in 1998. And it is not only the tabloid newspapers or the rather sad creatures of the men's movement who overreact to any real or imagined change in gender shift. The 'women are taking over . . . men are emasculated' thesis is everywhere.

Piers Paul Read, an author in love with traditional values, complains about the lack of a role any more for men and the increasing role for women. Richard Gott – formerly the *Guardian*'s literary editor – observes that both his literary agent and his publisher are now women, whereas thirty years ago both were men, because 'publishing is one of many industries that now seem to be almost wholly dominated by women' and men have been 'relegated to the status of also rans and drones'.[26] The same kind of observations are made in many other fields, but when the evidence is properly analysed the myth of female domination evaporates. It may be true that women in publishing are now no longer entirely confined to making the tea and PR small talk; in recent years a few have reached more senior positions. Yet to deduce from this that women have taken over and now run all the major publishing conglomerates is far from the truth. As for literary agents, there are more women agents today, but they are often running their own small-scale operations, having left the corporate mainstream after becoming disillusioned. This is precisely the type of Me & Co activity that women can embrace when corporate life no longer works out. It is hardly comparable to running ICI or BP. The scale of the 'women are everywhere' complaints gives the impression that women are storming City boardrooms and occupying more than their fair share of senior positions (maybe 50 per cent). Yet at the end of 1996 women reached the dizzy heights of constituting 1 per cent of chief executives of the FTSE top 100 companies. Marjorie Scardino, who became the boss of the media conglomerate Pearson, is the first (and so far the only) woman ever to achieve such a position.

Confusion and inaccuracies arise because a woman in a senior position is so much more visible than her colleagues. When a woman is appointed to a high-flying job, we are immediately told

all about her, and especially about her looks, her clothes, her
domestic life. Marjorie Scardino's appointment merited major
profiles everywhere, even in the middle-market papers like the
Daily Mail, along with loaded questions as to whether she was
really up to the job. A lengthy profile in the *Independent on Sunday*
included remarks about whether she would now have to sharpen
up what was judged as her hitherto inadequate clothes sense.
When Pearson's share price slid 11p on her appointment, a City
analyst muttered that 'this was because she was an unknown commodity'. A few months later when Pearson announced excellent
results, the press coverage made very little reference to the gender
of the boss. But shortly afterwards when Ann Iverson was ousted
from the top of Laura Ashley because of poor results, extensive
amounts of newsprint were devoted to detailing her domestic life,
appearance, love affairs and asking the question 'Is a woman really
up to all this?' Meanwhile most of the other 99 FTSE-100 chief
executives (Richard Branson does *not* head a public company)
stay firmly hidden in the business pages, their clothes sense and
domestic arrangements of interest to no one.

   This same phenomenon of the media treating women as a freak
show happens again and again. If a man moves from one faceless
City institution to another, or is accused of poaching some junior
pension management staff, it may conceivably make a small paragraph on an inside page of the *Financial Times*, although the news
would more likely be confined to a trade paper. But in January
1997 when Nicola Horlick did this, the story was splashed repeatedly over front pages large and small. All the usual columnists –
tabloid and broadsheet – weighed in with observations on her
actions, appearance and lifestyle. A lengthy special report on
ITN's *News At Ten* provided details of Ms Horlick's domestic
arrangements, including who did the hoovering and the laundry.

A man would have to be a celebrity or football superstar to merit this kind of attention when he left his job. The star presenter Chris Evans made a highly acrimonious departure from BBC Radio 1 in the same week that Nicola Horlick left Morgan Grenfell, but he received slightly less coverage, and no one expressed interest in whether he did any hoovering. The excessive and noisy coverage of stories such as Nicola Horlick's superficially reinforces the impression that 'women are taking over'. A simple headcount tells a different story. It is the *potential* of women to occupy more powerful positions that causes so much concern – the reality is still a long way off. As the American writer Susan Faludi observed, 'Nothing seems to crush the masculine petals more than a bit of feminist rain – a few drops are perceived as a downpour.'[27]

A handful of exceptional women have reached senior positions in some fields. But the reactions to such achievements are out of all proportion to the reality of what has happened. At its extreme this resentment about the perceived and potential advance of women has manifested itself in acts of violence. The Central Park Mugger in New York targeted apparently successful yuppie women whom he blamed for his inadequacies. According to traffic police in the US and the UK, some incidents of road rage are the result of men becoming incensed at the sight of an apparently successful woman driving an expensive fast car. In 1995 the US writer Thomas Edsall Jnr even attributed the murderous anger of the Oklahoma bomber Timothy McVeigh to women's rising expectations and opportunities on the basis that a seismic upheaval had left men with a poor economic future. According to Edsall, men are left with 'a private sense of siege, voiced most often only in quiet tones at lunch or more angrily over beer after work'.[28]

Even when the backlash does not explode in violence there are strange reactions amongst certain American men. In the last few years some of the biggest political demonstrations seen in the US have been the Million Man March and the hugely popular all-male movement of the Promise Keepers, both of which are manifestations of men wanting to return to traditional values. The quid pro quo in this desire for return is that men will only keep to the straight and narrow, fulfil their promises to their family and society, if they are once again the undisputed boss – both in public and private. In order to behave properly, men need the 'patriarchal bonus'.

Men's Work, Women's Work

Men have lost a role and women are taking over. These are the thrusts of the backlash that urges a return to 'old values'. Yet the men who have really lost out – uneducated young unemployed – have not suffered because women have taken over a few key jobs. This is another inconvenient fact that is frequently avoided. During the 1980s, President Reagan asserted that the ideal economic scenario was for men to be paid a family wage and for women to leave the labour market and stop competing with men for work. Similar arguments came from other parts of the political spectrum. In the UK, Frank Field, the former Minister for Social Security, argued that in the contemporary labour market women are finding jobs at the expense of men.[29] On the left, concerns that at the very least women are undercutting pay scales because they will work for less, are not uncommon.

The truth is rather more complicated and uncomfortable. The types of job which are traditionally considered women's work – frequently service sector occupations – have often been regarded as marginal. In many cases they were not unionized at all, particularly in areas such as the catering industry. Even when there was some union involvement these were seen as pin money jobs, part-time and not significant like the 'real' occupations which brought home the 'family wage'. Male-dominated unions were not unduly concerned with achieving good pay for mere women's work and frequently opposed the notion of equality 'because it might threaten the family wage'. Until the 1970s women barely featured in mainstream trade union activity. Baroness Brenda Dean, who was a powerful force in the union movement over several decades in an atmosphere that was loath to address women's priorities, now sees that the men whose concerns dominated the union agenda eventually found themselves marginalized and downgraded in a new industrial landscape.[30]

Today the tale of two workforces has changed. The heavy industries that provided the 'real' and historically well-paid jobs have shrunk. Meanwhile the service sector and the traditional areas of women's work have expanded and will continue to grow. Over 90 per cent of new jobs on offer nowadays are in the service sector. But frequently the response from unemployed men is that they do not want to do women's work and they will not work for 'rubbish' women's lower wages. An ICM Research poll in 1996 found that six out of ten unemployed men would not apply for what they considered a woman's job.[31] And on average when they were asked about how much they would settle for above the benefit level – what economists call the reservation wage – men wanted 25 per cent more than women to give up benefit and take a job. Interestingly this almost coincides with the average differential between men and women's pay.

In 1996 the Channel 4 programme *Genderquake* set up some unemployed Merseyside men with the kind of stereotypically female jobs – dinner lady, receptionist, chambermaid – they would never previously have considered. Although some, but not all, of them coped quite well with the traditionally female tasks and the female working environment, all agreed in the end that it was not worth carrying on working for wages that were only marginally above the benefit level. Yet it is largely low-paid service-sector jobs, requiring nimble fingers or people skills, that are on offer in areas of high male unemployment.

Many of the Far Eastern companies that have opened factories in the UK have predominantly female assembly lines, the women workers arranged in neat rows wearing white overalls and elasti-cized hats. In areas such as Merseyside by the mid-nineties there were already more women than men in work. Does this mean that the future is female and that the men's movement, and all their associated hangers-on, were right after all? The catch is that this is not a future of empowered and successful women striding into the top jobs, but a future of poorly paid, low-status, mainly service-sector employment. The criticism of women 'taking away men's jobs' or 'bringing down rates of pay' is sadly misplaced. The men's jobs have gone and it is women's jobs that are now left.

Men who have been displaced from the labour market are often in a state of collective shock. They search in vain for another 'male' job, in anticipation of the wages they earned in their old position as a shipyard worker, say, or a miner. Frequently what is on offer at the Job Centre is very different and at vastly lower rates of pay. Even where there are still 'male' jobs available – typ-ically vacancies for security guards – the pay and conditions are very different from what a former coalface worker is used to. Those former miners in the early 1990s who were lucky enough to find work saw their wages drop on average by 30 per cent.[32] A man used to earning up to £400 a week finds it hard to come to terms with the fact that in 1997 the starting wage for a security guard was sometimes as low as £2 an hour, along with minimal sick pay and holiday entitlement because of the nature of the 'temporary contract'; in some cases the employee had to buy his own uniform. A Job Centre, advertising for a security guard near Barnsley, listed an additional requirement: 'Bring your own dog.' Many redundant men seek retraining courses in trades like painting and decorating, with the result that some former areas of heavy industry, like south Yorkshire, are now full of painters and decorators with no customers.

The adjustments are not just in the labour market. A man who is no longer the principal family breadwinner frequently has to invent a new identity in the home. Some can adapt to this, but others find the stereotypes too deeply ingrained. Gary, a former Nottinghamshire miner unable to find another job, has come to terms with looking after his working wife and child. 'It's only when I see myself through other people's eyes, like when a travelling salesman rings the doorbell and I answer it in my apron, holding a duster, that I feel embarrassed that he'll think I'm not a proper man.' David, in Lancashire, has also had to adjust to being a father at home, but he experienced a crisis of machismo at the beginning when 'meeting a friend and having to tell him "I do what your missus does – I wear the skirt in this family"'. For those not in a stable relationship when unemployment strikes, the tendency is to stay at home, looked after by mum. This is another way in which the economic landscape has infantilized men. The numbers of people in their twenties still living in their parental home has risen in the past ten years, and boys of this age living at home substantially outnumber girls. In 1996 nearly one in four men aged 25–29 was living with his parents, compared with one in five in 1991. This is the first time the figure has risen since records began twenty years ago. And even amongst men 30–34 years old, one in nine of them is still at home being looked after by mum – which is 20 per cent more than five years ago.[33]

Back to Basics

The inconvenient facts about the current changes in the labour market and the deskilling and disappearance of 'men's jobs' are pushed away in favour of a narrative of return. If women would return to being women, to staying at home and looking after children, men could be men and go out to work. In one stroke unemployment would be solved and children would once again be properly cared for, instead of roaming the streets and getting into trouble. Serious academics like Francis Fukuyama argue that there is a close correlation between working women and the breakdown in the family, which in turn is linked to 'a host of related social pathologies'.[34] Nevertheless, Fukuyama agrees that it is probably impractical to turn the clock back and remove women from the labour market; he agrees that it now makes more sense to look at changing male behaviour.

There are plenty of others who take a less measured approach, insisting that men are incapable of change and can only remain civilized if things go back to the way they always were. The threat is that if we do not put men back in charge and assure them of status in the workplace, the future will be nasty and brutish. This is the story told in *The Frog, the Prince and the Problem of Men*, written by Geoff Dench and published appropriately by Neanderthal Books in 1994. Men have a greater moral right to work, Dench argues, and must be rewarded by higher public status because 'if women go for freedom, men will just take even more freedom for themselves and that way lies the dark ages'. But, he adds, women secretly want men to have additional rewards and be in charge too, as 'the nature of society is such that the chains of sacrifice originate with and are initiated by women'. So the answer according to Dench is to withdraw state support and benefits from women and 'water the roots of male motivation', because expecting men to take on any different role is quite impossible. Men don't 'do' childrearing and domestic duties; their role is earning a family wage.

There are many who nod vigorously at this analysis and argue that the solution must be to try and remove women from the workforce by making it more difficult for them to work outside the home. The more extreme hint that too much education led women to be dissatisfied with their lot in the first place, and that if women do not return to their true role then society will pay a terrible price. Some of these warnings have echoes of science fiction about them, with talk of the 'sex change state' raising the spectre of a grim, genderless future if men are unable to be 'properly male' and are emasculated by too much domestic caring. Like all backlash rhetoric the facts are ignored in favour of gross exaggeration.

At its extreme this scenario completely fails to understand the economic restructuring that underlies why many women are working in the first place, often in jobs that men do not want because they are demeaning and underpaid. In the era of so-called 'flexible markets' it is probably too late to demand better pay and higher status for these jobs, beyond the implementation of the minimum wage, which is hugely significant for women. Moreover, employers may (illegally) prefer to hire women. When guaranteed anonymity some employers will admit that they prefer women because they are more docile, conscientious, personable and, of course, willing to work for less.[35] Just as in the early nineteenth century employers were prepared to use women or even children as a useful source of cheap labour in the mines or the factories, some economists argue that the female labour force today functions as the soft underbelly.[36] In contemporary jargon, globalization often means employers transferring production (and even some services) to countries like China or India in order to benefit from an uncomplaining workforce accustomed to low pay and meagre conditions: a wage of 20p an hour is not uncommon for making greeting cards or plastic bags. The workers share beds in a grim dormitory and there are no problems like sick pay or similar overheads. A company relocates its less complicated production and the bill for labour is transformed. When this transfer abroad is not feasible, employers have found that using a female instead of a male workforce is another way of reducing labour costs.

The recent fate of the Liverpool dockers was an extreme case of this pattern of changing labour markets. Unlike many other blue-collar male labour forces, the UK economy still has a need for dockers (albeit far fewer of them than in the past). Historically this was an industry where trade unions were highly organized – achieving enviable wages and conditions for their members. By the 1990s the port authorities wanted to reduce labour costs, but in this case they could neither transfer the work abroad to benefit from cheap foreign labour, nor substitute local women. The only route for cutting costs has been to squeeze the existing male labour force hard in a context where male manual employment opportunities were at a premium. Dockers' pay and conditions were dramatically reduced which led to a lengthy and bitter dispute on Merseyside – much to the embarrassment of the Labour Party before and after the 1997 general election (in the name of the dockers the pop group Chumbawumba drenched the deputy prime minister John Prescott with the contents of an ice bucket during the 1998 Brit Awards). The same attack on pay and conditions has occurred in many other industries but where it did not happen so directly, there were fewer opportunities for industrial action.

The transformation in the labour market since the last recession is different from previous economic cycles. From the start of the 'family wage' in the nineteenth century, women were regarded as a 'reserve army' of labour. When they were required, in boom periods or particularly in wartime, conditions were magically created that allowed them to work. During the First World War the female labour force rapidly expanded to undertake a wide range of occupations. After 1918 these women were no longer needed, and during the Depression years they were seen as threatening jobs that rightfully belonged to men. The result was a formal ban on the employment of married women in certain fields, such as teaching, nursing or the civil service. Women were dismissed upon marriage, so that jobs could be available to men and single women. There were special appeal panels where women with incapacitated or alcoholic husbands could plead their case to be allowed to work. Retired midwives still recall removing their wedding ring when they went to work, in order not to betray their married status. Interestingly when the BBC introduced its marriage ban in 1932 it generously agreed that charwomen and lavatory attendants would be exempted because 'it was a normal custom for women of this class to have outside employment'. The marriage ban was an effective instrument in exiling those women who were no longer wanted from the labour force.[37]

During the Second World War women were once again in huge demand. Nurseries were set up. (There were more nursery places in 1945 than in 1997.) Using daycare and going out to work were socially acceptable, even to the leader writers of the *Daily Mail*. Women were encouraged to occupy a range of jobs, albeit at rates of pay that were sometimes as low as half of that earned by an equivalent man. Strict union agreements helped to make sure that women were not given the same status and remuneration as men. When the crisis was over and women were no longer required they were simply dispensed with. Some nurseries were shut down overnight, without warning, after VJ Day. Women were exhorted to stop working and go home to fulfil their real function. The popular media echoed the words of the psychologist John Bowlby in his well-publicized work on the serious effects upon young children of maternal deprivation. Those who quoted Bowlby's evidence about the consequences for young children of not being looked after by their mother usually forgot to mention that his studies were principally of the highly disturbed inmates of children's homes, typically war orphans, not of children whose mothers returned home to them each afternoon. The way his work was interpreted made some women fearful even of leaving a child with someone while they did the shopping, in case this caused irreparable psychological damage. According to the novelist Fay Weldon, 'he wrote about the trauma of mother–child separation so forcibly that he terrified a whole generation of middle-class women into clutching their children's hands every minute of their dependency'.[38] In this climate there was no danger that women in the postwar period would stray back to work.

Today women are no longer treated as the reserve army of labour, and when jobs are tight they are not being laid off in favour of men. In areas of high unemployment there is no evidence that women are leaving assembly lines or service jobs so that men can take their place; instead the opposite has happened.

Part-time, low-paid women have tended increasingly to substitute for the full-time army of men. The modern economy has created jobs for which women are preferred. The stereotypical image of a modern workplace features rows of women with headphones answering queries or selling services at a customer call centre, instead of men in overalls smelting steel or mining coal.

Will this be a permanent feature of the labour market? Some economists believe that eventually men could be forced to accept the lower levels of pay and conditions, partly through restructuring the benefit system. Effectively their 'reservation wage' – the level below which they are not prepared to work – will drop. The notion of 'women's work' will then disappear. Men will have to adapt, and a whole new breed of male service worker will emerge. There may even be dinnermen serving school lunches and chambermen making the beds in hotels. At that point women's function as a kind of Trojan horse will be complete and they will again be displaced from the workforce, by means of the advocacy of a return to traditional family values from a chorus of voices. Others argue that we have come too far, and the prospect of now displacing women and sending them home is like putting the toothpaste back in the tube; in a highly segregated workplace, therefore, these jobs will remain women's domain.

These arguments can produce some funny bedfellows. Just as Ronald Reagan and Frank Field both lament the decline in male breadwinners, theorists of the traditionalist right find themselves siding up with old-style trade union arguments for a family wage. Patricia Morgan of the Institute of Economic Affairs urges mothers to stay at home and do their real job. She is, however, tacitly aware that preserving the necessary male 'breadwinner' wages means going hand in hand with effective wage bargaining by trade unions – which is of course an anathema to the right.

The right-wing journalist Peter Hitchens rants about working women as the source of major social decay, but he also acknowledges that it is largely market capitalism and the desires of business – the traditional sacred cows of the right – that are responsible for creating the demand for a female workforce, by changing employment patterns and fuelling the consumerism that drove many women to work in the first place. Some economists argue that the whole concept of 'in work' benefits like family credit is a dubious one, designed to re-create for low-paid men the illusion of the 'family wage' of old, through subsidizing wages.

Not all policy makers are aware of the huge inconsistencies in this area. Mrs Thatcher sharply criticized women who went to work and neglected their children. Yet she more than anyone wanted to crush trade unions and bring in the flexible labour markets that lay behind many women's need to work. The last Conservative government elevated 'scrounging' single mothers into the number one scapegoat of social ills. Yet if all proper mothers are supposed to stay at home, how can those whose partner has absented himself exist, except on benefit? The Conservative election manifesto in 1997 promised a modest tax break to mothers who stay at home, despite a rhetoric about increasing women's opportunities and professional advancement. As in so many areas of modern political debate, the imperatives of the deregulated market sit uncomfortably with the general desire for social cohesion.

To find where the straightforward narrative of return might lead, a good place to look is at countries like Japan. Everyone knows about the postwar wonders of the Japanese GNP (at least until Asia got the jitters in 1998), but Japan also offers a paradise of traditional values: a tiny number of single mothers, high marriage rates, a low and declining crime rate and a labour market that is essentially for men only. According to Japanese labour laws discrimination against women is still not subject to sanctions. Women are educated and receive degrees, but when they enter the job market, it is very often as underemployed 'office flowers' – making the tea and greeting visitors – who gracefully bow out after marriage. Japanese men work extraordinarily long hours, or they at least 'attend work' for a large part of the week, as much of their time involves socializing outside the office. Some sociologists believe that this highly traditional pattern, stressing the vital role of a man as a worker, woman as homemaker and wife, underpins a cohesive and well-ordered society.

When other Far Eastern leaders stressed the need for economic development against a background of 'Asian values' they meant that they want to avoid the patterns of social deviance associated with advanced industrialized countries in the West and instead to follow the model of Japan. Francis Fukuyama is clear that

> . . . the core value that differentiates many Asian societies from those in the West concerns the status of women. The reason that Asian societies, beginning with Japan, have been able to avoid the kinds of social problems facing North America and Europe is that they have more strongly resisted female equality.[39]

The problem for Japanese society is that Japanese women are starting to grumble, and there are signs that the traditional arrangements where 'men are men' will not last forever. Furthermore the declining birth rate and the age structure of the population means that in the long term there will be growing economic reasons, quite apart from their own frustration, for women to enter the workforce.

Perhaps in twenty years Japanese men will face the same questioning and dilemmas as their fellow men in the West, and the market for men's studies will expand and diversify eastwards. By then some of the responses of Western men might be rather more sophisticated than those currently voiced in popular culture. For here the solution to the question 'where are men going?' has been the kind of dismal withdrawal into hardened stereotypes exhibited by the nineties cult of laddism. Of course, at the margins some men have taken on some caring tasks, and New Man has allegedly been sighted, but the most enduring symbol of the nineties male culture has been the emergence of the New Lad, the deliberate reverse of New Man. What seems to have happened is that as women's identities have broadened and encroached upon male territory, instead of a swapping and merging of identities, men moved further into the traditional heartlands of male identity – the drinking, shagging, sporty stereotype. As feminism went mainstream, its subtle presence pervaded every ad campaign, every TV programme and the consciousness of every woman in the West – so men felt threatened. It seems they felt lost in a morass of sinking opportunities and rising expectations from women who wanted Mr Perfect or nothing. So they went on the offensive and liberated themselves from the chains and shackles of women's anticipation – to be themselves. They joyfully revelled in the right to scratch and belch and love football more than anything else in the world, to get pissed and leer at women with big breasts. The message was 'Stop patronizing me; I understand the equal rights thing. Now let's have a laugh for Christ's sake.' The TV comedy series *Men Behaving Badly* about the life of some nineties lads and lasses (the same show in which the actresses were annoyed at their unequal pay) achieved cult status. On the shelves of the newsagents a whole new genre of 'men's-interest' magazines emerged, with the staggering success of *Loaded, FHM* and *Maxim*. Articles on health, cars, football and computers were spiced with a liberal sprinkling of soft porn babes and tips on the latest chat-up lines.

For many women the most disturbing aspect of all this was the boys' own gang mentality that laddism encouraged. If you were not prepared to enthuse about Page 3 girls, living off lager and chips, and toenail clippings on the sofa you were dubbed uncool, uptight and a bad sport. And at its worst, laddism meant the oafish behaviour of the football star Gazza – the national hero who cried on the football field but also physically abused his wife – which caused James Brown, former editor of *Loaded* and father of laddism, to protest that he had 'always said there was nothing big about beating up your girlfriend'.

Perhaps laddism reflects the male response to an unrealistic role model: just as women despair of ever being 8-stone cover girls, so the lads shout when asked to feminize. The argument that political correctness had gone mad and transmuted into some kind of Stalinist monster was one that the nineties generation felt instinctively – for these men analysing the feeling would be too wimpish. Going on the offensive proved a psychological triumph. It's a great trick: men make their imperfections part of the attraction and by saying 'Love me, love my warts,' simply echo what feminism was saying thirty years ago. Laddism was defined as finding a space where men can be comfortable. The key ingredients became machismo – that is, anything that differentiates men from women, humour, and a rejection of all self-conscious agonizing about what men are for. Finally it included a large dose of nostalgia exemplified in boyish lists of likes (ketchup, fast cars, collecting things) and dislikes. (Market research confirmed how popular lists are with men, and the editor of *FHM* attributed his eventual outselling of *Loaded* not to more nipples but to the publication of interesting lists, evoking nostalgic memories of anoraks on station platforms writing down engine numbers in their notebooks.)

Like all the media complaints about women taking over and leaving men behind, laddism has nothing to do with the men who have really seen their expectations devastated. The prototype New Lads – like the gawky redhead Chris Evans who still manages to pull the birds, the *Men Behaving Badly* heroes Martin Clunes and Neil Morrissey, or other typical products like Skinner and Baddiel – are far removed from the real male losers. The most that they have to worry about is reminiscent of the character in Nick Hornby's novel *High Fidelity*, who moans that he is now expected to do his share of cleaning the toilet, a task that his dad in the 1950s never had to perform. Laddism has nothing to offer those men whose whole reason for existing has been undermined by the loss of potential livelihood and consequent social position. Indeed the stars of New Laddery are symbolic of the problem. Comedians, footballers and pop stars are very much part of the winner-takes-all society of sharply rising inequality, where the incomes of the top earners have soared to the stratosphere. The economics of the star system has spread into many other areas, so that rewards to those at the top (most usually men) are out of all proportion to the rewards to the rest.[40] Each Christmas in the late nineties Santa brought bonuses totalling a billion pounds to the Square Mile. The highest earner of all in 1996 with his salary of £54 million was Bernie Ecclestone of Formula One, racing being the quintessential New Lad activity. The rapid divergence in male wages is one of the most dramatic rising indices of inequality since 1979. By the mid-nineties the gap between the income of the poorest 10 per cent of male workers and the average male wage was wider than at any time since 1886 when data was first collected.[41] In every region and age group inequality has risen. While the highly skilled and educated command vastly higher incomes than their counterparts twenty years ago, those with the least skills and education, if they are working at all, are earning much the same wages.[42] When housing costs are included, the poor are worse off in real, as well as relative, terms.

Yet the rhetoric of the lads articulates something more than a glorifying oafishness. There is an underlying worry as to what the goals of manhood are supposed to be. This has all become part of a general masculine panic over work, relationships and even declining sperm counts. Above all there is confusion. As girls and women have slowly expanded their repertoire, discovering that ambition, competition and desire are no longer out of bounds, men have simply stayed the same as they always were – and laddism offered the temporary solution of regressing. In 1996 a book appeared with a title that summed it all up, entitled *The Stronger Women Get, the More Men Love Football: Sexism and the Culture of Sport*.[43] In its own way laddism is just as much a narrative of return as all the family values and 'women stay at home' rhetoric, except that it promises beer and sex as well. It offers a retreat into a familiar setting instead of a way forward into a new era of gender understanding.

Changing Masculinity

Angela Phillips in *The Trouble With Boys* observes that it is difficult to expect men to change when they suffer from such an inherent imbalance in their upbringing.[44] Girls watching their mothers have a constant clear role model, but for boys their adult role model is often absent from the home and daily routine, so they have the more complicated task of imagining what he is up to. Motherhood is a self-perpetuating institution. If the only available role models are the same traditional ones, we first need to break the circle to offer a different set of possibilities. Men need to apply themselves to parenting with the same diligence with which women have applied themselves to work. This in turn would lead to a more balanced world. For the American feminist Dorothy Dinnerstein, author of *The Rocking of the Cradle and the Ruling of the World*, the position is more uncompromising.[45] She argues that

> . . . no societal compromise which changes other features of woman's condition while leaving her role as first parent intact will get at the roots of asymmetric sexual privilege . . .
> because it is this arrangement which stops men from growing up emotionally and stops women from developing as full adults in the public sphere.

Or as Ann Oakley identified twenty-five years ago, 'men and women cannot be equal partners outside the home if they are not equal partners inside it'.[46]

The truth is that, as with any revolution, the old order dislikes the idea of change, which will be uncomfortable. Men cannot stay the same while all around them everything else is changing. Yet accepting new versions of manhood is not impossible, just as we have seen so many other huge cultural and attitudinal changes. Women have changed their expectations and values in a generation. It is not inconceivable that there could be a new set of worthwhile goals for men. Some men say that they would genuinely like to embrace a new, flexible and balanced role, so long as they were not the only one. It is perfectly feasible that the traditional male deal might rearrange itself – except that the time may not be right.

A small number of men talk about the wonders of being able to expand their horizons and embrace both private as well as public roles, mirroring how women have changed. Many gay men, in particular, are interested in considering new versions of mas-culinity and fathering. But these views are mainly held by those who have the luxury of choice and the confidence and imagination to embrace change; their backs are not economically against the wall. There is a world of difference between middle-class writers describing the pleasures of being a dad and the desperation of a redundant man who spends his days wheeling a buggy around an impoverished housing estate. Jack O'Sullivan, a journalist who is full of the joys of fatherhood, and the author of a 'Manifesto for Men', admits that he might not change nappies with such enthu-siasm if he was not also secure in his identity as an assistant editor at the *Independent*.[47] The men most open to change are inevitably those with more autonomy over their lives. In Sweden the partners of professional women are more likely to take up the generous parental leave entitlement and share in childcare. Blue-collar workers in insecure jobs will tend to opt for traditional gender roles. If it is those in secure jobs which provide the necessary space who are more likely to accept newer versions of manhood, there is a further problem if the opportunities for these kinds of lifestyle are declining.

Requests for adjustment and new expectations have probably come too late. This kind of change of culture works best in an atmosphere that is unthreatening and not economically hostile. The contemporary labour market with its frantic and relentless demands and unforgiving pace is the least favourable climate in which to ask men to reorder their lives and look at beneficial changes. Had the economic climate of the sixties prevailed, we could now envisage a more satisfactory reordering of working life and gender roles. Instead there is a deafening rush towards the bunker. And where does that leave women?

6

Choice, What Choice?

If the truth about heterosexual men is that there is only one way to be male, the myth about women is that life is all about making choices. Once upon a time little girls, unless they were budding Jane Austens, could plot only one route into adulthood. Should the key objectives of marriage and motherhood not materialize in time, they imagined themselves sadly gathering dust upon a shelf. Now that anything is theoretically possible, women are presumed to be making active choices about work and positively constructing their private lives and reinventing their identities from a dizzy variety of combinations. Modern woman is portrayed as a prototype customer at the pick 'n' mix counter of available lifestyles.

The trouble is that many of the myriad alternatives apparently on offer are often not real options at all. The choice allegedly open to women between children or childlessness, work or home, full- or part-time employment, is often just an illusion of real choice. The woman who returns to work after pregnancy only to find herself sidelined and her role downgraded because 'mothers lack commitment' may feel that her choices are pretty limited. Equally the poverty trap, where benefit losses outweigh potential wages, limits any real choice for many women. Anyone who cannot earn enough to afford adequate childcare is not in a position to choose to work.[1] The majority of single mothers with children under five have been in this position, and this is a group which has grown dramatically in the past twenty years, so that single mothers overall are the only category of women less likely to be working today than in 1979. Tax changes in 1999 will make work a more likely prospect for poorer women, but the single mother who feels that to avoid poverty she has no choice but to work – despite having to resort to unsatisfactory childcare – may also feel her 'choices' are deeply unsatisfactory. As the Swedish Ministry of Labour expressed it, 'If children cannot receive good care while their parents are away working the right to work becomes illusory.'[2]

Even for women with a working partner, choice is more restricted than it might first appear. If social mores obliged the fifties mother to stay at home, her modern counterpart is meant to be able to decide freely whether or not to work. Yet the fifties mother could only stay at home because the fifties father was earning a family wage: during this brief period of postwar recovery more men than ever before or since earned enough to support a wife and dependent children. A self-respecting family could live comfortably off the earnings of a skilled worker, a middle manager or even a teacher or lecturer. It was modern capitalism, with its endless urging for more consumption and more consumer choice, that lured women into work. Once a stream of new consumer goodies became mandatory for a decent life, someone had to earn the extra money to pay for them. The initial impetus for so many women to return to work was the desire to boost their families' living standards so that they too could aspire to the washing machines, videos, cars and holidays.

Gradually the definition of poverty has become a relative measure. A UK household on less than half the national average income (a common measure of poverty) may be unable to afford those items that have become part of the social norm – like a television. Yet relocate that same household to an Indian village and its access to running water and electric light would place it beyond the most luxurious dreams of the surrounding inhabitants. The fashionable expression 'social exclusion' is the contemporary term to describe poverty, for once basic needs are fulfilled then being poor means not being able to participate in what society considers a regular way of life. As the norm has become more complicated and consumer opportunities have expanded, households have required a greater income in order to keep up what feels like an average standard of living.

In the United States average wages, according to some indices, have barely kept up with inflation, never mind being able to cover all the extra 'necessities' which were once luxuries. Similar trends are apparent in Britain, where the bottom 20 per cent of the population have seen no measurable rise in their earnings. In the US 'the stagnant incomes of the majority in "winner takes all" capitalism' mean that average hourly wages are below their 1973 levels, even though in the same period profits have soared (and the proportion of profits to turnover has also risen).[3] One US economist has calculated that, adjusting for inflation, in 1988 two salaries brought in only 6 per cent more than one salary in 1973 . . . due to the eradication of stable full-time, long-term jobs: 'one well paid smokestack job with health insurance has been replaced by two service jobs without benefits'.[4] A combination of changing work patterns, sluggish wages and a redefinition of consumer 'needs' have made women's earnings a vital part of family budgeting, so that in more and more cases it is the woman's wage that keeps the family out of poverty (defined as half of average income). In Britain it was nine times more likely in 1989–91 that a male-breadwinner family would be in poverty than a decade earlier. And a family with only a male earner is ten times more likely to be poor than one where both partners work: only 1 per cent of dual earner families in 1989–91 were poor. Even though their rate of pay might be miserably low, it is indisputable that many women now contribute much more than 'pin money' to the family income.[5]

In 1963 Betty Friedan published the classic *The Feminine Mystique*,[6] about the relentlessly middle-class college-educated women of the US suburbs who dutifully gave up work in favour of marriage and children. She painted a miserable picture of empty lives in perfect houses where women had no identity beyond their role as wives and mothers. This was the so-called 'problem with no name' that they fretted about as they lay awake contemplating the lack of meaning and purpose in their lives and asking themselves 'Is this it?' Today there is another 'problem with no name' confronting frantic, juggling working mothers as they race from office to childminder to supermarket to bulging briefcase in the midst of tightly organized schedules, women who may barely have time to ask the question 'Is this it?' The nineties hyperwoman is more likely to lie awake at night compiling endless mental lists of all the things that need to be done the next day; in the words of Erica Jong, women have won the 'right to be terminally exhausted'.

Despite all the newspaper babble about high-flying supermums, in the eighties and nineties it is women from lower- and middle-income families who have gone out to work more than women from high-income families. These are women who have to cope without the cushion of elaborate support staff, women for whom paid work is far more likely to be a necessity rather than a matter of choice. Any woman (following the pattern that men have followed for generations) who combines paid work with having a family is bizarrely described as 'having it all'. But as Margaret Cook observed when her dual-income marriage to the Foreign Secretary, Robin Cook, was abruptly terminated, the phrase is really far more applicable to men. 'It's selfish that men should expect it all. They are quite capable of sweeping the floor, sending Christmas cards, buying birthday presents – they are quite capable – they don't have to have it all, they just like to have it all.'[7] If men are having it all it is because women are usually doing it all – the private, unpaid role is indivisible from her sex and the public, paid role is simply grafted on top. The stereotypical media image is of the glamorous executive whizzing between boardroom and maternity ward, but she is not that common in flesh and blood. Statistically the woman who allegedly 'has it all' – employment and a family – is much more likely to be a shop assistant, nurse, cleaner or office worker: reliant upon childminders, neighbours and other patchwork childcare with no domestic support, unable to choose because her income is not an optional family extra. But the scenario of the woman fitting in the ironing on Sunday afternoon or returning from a long night shift to butter sandwiches for the school packed lunches rarely makes the features pages.

The question of whether families *need* two incomes to survive is a contentious one. Amitai Etzioni, communitarian philosopher and a favourite New Labour guru, worries about the 'parenting deficit', arguing that too many families are driven to acquire material goods when they would really be enriched by having less luxury and spending more time at home interacting with their children. He agrees that the poor have little scope for choices but insists that the income level at which there is a genuine choice between earning more and caring for children is below that which conventional wisdom dictates. Etzioni mocks the family that 'needs' the income of two lawyers – with its skiing lodge, summer house and designer clothes. The problem in his view 'is that culture and community have changed what are seen as essentials'.[8]

It has become increasingly difficult, especially for parents, to jump off the consumer bandwagon. But the problem is not just the shopping society and having to run harder and spend more to keep up with the Joneses. There is also the growing unreliability of the long-term family income stream. If father no longer has a guaranteed job for life, it may be vital for a family to diversify its sources of income. Ron, a junior manager, feels that 'Although we could probably live off my income, even if it would mean fewer holidays and luxuries, I am in such a volatile sector that my wife has to continue teaching full-time just in case the worst should happen – even though it means continuing stress and juggling complicated childcare arrangements.' He feels a current of disapproval from his parents at their pressured lifestyle, 'but then they have no conception of the insecurity at work'. This combination of shifting income patterns, shifting labour markets and perceptions of insecurity means that economic pressures preclude a meaningful choice for an overwhelming number of mothers. 'At college we were told to go for it and sent forth into the job market, promised a golden future,' said Ellen, who is contemplating motherhood. She works as a costume designer on a moderate income, with a partner earning much the same in a similarly insecure job.

But now I feel as if we were sold a pup. At work things are
still not equal and women face a more difficult time, and yet
there is really no alternative anymore to work because we
could not survive without my income. So I will have to work
when we have children and I would really prefer not to, for at
least a few years. I am in an occupation where irregular,
unsociable hours and insecurity are a way of life – it is clear
from watching my colleagues that trying to accommodate
employment with adequate and affordable childcare
invariably brings friction.

The concept of mothers who freely choose paid employment,
even when they do not have to economically, is a strange new
idea. Earlier in the century the distinct alternatives were, for all
but the poorest, much more clear-cut. The majority of women *à
la Feminine Mystique* had a family by their mid-twenties. Once
the children were older they might return to a little light or voluntary work. The combination of peacetime, economic stability
and low divorce rates meant that the breadwinner would provide
for life and social pressure was firmly against mothers who went
out to work. The poor muddled along doing both – 'having it
all' – and a small group of women, often well-educated or those
whose potential partners had died in battle, consciously or
unconsciously 'chose' work. Betty Boothroyd, the first woman
Speaker of the House of Commons, has a formidable public aura,
but when the mask slips she talks poignantly, as an only child and
a single childless woman, about the emptiness of life without
close family, something that she has become more aware of missing as she has grown older. When she dies there will be much
pomp and circumstance at her passing but she feels sad that there
will be no one who will really miss her in a personal sense. Yet she

is well aware that her remarkable professional achievements would have remained unrealized had she followed a conventional domestic pattern.[9] Her 'choice' mirrors the stirring dilemma described by the innovative feminist thinker Charlotte Perkins Gilman at the turn of the century, when she called for a grand domestic revolution, a complete rearrangement of work and home, because

> . . . we have so arranged life that a man may have a house, a family, love, companionship, domesticity and fatherhood yet remain an active citizen of age and country. We have so arranged life on the other hand that a woman must 'choose': she must either live alone, uncared for, homeless, childless, with her work in the world for sole consolation; or give up world service for the joys of love, motherhood, and domestic service.[10]

Like Betty Boothroyd, thousands of other women – teachers, academics, professionals – followed the same pattern on the basis that public achievement was incompatible with raising a family. Dame Pauline Neville-Jones said that if she had had a family she would never have risen so high in the Foreign Office (paradoxically, though, it appears that one of the factors that counted against her final promotion to a senior ambassadorial post was her status as a single woman – without a wife). Baroness Dean acknowledges that she would never have risen to the top of a trade union if she had been diverted by children. A small number of women brought up children in the immediate postwar period and worked because they wanted to, but they were the exceptions. The composer Elizabeth Lutyens gave an interview to *Woman's Hour* about her life in the late 1940s.

> There came a time when I wanted to marry and have
> children. You cannot marry and have a career they said.
> These 'theys'; these ogres. I thought naïvely men marry and
> work and have children. Truly they said, but you are not a
> man – choose either or. What ghastly tyranny – this
> choice. . . . I know of no other woman who combines
> composing, family and earning a living. I can only say to thine
> own self be true.[11]

Others were equally steadfast, like the part-time GPs, teachers or occasional exceptional professors such as the philosopher Elizabeth Anscombe – mother of eight children – or the remarkable Nobel Prize-winning Dorothy Hodgkin and her erstwhile student Margaret Thatcher, who of course was not one to follow 1950s convention. Yet for the overwhelming majority, the pressures to be a proper mother and not to work were enormous, regardless of their education or potential. It is illuminating to listen to mothers, now in their late sixties or seventies, who feel they were born too early: they were educated and given some intimation of their potential, but children were still firmly regarded as 'the enemies of promise'. One university-educated wife of a prominent politician, with achieving professional daughters, says in a tone of regret, 'I was probably cleverer than all of them, but instead spent a lifetime stuffing washing machines.'

A fault line runs somewhere through the early 1950s on these issues. For those born earlier the combination of fulfilling work and having a family was highly unusual and only for the most determined, but gradually the climate altered as girls' expectations and ambitions shifted. Even though economic reasons were the real motivation behind larger numbers of married women and mothers entering the workforce, the status and importance of paid work as a source of identity and social meaning became more significant for women. Thirty years ago a full-time mother may have felt frustrated, undervalued or unfulfilled but at least she was 'doing the right thing' and socially sanctioned. Disapproval was heaped upon those who 'neglected' their children. Slowly this emphasis changed so that women who gave up all paid work and stayed at home now felt on the defensive. As Penelope Leach observed:

> . . . the woman who sees herself as 'only a mother' even if she enjoys a high material standard and mothers with excitement and devotion is likely to feel herself stranded in a backwater missing the mainstream current that is rushing everybody else to the real focus of aspiration and achievement and social acknowledgement of both: the workplace.[12]

And yet the image of the selfish woman, who chooses work when she does not *have* to do it, remains equally potent. Mothers who work either because they enjoy it, or because they perceive it as the only source of public status and no longer regard marriage as a guarantee of lifetime security may still have to justify their decision.

Financial necessity, whether this means paying the mortgage, food bills or school fees, legitimizes women's decision to work. In 1997 during the Boston trial of Louise Woodward – accused of murdering baby Matthew Eappen – opprobrium was heaped upon Deborah Eappen for going out to work and leaving her children. When it eventually emerged that she went to work as an eye surgeon for financial reasons – in order to repay graduate school loans – the focus of anger suddenly shifted. The effect of her working was exactly the same but *she* was no longer considered such a villain if she *had* to work. It was the possibility that she might be choosing to work, in order to fulfil herself or simply because she wanted to use her talents and capacities outside the home, that upset American public opinion.

With the aid of middle-market tabloid cheerleaders the stand-off between mothers who do and mothers who don't has become one of the most contentious areas of modern life. According to Harriet Harman, erstwhile Secretary of State for Social Security and Minister for Women:

> Inside every housewife is a career woman, inside every career woman a housewife and both are struggling to get out. Whatever decision women have made about work many fear that they have made the wrong decision and resent other women who might have made the right one.[13]

The *Daily Mail* gleefully talks about the mothering wars, and like many other newspapers it loves nothing better than when one of the have-it-all mums leaves her juggling act and returns home to spend more time with the family. When women like Coca-Cola boss Penny Hughes or Linda Kelsey, editor of *She* magazine ('for women who juggle') leave their high-paid and visible positions, pages of predictable stories and live studio discussions are sure to follow. Even the *Guardian* wrote excitedly about the 1997 resignation of mother-of-three Pepsi boss Brenda Barnes under the headline 'Superwoman's coming home to the family'.[14]

These stories always feature the same caricatures – from the ambitious high-flier to the cosy vision of the stay-at-home mum. They rarely capture the complexities that such choices entail or the sense in which many women feel disenchanted in the long term by the rigid expectations of a corporate workplace, which is governed by an all-or-nothing commitment. Brenda Barnes said upon her resignation:

> I hope people can look at my decision not as 'women can't do' it but as 'for 22 years Brenda Barnes gave her all and did a lot of great things'. I have struggled with this for a long time. Hopefully one day corporate America can tackle this.

For Penny Hughes too the reality was far from the media stereotype: women can't hack it. She swiftly went on to build up a successful part-time role as a non-executive director which gives her the ideal balance and quality of life that she was looking for. Yet the prestigious part-time portfolio work is only there as a result of her eleven successful years at Coca-Cola. On closer inspection she provides a far more satisfactory role model for most women than the madly juggling full-time executive, but it is a subtle, complicated story and Hughes is aware that it needed confidence to say that she wanted to make the change. 'I often say that I hope that if I had been born a man I would have had the confidence to make the same decision, but men just don't.'[15]

The Mother of All Differences

Once upon a time there was only one way to be a mother. Today she can express breast milk in the executive suite, do an evening shift as a taxi driver, climb mountains, or be at home baking bread. One way to portray this diversity is by looking at it from the perspective of children. In the 1950s not only was there less income inequality between families, but there was also far less scope for alternative parenting styles. Children were more likely to have the same 'Janet and John' experience of going home to mother in the afternoon, whilst father probably returned home from work sometime later in the day. Amongst today's primary school children there is a much wider range of possibilities: some will still be collected by their mothers, while others will be met by a childminder, foreign au pair or nanny. A growing proportion will transfer to an after-school club, but others may go home alone to a neighbour or to an empty house. A tiny number will find father at the school gate. The chances are that a few of them will see a parent only briefly, if at all, before bedtime, and many children will have a shifting combination of alternatives depending on which day of the week it is. A child will stand in the lunch queue or change for gym next to someone who has totally different parenting and caring arrangements; moreover, this divergence is not simply a function of economic pressures. The investment banker's children will see far less of their mother than the part-time cleaner's. Joint custody arrangements, complicated childcare, and the needs of flexible working patterns mean that there are multiple ways of negotiating all these roles and such multiplicity breeds uncertainty and confusion about who is getting it right.

The widening polarity of styles of mothering – from the mother who spends less than five weeks a year in sole charge of her children to the mother who spends every possible minute devoted to her offspring – can produce resentment. There is social and peer permission to work, yet women are said to 'feel inadequate if they do not work and profound anxiety and stress if they do work'. The polarizing of mothering styles so that even women who are from similar backgrounds approach their roles quite differently is an endlessly debated topic and has even become the subject of vigorous and sometimes ill-tempered academic controversy. In 1995, Catherine Hakim, a senior research fellow at the

London School of Economics, declared that women divided into very different camps and that only one quarter to one third of them would really want to undertake paid work if they did not have to.[16] Women were far less committed to work, and more than half would prefer to fulfil a more traditional role. She said that feminists had distorted the facts and created myths about women's employment to suit their own narrow agenda, and she criticized the European Union policy analysis, which assumed that all women wanted to combine lifelong employment, because 'national surveys across the world demonstrate that many women, often the majority, actively seek and accept the homemaker role'.

A range of eminent sociologists lined up to pour critical scorn upon Catherine Hakim.[17] They attacked her analysis as a caricature, her use of statistics as cavalier, and they pointed out her failure to distinguish between the nature of jobs and the characteristics of their occupants, and her unwillingness to accept that difficulties in finding suitable childcare played a part in women's employment constraints. They identified a different polarization: between women with better education and qualifications, 'an elite minority who have the financial resources to buy exemption from some of the effects of motherhood on employment' and 'the majority . . . trapped in a vicious circle of low pay, inability to afford full-day childcare and part-time employment'. Hakim replied with more evidence and criticized her opponents for regarding women as 'an undifferentiated mass of mindless zombies' rather than real individuals capable of making choices and reasserting the picture of growing female heterogeneity.[18] The argument spilled over into the popular media: television, radio and even the tabloid press joined in. It is rare indeed that the worthy articles of the *British Journal of Sociology* receive such wide exposure but it was a sure sign that Hakim had touched a raw nerve, even if her analysis and reasoning were open to wide disagreement.

American sociology had already observed these widening variations. *Hard Choices* was a study looking at what propelled women into following traditional or non-traditional patterns; it concluded that

> . . . structural changes in the economy, the organization of the workplace and the nature of private life have combined to create new avenues for women outside the home, to erode the supports for female domesticity and to *intensify the split* between those reproducing old patterns and those riding the currents of social change. Women develop differing choices and orientation toward motherhood and work . . . some have been exposed to structural changes whiles others have been insulated from them.[19]

For some women all kinds of new combinations might be possible, but the endless anxiety about who is doing the right thing amongst this growing 'variety of life patterns' shows no sign of receding.

Even women with the best academic preparation may feel surprised when they encounter these conflicts. Many are so convinced by the message that everyone is equal now that any contradictory experience feels like a personal failing. Careers advice is simply about finding a good job. Josephine, aged thirty, is a corporate lawyer. Until now her professional life has been unproblematic, but having watched the experiences of colleagues and friends she is all too aware of the kind of difficulties and choices that will face her in the next few years. She is critical of her high-pressure all-girls school for not having alerted women like herself to the conflicting pressures that can accompany educational and professional success.

> The message was always if you work hard, pass the exams, you will find a good job and your talents will be recognized. There was never any discussion of how to negotiate the various roles and the awkward compromises that might arise, because of the way the workplace is structured.

The schools' defence is that building up their pupils' expectations and ambition is difficult enough without alerting them to problems or ambiguities that could lie ahead. Schools are reluctant to accept that it is misleading not to alert their pupils to the wider picture, or that in many ways it is like sending someone out on a long journey with incorrect maps and false directions.

Helen is a doctor, of the same generation, who after having three children in quick succession felt unable to work more than a few hours a week as a locum. It took her several years to stop feeling guilty about not working more. She too blamed her academic girls' school for conveying the message that fulfilment would only come through an absorbing career and any one who did not single-mindedly pursue work was failing. 'Children and family life were not really mentioned when we were discussing our career plans. They were never excluded but assumed to be something that could be effortlessly fitted in on the side.'

There is evidence that these issues are officially sidestepped in higher education. A study of 900 women who were once high-flying Harvard graduates concluded that 'no one in graduate school or by professional example had alerted them of how heart wrenching their individual choices would become'.[20] One American academic recalls listening to her former students wonder

... 'why in my last year in University the women's centre on campus was more likely to run a talk on matriarchy in Finland than on parenthood and careers' ... for the perception of these young women was that working out how to deal with their double burden might be the central problem of their adult life.[21]

But it was not a feminist issue. There was no support or acknowledgement as women tried to integrate the two models of dedicated eighties worker and dedicated fifties mother.

The Origins of Choice

The novelist Margaret Forster, investigating the early roots of feminist thought in her book *Significant Sisters*, showed how in the course of the nineteenth century the original ideas about fighting for rights and justice gradually gave way to the issue of choice, to enable women to use their rights and break out of their traditional roles. When in 1849 Elizabeth Blackwell became the world's first trained and registered woman doctor, she realized this desire. (Blackwell was an early example of the queen bee syndrome, believing that most other women were too weak and inadequate to do anything beyond their domestic and mothering role. She, however, even managed to combine work as a doctor with the adoption, late in life, of a daughter.) A small but significant band of women began tentatively to plot a course that led them away from the traditional female role model. The noble ideal of the accomplished professional woman, like Florence Nightingale, who chose to dedicate her life to her vocation opened up a whole new world, but also a risky one. As Forster grimly observes, 'Choice even then began to look like a trick, although it was not until the twentieth century that the full extent of the trickery became evident.'[22]

Historically feminism did not have much to say on the subject of choices – it had more to contribute on abortion rights than on the right time to have a child. The theme in the 1970s was women getting out of the house and into the wider world, although Germaine Greer, amongst others, would add that feminism was always meant to be about liberation – changing the world for everyone – and not straightforward equality.[23] Nevertheless the novelty of joining the workforce and forging a public role was quite enough to be going on with: any ideas about simultaneously reinventing the values and attitudes of that workplace would have to wait. Late in the day American women, in particular, have realized that simply accepting the existing structures of work without any change was a mistake. A succession of books including Mary Ann Mason's *The Equality Trap* and Sylvia Hewlett's *A Lesser Life* discuss ruefully how women have embraced work on the wrong terms, pointing out that they should instead have tried to change things. Blame is laid on some of the early feminist attitudes which asserted that women should be interchangeable with men in developing their public role and that being a mother was not part of the plan. In *When Work Doesn't Work Anymore* a former publishing executive, Elizabeth Perle McKenna, describes the midlife agonizing of corporate American women who are choosing to opt out of their frantic lifestyle.[24] She argues that the reason the women's movement had such rapid effects was 'because it didn't change the values of the success culture; it strove to make them equally available'. In the end this made women like herself, who strived in that culture, profoundly dissatisfied with their lives. Or as the colourful *New York Times* columnist Anna Quindlen put it, 'We did the guy thing and the guy thing sucked!'

If feminism as it developed in the 1970s was not interested in discussing dilemmas of choice or balancing roles, it was because in the urge to leave the kitchen, continuing to accept the burdens of child rearing was just not part of the plan. While equality feminism was in the ascendancy, anything that accentuated women's differences from men – like giving birth – was not to be encouraged. The extreme attitude was that anyone who, in spite of the pill, voluntarily undertook the constraints of children had only themselves to blame; most pitiable of all were those who gave birth to males. Erica Jong recalls that she was once booed off the stage for reading a poem about breast-feeding to a feminist audience. Germaine Greer helpfully pointed out to women that all the agonizing about mothers bringing up children was quite misplaced. Why should they need to be 'brought up' as they would anyway grow up themselves? And other prominent (childless) feminists simply repeated the mantra of free twenty-four-hour nurseries as the solution to all possible conflicts. Today there is all-night childcare in the United States for women who work shifts, and in London a version of that exists: there are 'children's hotels' complete with internet sites linked to cameras so parents can log in and keep watch. Even if such institutions were afford-able and widely available, they would probably not catch on; despite feminism's impatience with childbearing, plenty of women still want to be mothers and to be involved in their chil-dren's upbringing. But the complicated and tricky truth is that they would like to be not only but also a mother. Margaret Forster quotes the suffragist Elizabeth Cady Stanton's observation that 'The woman is greater than the wife and mother and in consent-ing to take upon herself these relationships she should never sacrifice one iota of her individuality.' But Forster adds ominously that 'Women may wish to agree but come the testing time and the woman is rapidly submerged by the wife and mother, sometimes never to reappear.'[25]

Childbirth has become the key turning point in women's employment, whereas before it used to be marriage that marked women's changing status in the workforce. It is almost as if there are three categories of worker: men, women and mothers. The genderquake argument that the new generation has 'androgynous values' does not extend to parenting and motherhood. The optimistic picture of merging values and similarities between the sexes breaks down for many women in their thirties once children arrive. Women who delay or avoid childbearing can sustain the illusion of merging values and interchangeable personae at work. Despite all the rhetoric, mothers who want to preserve their position in the workplace find that the unchanging assumptions about gender roles, when combined with the demands of a job, can put them at a disadvantage. 'Women in this position may "have it all". They have their children and they have their careers. . . . The cost is simply a reasonable way of life,' concluded Terri Apter in her memorably titled book *Why Women Don't Have Wives*.[26]

If a woman with children does not want to 'drop out' of the race she frequently has to pretend that nothing has changed and treat her family as invisible while she is at work, just as men have always done. This is the problem: women who were for so long excluded from the workplace, have embraced the work culture and contemporary working life on its existing terms. Starting with the women under 24 working the longest hours of all groups, they bought unquestioningly into the existing structures, because they were grateful to be allowed in at all. This is particularly evident in the US, where there is no official maternity provision or 'special concessions'. Women executives make the same frequent relocations, work the same hours, receive two weeks' annual holiday and suffer the same disruptions of an all-embracing work culture as their male colleagues. In Britain for the lucky ones there is maternity leave, but a lifetime of complicated juggling and role play begins six months into motherhood, if not before.

Once again the prospect of choice is illusory. In the modern workplace, where working life is foreshortened, the leisurely prospect of taking years out and eventually returning to work is fraught with risks – for both sexes. Many women want to work fewer hours or take more unpaid leave, but serious players take only the briefest of breaks and do not return to the part-time ghetto of the mommy track. The structures of work and especially 'careers', the unbroken span of years, the assumption that real jobs require far more than a minimum of full-time hours, were invented by and for men – preferably with a supportive wife at home.

Future Choices

The lives of many contemporary women living without a map and holding together a novel and shifting combination of roles raise interesting questions for the future. The feminist movement told women to get a life, and as a result many women were determined to find a public role through work in reaction to their own mothers' empty lives; indeed some were even urged on by mothers who felt that they had never fulfilled their own potential. The most determined of all were often those who had seen their 'displaced homemaker' mothers left stranded after divorce in middle age, struggling to pick up the threads of work. Yet the influence of today's mothers as role models is less predictable. A sixth-form careers teacher from a large girls' comprehensive notes the differing effect of diverse mothering styles amongst her pupils: 'Everyone seems influenced by how their mothers treated them but the reactions are completely split; half want to do things the same way because they perceived it as OK and half want to reject it and do the complete opposite.' Whilst schools may not provide guidance on how to balance different future responsibilities, interesting messages are being passed on to girls at home. The conventional wisdom has been that girls benefit much more than boys from a mother who works and provides a clear role model of a woman finding fulfilment beyond the home. Everyone agreed that girls would be inspired to follow the example. Yet in some cases the careers teacher observes a very different pattern emerging: girls may reject the frantic pace of a mother living by the clock. The US study *Hard Choices* revealed that the experience of living with a very stressed working mother could make a daughter less ambitious, instead keen to establish 'a calmer life' for herself.[27] Children who have seen 'dual career' families from the inside might reach their own conclusions, like the daughter of one very senior executive who announced to her mother's astonishment that she wanted to be a 'real mummy' when she grew up. The upmarket agony aunt Virginia Ironside is unusual, for her generation, in having had a career mother:

I hold pretty feminist attitudes and yet when it comes to women working I find myself becoming remarkably stuffy. Probably because I was the daughter of a high-powered professor . . . and despite the fact that she had her holidays free, I just didn't like it. The rushed meals, the latchkey round the neck, the feeling that my mother's mind was always somewhere else, the ruined weekends with extra work always made me feel second best.[28]

In 1997 the think-tank Demos held a conference, entitled 'Tomorrow's Women', which aired some of these issues. A young assistant features editor said she had no intention of following in the footsteps of her continually fraught and harassed senior colleagues who tried to balance both family and serious professional responsibilities. A partner at a top London law firm noticed how her younger female colleagues were put off by her stretched lifestyle, telling her that if they had children they would prefer to leave rather than feel continually torn between work and home. 'The truth is,' she admitted, 'that in many ways I would not wish my own daughter to end up like this.' Meanwhile the recurring message from many of the younger women, the sixth-formers and students, was that they could not see how they could have a fulfilling occupation and also have children. 'I could not be there with them enough and children really want their parents around.' This is the latest twist in the story of apparent choices. The juggling frantic 'superwoman' is not only turning her daughter off childbirth in the future, but she is also influencing the decisions of her immediate contemporaries.

An Australian study on couples who are childless by choice concludes that it is

> . . . often a response to the material demands of
> parenthood. . . . women were aware of the sacrifices that
> mothers make, especially where those sacrifices intersect with
> paid work. . . . voluntary childlessness is a response to the
> unfair way in which we have organised family life rather than
> a manifestation of anybody's selfishness.[29]

Mothering might be venerated in theory but it is unsupported in practice. A US study found the same:

Many women report that in an ideal society they would like children but given current attitudes to mothers, lack of childcare provision and unresponsiveness of employers to parents they decide to avoid what they see as an untenable situation rather than try to modify it.[30]

The childcare dilemmas, the stress of trying to balance conflicting roles, the need to make mothering invisible at work, the difficulty of competing in a workplace where families make the playing field unequal for women – all the things that working mothers obsess about – have not gone unnoticed by their childless friends and colleagues.

The Baby Gap

In the generation that grew up in the 1950s and 1960s, marriage and motherhood were still accepted as the destiny of the overwhelming majority. Work was becoming more significant to a growing proportion of mothers, either for financial or other 'self-fulfilling' reasons. For them the question was how work and public status could be incorporated into their private commitments, and everyone sought their own particular compromise. Today the situation is exactly reversed: the need to work has become paramount and the dilemma is whether and how children will fit into that framework. A minority of women – Betty Boothroyd and her high-achieving contemporaries – have always faced this predicament. Their professional advance left no space for much private life, even if they wanted children 'one day'. Around 10 per cent of women born in the 1940s did not have children. Today the pattern has altered. According to official government forecasts at least 20 per cent of women born in the 1960s will not have children, rising to nearly one quarter of those who were born in the 1970s .[31] There are even some more tentative survey projections that if the rate of increase continues at this pace by the year 2010 one third of women will eventually be childless.[32]

A small proportion of women are childless involuntarily because of fertility problems and the current tend towards delayed motherhood means that many women are deciding to have children when their fertility is already declining. According to Sue Rice, head of ISSUE, the national fertility association:

> Women are in a no-win situation. If they stay at home and don't go out to work they are criticised. If they have a career and don't have children they're criticised. If they have children on their own they're criticised. If they get married and set up home first and wait for children they're criticised. They are told: well you are suffering from infertility because you left it too late, you should have started earlier.[33]

In contrast to the infertile are those women who positively state that they do not want children – and the most certain of those are the women in their twenties who undergo voluntary sterilization. Ten years ago a mere handful had the operation, and in the public sector there is still opposition to the idea because doctors are concerned that a relatively young patient could always change her mind later on. Even so, in 1996 an estimated 400 childless women under thirty had the operation on the NHS, and many more had it performed privately. When interviewed, young women who want to be sterilized describe a future identity that is focused upon their work and declare that they do not want to be distracted or diverted.[34]

The number of women who see children as a distraction from their work, or want to have unfettered leisure time has grown steadily. Until the 1960s uncertain contraception made children an inevitability for most women. With contraception, childlessness is a choice which has become both physically and even socially acceptable, at least in some circles. Female columnists such as Linda Grant or Joan Smith have written about their satisfaction in choosing deliberately to be child-free. Joan Smith says that she never believed in a universal maternal instinct and now no longer feels a freak in preferring to remain childless. She sees the emergence of a group of intentionally child-free women as a revolution in expectations comparable with the discoveries of Galileo.[35] The subjects whom Jane Bartlett interviewed for her study *Will You be Mother? Women Who Choose to Say No* indicated that they were also discovering 'a way of being female that was not necessarily entwined with motherhood'. And the survey responses showed that their work identity was as important to them as any man. Education and satisfying work are usually the *sine qua non* of voluntary childlessness. Fertility rates amongst women without qualifications have not changed.[36] Nobody is forgoing babies in order to remain at the supermarket checkout. The recent decline in childbearing has been amongst women who are educated to A level and above. It is those women who have discovered a different identity who are starting to mutiny against the dictatorship of procreation.

The link between achievement and childlessness is obvious – ambition is the best form of contraception. Not every one will aspire to be the Speaker of the House of Commons, but the principle that a busy working life leaves less room for children is now recognized a long way down the occupational hierarchy. Mothers are especially scarce in those areas of employment that are the most demanding, the most insecure and allow the least private space. The British Film Institute report on the television industry found that amongst older women working in this field 53 per cent were childless, compared with only 15 per cent of men.[37] At the very senior levels in television the numbers of mothers were well within single figures. In the City a survey for the *Guardian* on women in the Square Mile found the same patterns, encapsulated in its profile of a 32-year-old female investment banker who worked a six-day week and most evenings. She loved her job and was proud of her achievements but said:

> I know I could not do this job and have a family. I can't have it all, it would be completely impossible. But it would be possible for a man to do my job and have a family. Is that really equality?

The Institute of Management reported that 63 per cent of its female members were childless compared with 30 per cent of men.[38] And in a *Wall Street Journal* survey of women executives with the title of vice-president or higher 52 per cent of the 722 women were childless compared with 7 per cent of comparable men.[39] In May 1997, when the *Guardian* profiled the 'Fifty Most Powerful Women in Britain', 40 per cent were childless. Marriage and children are taken as signs of a stable and dependable male employee, but in relation to women employees they signal unreliability. Yet paradoxically older childless women complain that they are regarded as 'weird' and 'unnatural' by colleagues at work.

The continuum of the voluntarily childless stretches from those who have made a conscious choice to do other things and see no place for children in their busy lives, to those who might perhaps like children but simply cannot figure out how and when they

could be fitted in, and also to those whose dedication to their
working life has left little or no time for building relationships, let
alone reproducing. In marketing-speak these are the 'lone rangers',
the singletons who have the demanding job, car, flat but not a
worthwhile man.[40] One million women in their thirties (nearly one
third of the total) are single. The 1995 General Household Survey
found that four out of ten single women were not even in a sexual
relationship. Business at dating and introduction agencies is
booming as women (more than men) ring in to search for a partner who can meet their expectations. According to the dating
agencies, the control and achievements women have discovered
through education and work mean that they now have higher standards in looking for the right man and less leisure time in which to
find him. Straightforward criteria like finding a provider or a
breadwinner are no longer relevant when so many women earn a
reasonable income through their own efforts. At the same time the
stereotype of women wanting to marry up persists and so as they
rise higher they find themselves chasing an ever-diminishing pool.
Equally, many men may not be ready to accept a woman who
earns more than they do and is equally ambitious. So even if a
woman might not have chosen to be a lone ranger – and would
willingly embrace a different lifestyle – it may be assumed that she
has made a choice. 'The reason I am not married,' said one forty-
year-old senior public sector manager, 'is because all the men I
have been close to in the end really just wanted a wife and I was
not prepared to end up only as "somebody's wife".' She is the
typical product of a mother whose horizons were sharply cur-
tailed by domestic duties and who urged her daughters to succeed.

I remember feeling as a teenager that the equality legislation
of the seventies would herald a bright new dawn, but twenty-

two years later so little seems to have changed. Despite the high expectations and professional breakthroughs, in the end men were not prepared to travel the same road with us.

The advertising world has identified a valuable new category of long-term-single, financially solvent women, whilst the film makers have been busy telling the wistful stories of this emerging social phenomenon. In 1997 the director Mike Leigh did a powerful job with *Career Girls*, whilst TV documentaries with titles like *On the Shelf* or *Singled Out* told the factual tales of high-earning, hard-working women – patrons of dating agencies or readers of the personal columns – many of whom would like to find a partner and have children, but meanwhile were doing quite nicely without. For one attractive, vivacious thirtysomething with a very grand job in advertising, the moment of realization came when her parents presented her with a toolbox for Christmas – confirmation that, after five years without a boyfriend, for the medium term at least she was likely to be unattached.

The rising number of women in the UK who are childless is part of the pattern of overall declining fertility. The size of a completed family (or live births per woman) dropped from the famous 2.4 children per woman in 1981 to 2.04 in 1995. At the same time there has been an increase since 1981 in the number of two-parent families which have only one child.[41] The single-child family – Chinese style – might be the compromise for the busy two-career couple who come late to child rearing. So future generations may see a whole new pattern emerging in which the nuclear family is even further pared down as fewer children have siblings or cousins and family is increasingly understood as a vertical relationship with parents, grandparents and even great-grandparents.[42]

All across Europe motherhood is going out of fashion. In many countries fertility has dropped below the replacement rate of 2.1; in Catholic, family-loving Italy the total fertility rate stands at 1.2 births per woman, which along with Spain's is one of the lowest in the world.[43] The Italian prime minister, Romano Prodi, called the 'anti-baby boom' a 'demographic catastrophe', not least because of the burden it will place upon the national pension funds. The 'pay as you go' concept of funding retirement provision starts to look very precarious. In 1996, 521,000 babies were born in Italy. Thirty years earlier the figure was over 1 million. One detailed study that tried to explain why Italian women are not procreating identified the 'unfair distribution of house-work between partners' and the 'frightening insufficiency of state provision for childcare services, as well as the conditions of job uncertainty'.[44] The report stresses that contrary to the general perception, female employment is not particularly high in Italy and it is therefore unlikely that a low birth rate is simply the result of women going to work. Indeed Sweden has the highest rate of female employment in the OECD, yet in contrast to nearly every other European country it has seen its birth rate increase back above replacement level.[45] In the 1970s the Swedish birth rate was 1.59, but since then it has risen to 2.3, and with the exception of Ireland and Iceland it is the highest in Europe.[46] In Sweden many of the anxieties about childcare and parental responsibilities have been alleviated. This is the result not simply of adequate nursery provision or day care – there was plenty of that in the communist states of Eastern Europe, like East Germany and the Soviet Union, although they nevertheless dis-played stubbornly low birth rates[47] – but also of a wider culture that encourages working parents to share some of the responsi-bility across the sexes, and that does not devalue caring and parenthood or discriminate against part-timers. For working parents Swedish provision is a nirvana: guaranteed nursery care, parental leave, reduction in hours. Politicians in other countries point out complacently that Swedish social provision has led to grave economic trouble and that nowhere else could possibly afford such luxury. But if the falling birth rate in many countries is a real crisis, the Swedish example cannot be dismissed so readily. Penelope Leach is a persuasive advocate of the Swedish model which allows individuals to parent and to work without conflict, in stark contrast to Britain:

> As long as we do not differentiate between what mothers are in relation to their children and what they do, motherhood will continue to be presented as an either or choice . . . women cannot choose between their relationship with their child and their individual adult identity, vested in a salaried or wage-earning role . . . both are essential . . . to suggest that she cannot fulfil the role of mother unless she is with her child, or work unless at her desk 7 or 5 days a week is idiotic . . . it is like choosing between food and drink . . . only flexible integration and sequencing of people's various roles can defuse the conflict between parenthood and paid work.[48]

Italy is not the only country where babies are going out of fashion. Another, very different society is seeing a 'silent revolution' by women whose 'bellies are on strike' – Japan. In 1989 there was talk of the '1.57 crisis' when discussing the falling birth rate, yet by 1996 the birth rate had fallen still further, to 1.43 live births per woman, and there is concern that in the twenty-first century Japan will have the world's oldest population. Japanese society shares some of the features that distinguish Italy from

Sweden. Certainly the falling birth rate is not a result of women working. Japanese women are discouraged both by employers and social pressure from working beyond childbirth, and sometimes give up after marriage. They face a male working culture that exhibits all the features that cause extreme difficulties for anyone with a meaningful domestic life – insanely long hours, arduous commuting, relentless presenteeism with a round of compulsory extracurricular 'socializing' in the evenings and at weekends. This is the world of the Japanese 'salaryman' which partly explains his reputation as a totally unreconstructed man about the house. Japan has been described as 'a fatherless society' so minimal is the average father's involvement with his growing children. The domestic division of labour here starts from a totally different baseline. Far from making any contribution towards childcare and other tasks, Japanese men themselves expect to be waited upon by a willing spouse, but educated Japanese women are no longer so keen to fulfil this role. This has precipitated the growth in a 'wife trade' – the importing of women from other Asian countries who are less educated and more biddable marriage prospects.[49] The expectations of mothering are higher in Japan than in Western countries; paediatricians exhort women to achieve unrealistic standards in nurturing their young. Mothers must provide devoted babycare in the early years, and later on produce the highest-achieving schoolchild. The use of disposable nappies is seen as bad for baby, so in 1986, 93 per cent of Japanese mothers were still using terry nappies that they washed themselves. Fewer than 2 per cent used commercial baby food, which is discouraged even though it is highly convenient. Leaving children in a crèche is frowned upon, so those mothers who do try to work find the social pressures and practical difficulties hard going. Japanese TV even showed a soap opera about a working mother whose children suffered and who made her children, parents and husband deeply unhappy. The climax of the plot came when she made the noble 'choice' to give up work and stay at home. Most mothers do not attempt to work, but then complain that motherhood is 'isolating, lonely, limiting and exhausting'.[50] They think hard before having a second, let alone a third, child. Of the annual half a million abortions in Japan some 70 per cent are performed on married women. The trend away from childbearing has caused official public concern as the median age of the Japanese population is predicted to reach fifty-four by the middle of the next century. The tricky political problem is that women, especially those who are well-educated, appear reluctant to choose motherhood under the prevailing conditions. There is criticism that women are too concerned with enjoying themselves and being independent. The former prime minister, Ryutaro Hashimoto, warned in 1990 that the harmful effects of education distracted women from their primary duty in life.[51] He was doubtless correct that it is women whose horizons have expanded who are reluctant to give it all up to have children in a society where the domestic burdens are so unequal.

Japan is perhaps an extreme case, but in Britain too – although it never used to be explicit – mothering is supposed to be about sacrifice. The outspoken Conservative MP Ann Widdecombe has warmly praised her mother, who lived 'the sacrificial life', giving up her own aspirations and ambitions to support her husband and children. Ann Widdecombe disarmingly likes to tell the world that she is a virgin, but she claims that had she become a mother herself, she would certainly have followed this route of sacrifice for the sake of her family.[52] In an age of go-getting individualism where everyone is urged to prove themselves in the marketplace, the idea of any kind of sacrifice, especially a lifelong one, sits uneasily. And the sacrifice today is far greater than ever before as many women have so much more to lose. The opportunity cost of an independent achieving woman in her thirties (or a government minister) turning into a Stepford wife may be unacceptably high. Quite apart from the negotiation over children and child rearing, the aspirations such a woman will have in selecting a partner will inevitably amount to something more than searching out a traditional breadwinner; hence the constant murmurs of dissatisfaction questioning why there are not enough good men available and the suggestion that having a baby by oneself might be the only alternative.

There are lurid newspaper accounts of the fashion for donor insemination amongst wealthy thirtysomethings who are worried about their biological clock and have the resources to comfortably go it alone.[53] Internet sites offer selections of sperm for artificial insemination, which is particularly attractive for single women who want to pick the best genes and wish to avoid awkward questions. The customer clicks on her choice and with a credit card payment the package of sperm can be despatched with full instructions, direct from California. This is for the tiny minority with the determination and financial means. They are too few to register in the figures. The more general trend meanwhile is the growing disinclination towards having children.

Naomi Wolf has sounded a warning that mothering and self-sacrifice are not mystically paired:

'Maternal instinct' has long been the margin of error that a sexist society has taken for granted. Society has assumed that it could leave women and children at the bottom of the heap; that for women a profound mammalian force would manage to overcome lack of income, health care and childcare and somehow nurture and socialize the next generation.[54]

Once the range of opportunities on offer to women is expanded,
even if the choices are not quite what they seem, all the previous
comfortable assumptions start to unravel. Outside totalitarian
states, the business of continuing the human race has, since the
1960s, become equated with a simple personal lifestyle decision
for individual women. But now that there is a danger that more
and more women will say 'thanks but no thanks' to procreation,
childless women are no longer referred to as 'sad' or 'unfulfilled',
but instead they are criticized for being egoistic or self-centred.
Even parents of only children are referred to as selfish. The veteran management guru Peter Drucker believes that the predicted
population decline in the twenty-first century and an ever-ageing
population structure are the greatest catastrophes facing the
West.[55] So if bearing children is suddenly recognized as a positive
social contribution, perhaps it is time that there was more support
for this activity from the other half of the human race and a more
satisfactory integration of family with the rest of working life.
The alternative is that an increasing number of women will
decline, either through conscious choice or through force of circumstance, to undertake childbearing. In the words of the
Japanese poet Taeko Tomioka, 'women who have nothing better to
do have a child'.

7

The Black Hole of Policy

If the most pressing question of our age is how a deregulated market economy can be reconciled with social cohesion, where do women fit in this conundrum? After 1989 the utopian vision of the global free market emerged triumphant. Of course some people might say that socialism like Christianity had never really been tried, but in 1989 what passed in its name was finally discredited and the trappings of a collectivist political culture were discarded. Likewise the criticisms that Marx had originally made of the capitalist system – the inexorable profit motive, the dangers of globalization, the widening inequality – were forgotten. The US model of vigorous unfettered economic competition became the template for the future, and the principles of the market reached their tentacles into more and more areas of activity. Ultimately every field of endeavour could be understood by its bottom line and the concept of the world as one gigantic marketplace of labour, money and ideas. National governments were charged with achieving the maximum possible competitive advantage in the global marketplace.

At the same time a growing unease emerged at the perceived decay in the social fabric. Mrs Thatcher famously declared that society did not exist and fell back on the family as the repository of values and decency. But the family itself was metamorphosing – and fast. That was hardly surprising: if the public world was all about thrusting individuals seeking their fortune and fulfilment, then an institution that depended upon unquantifiable values and non-market principles of love, dependence, lifelong loyalty, sacrifice and mutual support sat awkwardly in the new order. New Labour is very keen on the family, and it also believes in the ideal of 'community' – which is those same caring, sharing values writ large. Yet at the same time it proclaims the benefits and advantages of the flexible labour market. According to New Labour the answer to these contradictory forces is the elusive 'third way' that can synthesize both the market and community. But many observers wonder if this formulation is not spin doctor hype, citing J. K. Galbraith's dismissal of the middle way as a misguided search for a point between right and wrong, whereas the real task is to seek to repair the damage that the capitalist renaissance has done to the social fabric.[1] This is the fundamental dilemma that Western politics grapples with daily but fails dismally to resolve. And although the role of women is most affected by this paradox it is also the subject on which politicians have the least to say.

Political debate has fragmented, and women in particular have slipped through the cracks. On the one hand there is anxious talk about the family and the need to create the kind of stable homes in which children can thrive. Tony Blair has spoken about parents needing to find time for their children, to read to them and to help with homework.[2] His government's education policy includes proposals for the policing of truants and for making parents directly responsible for their children's behaviour; it supports contracts between parents and school with guidelines for minimum levels of homework – and since homework is supposed to begin at four years old it necessarily involves active parental support.[3] There is a Ministerial Committee on the Family trying to promote ways of re-establishing family and community bonds – like classes on parenting skills, curfews for youngsters, and other means by which good practice can be instilled into families and childrearing – because these are above all the necessary conditions for reducing juvenile crime. New Labour is clear that families 'should teach right from wrong and should be the first defence against anti-social behaviour'.[4] The Home Office, which is steering much of this agenda on the family, is also anxious to promote a 'compact' with the voluntary sector to encourage volunteering amongst a new and younger generation who are losing the habit.[5] For New Labour, 'voluntary activity as an expression of citizenship is central to our vision of a stakeholder society'.

MP Denis MacShane, who wrote in the *Daily Mail* about the 'unsung heroines keeping Britain together by staying at home', is one of several members of New Labour who go even further.[6] He has argued that housewives should be allowed a tax break (transferring their unused personal allowance to their partner) in return for doing this valuable work in the home – a policy taken from the Conservative Party's 1997 general election manifesto. Yet the caring-and-sharing rhetoric seems to contradict the parallel discourse of economic advance, the primacy of wage earning and the operation of deregulated labour markets. Here salvation is through wage earning, especially for single mothers (who would of course not benefit from a tax break for caring because they have no one to transfer the allowance to) and there is an accompanying assumption that women who work will fit into the existing capitalist structures of the economy, however demanding they may have become.

Insecure and casual work, short-term contracts, antisocial hours or long hours: familiar features of contemporary labour markets can make it more difficult than ever to fulfil the expectations of parenting and community. The problem is that in practice mothers *are* the community, and in some ways they need to contribute even more than they used to, since one fifth of dependent children now live in one-parent (usually lone mother) families. It is mothers who are more likely to feel themselves part of the 'sandwich generation': caring simultaneously for older and younger dependants, because in the vast majority of cases mothers are the ones who are assumed to be responsible for the disciplining, reading and the nurturing as well as for caring for the elderly or cementing the links in the wider community. Some of the doubters about Labour's 'third way' even describe it as 'a synthesis of market forces embedded in "community" which mops up the damage done by market forces largely through unpaid work done by women'.[7] Anna Coote, now a government advisor on women, has written eloquently of how the hidden threads of community and family networks are sustained by women.[8] Yet in relation to the labour market these are all unpaid and therefore invisible activities. Family itself is like a hobby, which is slotted into spare leisure time. Children are no longer as critical to parents' economic future as they used to be when they were instrumental in the ultimate well-being of the family, just as they still are in much of the developing world. Indeed, whereas children used to be seen as future profit centres, they are now perceived as cost centres, with frequent newspaper surveys, or academic reports, trying to measure the gross expenditure of bringing up a child over twenty years. At the extreme children are almost the ultimate fashion accessory –

which offer in turn a catalogue of commercial possibilities. (In his autumn 1998 collection the designer Isaac Mizrahi even used the concept to put babies on a New York catwalk so that he could model a range of mother's outfits with matching quilted baby carriers.) When the *Sunday Times* adds up the total cost of a comparatively well-heeled upbringing (from colour-coordinated nursery to riding lessons, the 'right' trainers, exciting holidays and private schools) and then compares it with the alternative purchase of a small yacht or a cosy thatched cottage, the subliminal message is that childrearing is really just another lifestyle option.

Amidst all the emphasis upon children as consumer opportunities, Penelope Leach feels strongly that in political terms 'parenting a child and particularly mothering a child has been squeezed out and made to feel an extra . . . whereas for anybody doing it, it is central. You are strapped for time and money.'[9] The sense of parenting as a peripheral activity carries over into political debate. In the 1997 general election campaign, despite the rhetoric, parenting and the family were treated as marginal issues. The Women's Communication Centre in its report on the campaign found that the concerns that women had about family life and support for parenting were largely absent from the visible agenda of political debate – despite the warm words.[10] At the most basic level, just as Anna Coote observed that politicians don't have much time for living in communities, they also don't have much time or space within their own lives – outside election address photos and kissing babies on the campaign trail – for creating the kind of family that they idealize. And in practical terms following through the policies that support parenting and families may well have financial implications and contradict the tides of change in the contemporary labour market.

The Cost of Caring

The withdrawal of benefits from lone parents at the end of 1997 was a straightforward example of the conflict between the official value placed on caring and the primacy of the paid work ethic. Even those most closely involved with the policy admitted that it followed an unnecessarily tortuous path.[11] Logically, a single parent has to expend more effort upon caring and sustaining family values, all those things that the Ministerial Committee on the Family worries about, but taking away some of her benefit meant that she had even less choice about work. And taking away the benefit from *all* lone parents – when the government's New Deal to assist lone parents into work was originally designed to help only those with school-aged children – made the policy totally indefensible. The government rushed in to repair the damage, although for a period new lone parents were left worse off, and the principle of the original benefit that it is more costly to bring up a child as a single parent was removed for good.

The resounding message was that for everyone the best route out of poverty was work, and it was generally assumed that taking women off Income Support and into work would reduce the burden on the taxpayer too. But sending poorly skilled single mothers with very young children back to work is not an exercise in saving money. The cost of quality childcare for babies and children under five is extremely high, way beyond the earning power of most single parents. In the 1998 budget there was a promise of generous help with childcare for the poor through tax credits. If the Treasury is largely paying for this care for the very youngest children, there will be no net financial gain from sending poor mothers back to work. The bottom line calculation is that it will cost the taxpayer more if a low-skilled single mother with young children is working at the supermarket checkout and receiving the working family tax credit and maximum childcare credit than if she is claiming benefit and looking after her own child at home. In the US state of Wisconsin, which has become a hotbed of social experimentation, 'welfare mothers' have no choice but to work once their baby reaches twelve weeks, while their children are given high-quality day care – but the total bill to the state is 60 per cent more than when they stayed at home on benefit.[12]

The policy of subsidizing registered childcare for low-income families who work involves a huge gamble by the Treasury. It is aimed at encouraging new entrants to the labour market who will be generously subsidized for using registered childcare – like nurseries or childminders. Currently the poor use very little official childcare – it is not financially viable. Under the new system if all the grannies and neighbours who informally look after children decide to register themselves, the government will start to pay huge sums in subsidy. Even if only those currently working were to take full advantage of the subsidies, the costs would soar to an incredible £4 billion (against the government's modest expectation that it will spend £250 million on childcare credit by the year 2001).[13] Any new entrants would push it up even higher.

It is not only the direct costs that will rise, but the associated cost of monitoring the expansion in care. Childcare inspection by local authorities is stretched under the present arrangements. Tragedies like the Norfolk childminder who evaded the system and later killed a baby in 1998 highlight the inadequate supervision; but if there was a major explosion in registration the cost to local authorities who regulate the provision would rise dramatically. Indeed there is even pressure to widen the net of inspection. The Labour Party in opposition promised to consider a proper nanny register, and in 1998 when a nanny was accused of shaking a baby to death in London it highlighted the alarming fact that there is more public regulation involved in a spot of angling than in private childcare. Meanwhile a government task force chaired by the businessman Lord Haskins decided against regulation of 'private' childcare.

If the government finds that it costs British taxpayers more to send some poor mothers back to work (through childcare subsidies and in-work benefits to compensate for low wages), the justification of the policy must be that paid work is in itself a more valuable activity for a mother than being at home with her children. When an activity receives a wage packet – from serving hamburgers to cold-calling on the phone to sell double-glazing – it becomes intrinsically more worthy. The neighbours who register as childminders and increase GNP by taking in each other's children become socially more acceptable, and individually better off, than when they look after their own children. The Fawcett Society, which campaigns on women's issues, was sadly disillusioned with such measures, commenting that the 'Prime Minister's talk about hard choices really meant easy targets', observing that 'it is like the old joke – sink into his arms and end up with your arms in the sink. Now it seems that under the New Deal for Lone Mothers, single mums may well find themselves washing up for McDonalds rather than looking after their children.'[14] There are echoes of the Stalinist reinterpretation of Marxism 'to each according to their work'; the economist Pam Meadows (one of the *Guardian*'s seven wise women) even refers to the 'Arbeit macht frei' rhetoric of New Labour.[15]

Paid work is the route out of poverty – but if the childcare available is substandard, the lone parent is in an almost impossible position, facing a miserable choice. Reconciling the responsibilities of parenting with the labour market becomes more tricky than ever. The lowly status and pay of many care workers highlights the paradox in this area. As in any other area of endeavour, well-qualified and motivated individuals will not magically emerge if the pay is miserly, and nor will low staff turnover. High-quality care from well-trained and committed individuals is inevitably costly, because it means paying the (mainly women) carers a reasonable wage commensurate with their responsibility. Everyone wants good-quality care but there is a continuing reluctance to value the individuals who are doing it, because the cost (to the parents) seems so high.

In the US, childcare has even lower status and is less publicly valued. It is typically the preserve of the huge armies of illegal domestics whose wages, conditions and suitability are totally unregulated. (This was the undoing of two potential female Cabinet appointees in President Clinton's first administration. No one examined how many (dozens?) of male Cabinet members had used similar arrangements over the years.) Even according to the official regulations an untrained au pair – the Louise Woodward scenario – may legally do forty-five hours a week of sole-charge childcare and is entitled to £80 live-in wages. The wages for nursery workers are also extremely low. Interestingly in 1990 the Worthy Wage Campaign involved childcare workers who tried to focus attention on their comparative worth to society as a way of raising the value of their work.[16] They defined work as an activity with a social purpose and against the entire trend of market economics, the higher the social purpose the higher the value – the nurse outstrips the currency trader – so caring for the next generation suddenly becomes a high-status occupation.

Under the New Deal the government will take 50,000 youngsters off benefits and allocate £750 each (one day a week for six months) to train them for work in out-of-school clubs or an expanded nursery sector. This may indeed provide a service that is needed, but it is not clear that it will result in high-quality care from individuals who really want to do it – which is a vital aspect in providing good care. The question of motivation may not matter much at the supermarket checkout or on the assembly line but in childcare it is paramount. The investment in out-of-school clubs may have other problems, because National Lottery funding will cover only the start-up and the first year (equivalent to £1.20 per week per child). After that, as in all the existing out-of-school clubs, parents must pay their own way, so the childcare tax credit will be an important contribution. Kids' clubs are usually not self-financing, and if the revenue from parents falls short of the outgoings, the club must supplement its income by the precarious means of looking for local hand-outs. Some existing clubs have opened and shut several times depending upon the current financial position and grants from local authorities and businesses.

For most people paying for good childcare has until now not been feasible. They tend to rely on informal networks which may or may not be adequate. In 1999 registered or regulated childcare for children up to eleven years old is due to come within the reach of many low-income parents through the tax credit. Today there are 800,000 latchkey children under twelve years old.[17] The campaigning group Parents at Work estimates that there are 100,000 among the invisible low-paid workers who are unaccounted for in terms of their childcare provision – like the cleaners who take their children to work with them. If the government's new schemes work as they are supposed to then the very poorest, providing they are within the tax system and they want to use officially registered care, will start to receive more help. They will be able to pay for childcare, but that does not mean that good enough and well-regulated provision will necessarily exist.

The Policy Clash

The divergence between the policies associated with unpaid caring and the labour market is a recurring theme. The Family Policy Studies Centre looked at some of these contradictions at a seminar in 1996.[18] It asked:

> How can we recognise the needs of children for security while the world is undergoing the greatest change since the industrial revolution? . . . There may indeed be costs to society of increased labour market flexibility. We all know of the short-term economic gains, resulting from contracting out, downsizing, lower wage bills and less favourable conditions but what if there are longer-term consequences in terms of family breakdown, higher crime and undersocialized young people?

These questions probe at the fundamental ways in which governments are organized and alarm politicians who are often uneasy about unearthing the social effects of economic causes. Once, the Conservatives vigorously disbelieved in any relationship between unemployment and crime, prompting Tony Blair's most famous soundbite ('tough on crime and tough on the causes of crime'). According to the Tory orthodoxy, individuals were entirely responsible for the morality of their own conduct, regardless of social conditions. A mountain of research later and William Hague agrees with what most of us assume to be obvious: deprived groups will tend to commit crimes because they see no alternative.[19] Now there is a new blind spot: the labour market and family cohesion. Britain has the most deregulated labour market and the longest working hours in Europe; it also has the highest rate of divorce and family breakdown – which at the most conservative estimate cost the Exchequer £3 billion in 1991.[20]

It is not easy for governments to balance these competing issues. The incoming Labour Party was acutely aware that policy must be coordinated across government – in order that the unintended consequences of actions or the multiple causes of a problem could be identified. They launched cross-cutting reviews on expenditure which sought to look at objectives independently of the various departmental interests. Historically this approach has been tried before. In the 1970s there was a Joint Approach to Social Policy (JASP), a ministerial initiative to coordinate the work of several departments in the field of social policy. Officials produced high-quality subject papers which were meant to provide the basis of consultation, but the exercise became bogged down in its own machinery.[21] The last Conservative government launched Health of the Nation as a cross-government initiative with ambitious joint departmental objectives, but that too petered out after much initial fanfare. It remains to be seen whether the present drive to reallocate spending priorities can succeed against the Sisyphus of Whitehall turf wars. If a spending review (following substantial US research) demonstrated that a combination of high-quality nursery care, family support schemes and holiday schooling could lower juvenile crime in fifteen years' time, it is still not straightforward for a government to implement that in practice. At the crudest level it might mean that a department like Education or Social Security spends money now to give the Home Office savings at some indefinite future date. This is a tall order and the unveiling by Tessa Jowell of the 'Sure Start' programme in 1998, targeting vulnerable pre-schoolers, represents a major breakthrough in this philosophy. Another potential objective is the 25 per cent of all prisoners who grow up in local authority care. A policy that gave intensive education, therapy and support to the 50,000 children currently 'in care' – so many of whom face the grimmest of prospects – may yield spectacular results, but again the pay-off of fewer prisoners and more productive adult lives for these youngsters would only come many years hence. According to the Association of Chief Police Officers, future criminals can be identified as young as seven or eight and potentially diverted from a life of crime. They estimate juvenile crime to cost between five and ten billion pounds annually. In the long term, identifying and thereby preventing youngsters from offending could have enormous savings, but the police chiefs feel that there is still insufficient cooperation between the multiple agencies involved for this to happen.[22]

Politicians tend to think in the short term while the government machine prefers to stick to its functional chimneys, both at the local and the national levels. Civil servants who are supposed to cooperate across departments find that 'invariably what matters is where you come from, not what you are trying to contribute to a discussion'. One familiar route to tackle wider questions and harmonize priorities is through Cabinet subcommittees, but this too has a patchy history. The most effective cooperation occurs when a group is formed with high-level political backing in order to solve a specific problem, unlike the more general Cabinet subcommittees which tackle wider subjects. For this reason high hopes are riding on Labour's Social Exclusion Unit – established in the summer of 1997 under Peter Mandelson – as a prime example of tightly focused interdepartmental cooperation, operating from the centre of government with the political power behind it to bang heads. But the subject of women is an example of a more wide-ranging issue conveniently allocated to tick over in a Cabinet subcommittee. The last Conservative government also had a committee on women, which met less and less frequently until eventually it was attended by the most junior minister from each department and became more form than substance. The current government's women's subcommittee is by contrast almost entirely composed of women ministers (an impossibility under the previous regime) but it is not clear that the results will be radically different.

Women are repeatedly at the mercy of political fragmentation. Just as Simone de Beauvoir identified women as 'other', they remain the 'other' of politics, still seen as a separate issue to be parked somewhere. In the last Conservative government they ended up at the Department of Employment. Under Labour they were transferred to a new berth in Social Security, although a series of turf wars meant that the crucial issues of equal pay and discrimination got left behind in the move. Yet this idea of putting them somewhere increases the danger that they will be sidelined. In most senses the issues are largely insoluble unless they are fully anchored in the mainstream. 'It is a classic mistake to label anything a women's issue,' said one knowing civil servant in 1997, who had seen it all before. Questions about organization of working time, trends in the labour market, and the attitudes of men towards work and parenting cannot be considered in isolation as 'women's issues'. They need to be tackled from within the centre and to cut across existing departmental boundaries. All the talk about 'mainstreaming' will only mean anything if the political will to mainstream these issues comes from the centre. 'Without dynamic political momentum in these areas the machine will just hum along as it always does. If there is to be a women's unit then it should be sited in the Treasury or the Cabinet Office to have maximum effect.' By July 1998 that message had reached the top and this time the Women's Unit migrated again – this time to the Cabinet Office. Quite apart from the problem of being sidelined, locating women's issues within a large-spending department like Social Security had meant there was always a danger of conflicting interests. Second-tier pensions are high on the social security agenda, but women have most to lose from the end of SERPS and the disappearing value of the state pension. It is elderly women who are most likely to live in poverty as their lifetime earnings are more erratic and total barely half those of men, making it difficult to establish any alternative pension provision. Similarly when the contentious issue of cutting lone parent benefits arose in 1997, despite all the back-bench agitation and angry women's lobbying, there was a deafening (public) silence from the Women's Unit because the policy might be bad news for women but it was good for trimming the social security budget.

If the Women's Unit is now situated in the most effective place there is still no recognition that this is a proper job. In summer 1998 Joan Ruddock was sacked and the women's brief tacked on to Baroness Jay's responsibilities. As Leader of the Lords, whose day job is to oversee the biggest ever constitutional reform of the second chamber, this hardly signals a high priority for women. The other part-timer is Tessa Jowell who was previously assumed to be fully occupied caring for the nation's public health. So political responsibility remains fragmented and women are still an extra-curricular activity. It was clearly too awkward to continue with the unpaid minister, but there was no interest in regularizing the position as a proper salaried post.

Another frequent suggestion – from both inside and outside the government machine – is the establishment of a Ministry for the Family (or a Minister for Children). That would enable children's interests to be coordinated instead of being looked at separately by half a dozen departments.

It is undesirable that links between employment patterns and child care regimes should fall outside the scope of every

department's remit, not least because it is then possible for
one department to advocate childcare policy which runs
counter to government aims in the sphere of family life and
child welfare.[23]

From a political perspective Patricia Hewitt has pointed out that

> . . . the work/family debate needs to move beyond the stage of
> enabling women to juggle their dual burden a little more
> successfully, to a new ideal which enables both women and
> men to be good parents as well as good workers . . . and there
> will be longer-term payoffs in policies which by enabling
> fathers as well as mothers to spend time with their children,
> improve the quality of children's lives and the chances of
> their educational success.[24]

This sounds a very simple proposition, but it would involve enormous joint effort across large areas of government and is unlikely
to emerge from a separate 'women's unit'. It requires coordination
and plenty of political energy behind it. In the meantime, the
fragmentation of these issues simply reinforces the fractured identity that so many women continue to feel about their lives and the
way their concerns are addressed.

Freud and the Spice Girls asked 'What do women want?', but
the really difficult question is, What does society want of women?
None of the big political parties nor the permanent institutions
can make up their mind about what role women are supposed to
fulfil. There is a jumble of messages. The benefits system is just
emerging from a Beveridge model of the traditional family where
the doctrine was that mothers needed support to 'ensure the adequate continuance of the British race'. Even the childless partner

of an unemployed man has hitherto been classed as a 'dependant' rather than someone who should also seek employment (and status). And paradoxically the benefit system has reinforced the illogical position that a woman who lives with an unemployed partner is herself less likely to be in work than a woman whose partner already works. Gradually the old template is being replaced so that women are becoming persons in their own right. Maybe one day men will regularly collect child benefit because they are classed the primary carer and their partner is the official breadwinner.

Now that women are no longer merely dependants, if they have no other means of support they will be expected to find jobs. Yet this ignores the fact that many women do not enter the labour market on an equal basis. Occupational segregation, much lower levels of pay and a greater burden in the home make their decision to work problematic and render their status as home-makers ambiguous. The present government is wary about offending women who wish to stay at home (so long as their partner is an employed man), but at the same time rejects the idea that lone parents caring for children at home are working (although if they were to care for someone else's children instead, it would be classified as work). From the end of 1999 it will be easier for poorer women to work. However there is also general concern about the disappearance of women's voluntary and communal efforts if they are too involved in the labour market. What sociologists mean when they describe the erosion of 'social capital' is the decline in communal and voluntary institutions as a result of women taking on paid work. The Conservative Party is worried about declining volunteer effort – an acute problem among its own ranks of envelope stuffers – and also reflects the ongoing tensions and contradictions about what women ought to be.

Tories believe (sometimes) that mothers (with the exception of single mothers) are needed at home to sustain strong families, and should not be taking away jobs from men, whilst (at other times) they delight in the introduction of independent taxation and the role model of the thrusting high-flier who succeeds in the workplace on equal terms. In 1977 the shadow Health and Social Security Secretary Patrick Jenkin (now Lord Jenkin) pronounced famously on television, 'If the good Lord had intended us all having equal rights to go out to work and to behave equally, you know he really wouldn't have created man and woman.'[25] And this was two years after he had himself been dutifully serving a woman boss, whom the party had elected as its first female leader. Today any parliamentary selection by a local Conservative association will still highlight these continuing contradictions of what a woman, wife or mother is really supposed to be.

The political tensions in the question 'What does society want of women?' surface each time a new scheme for taxation is floated. Furious letters appear in the newspapers, opening another front in the recurring mothering wars. Working mothers who feel they have no choice but to earn complain at the suggestion of a tax break (through the transfer of personal allowances) to help women to stay at home. Meanwhile mothers who are at home object to a policy that gives a tax concession to pay for the childcare of those who go to work. If they wish to provide their own childcare – sometimes in spite of considerable hardship – why should they be excluded from a subsidy? They complain that a two-earner household (which is frequently better off) already receives a greater tax subsidy through separate taxation, whilst the married couples' allowance has been left to wither away. And women who prefer not to use formal registered childcare but feel more comfortable using a relative or friend now object to being excluded from the subsidy net. Meanwhile most women are left trying to live some version of a fragmented identity, working and caring in varying combinations.

Family Values

Both the work-rich and the work-poor are having difficulty – for quite different reasons – in sustaining the kind of family life that politicians find praiseworthy because it helps to ensure good citizens. At the bottom of the scale a staggering one third of children now grow up below the poverty line.[26] Quite apart from the immediate disadvantages of material deprivation, their households must struggle to sustain the fabric of family life. According to Relate, the marriage counselling organization, low-income couples (coping on less than £10,000 a year) are the most prone to having serious arguments – and these are very frequently triggered by severe financial worries.[27] One Plus One – the charity that carries out research into relationships and marriage – says a man in social classes D or E (manual occupations) is four times as likely as a man in the upper social classes to get divorced. The difficulty of providing a stable and satisfactory environment for growing children is a key aspect of the familiar cycle of social exclusion. Frank Field captured this tension, albeit from a traditional perspective, when he said, 'Society cannot expect a mass of happy families in which to nurture children if the wage system is moving away from producing family wages.'[28]

The veteran social observer Professor A. H. Halsey believes that we face a crisis in the way that society cares for children. Together with Michael Young he issued a radical warning of the damage to society and children from widening incomes and the abandonment

of the third who exist below the poverty line.[29] They argued for a
'parent wage' which would raise the status of caring for children
and remove the stigma of not being in paid work; parenting would
thus be recognized as a valuable contribution. This is distinct from
the transfer of unused personal tax allowances, because it does not
differentiate between the care given by single parents or couples;
they cite Finland as an example of a society where the government pays a parental wage to parents with children under three. A
similar principle operates in Canada which provides the equivalent
of a very high (tapered) rate of child benefit for those with the
youngest children, enabling parents to employ childcare or to provide it for themselves, without facing poverty.

Halsey and Young are concerned not only about children who
face financial poverty. They also worry about the fate of family life
amongst the dual-income/work-rich, as women have entered the
labour market. According to One Plus One, parents who do not
build up a meaningful relationship with their children cannot build
up a 'family culture' that all can share. And it is the time-obsessed
parents amongst the better-off (as well as those who suffer severe
material poverty) who are least likely to be able to establish a
worthwhile family culture. Halsey and Young describe the tension
between the material economy, where contributions to production
and income are what matters, and the private, moral economy
where the currency is 'time available for other people'. They talk of
families experiencing time poverty where 'children get too little of
either parent and much too little of both parents together'. Their
goal is to relieve the financial pressures on time-hassled parents to
work and thereby relieve time-deprived children.

Denis MacShane, the MP for Rotherham, has taken up this
theme with a call for a 'politics of family time'. In place of the
vague outlines of the 'family values' debate, he argues for con-

crete, practical measures: making the tax system less hostile to families, strengthening provision on working time and parental leave, even giving financial assistance to couples on marriage; he also observes that 'admitting that parents who opt to work limited or no hours in order to stay at home to nurture children in their early years is a good thing, may be hard in a policy world where only work counts'.[30] He is not afraid to confront inconsistency and the contradictions between the triumphs of flexible, deregulated markets and the support of family life – but he borrows heavily from conservative rhetoric and, hard as he tries, it begins to sound as if he would ideally prefer to turn back the clock and restrict women's horizons. This is so frequently the unfinished, unsaid assumption from all parts of the political spectrum. If mothers worked less, families would be healed and children would prosper (except, of course, that salvation for 'parasitic' single mothers lies in paid work).

When the communitarian philosopher Amitai Etzioni talks of the dilemma of the modern 'parenting deficit', many readers invariably translate that as the 'mothering deficit'.[31] Etzioni always insists that he is not 'dumping on mothers' because he refers to the reduction in total parental time spent with their children. Nevertheless it is difficult not to draw this conclusion when he likens the changing nature of childcare to an industry that still expects the same output (a nation of healthy, well-balanced children) but where much of the workforce have walked out on the job in the past three decades. The deserting workforce he describes is, of course, a female one. It is mothers who have left their posts. And Etzioni points out, quite logically, that no other industry would expect to produce the same high-quality products (unless there was a transformation in technology) if most of its skilled workers disappeared. So the conclusion is left hanging in

the air – if women would go back and do the job they left, the
family would recover. Of course Etzioni in his measured and
deliberately gender-neutral way never says this aloud. There are
plenty of others to draw the conclusion – and the sentiment is not
confined to the predictable stalwarts of traditional values such as
Francis Fukuyama or Peter Hitchens, who says openly that he
would like to 'make work less family friendly and more difficult
for mothers'.[32] The last Labour prime minister, James Callaghan,
said that mothers who worked could cause delinquent children.
Even liberal columnists like Hamish McRae warn of the unpleasant social costs, the weakening of the family, which he is not afraid
to say is the direct result of so many women going to work. He
observes that it would now be difficult to reverse this process of
wider female horizons, even though he notes that Muslim societies, most dramatically Afghanistan, have managed it.[33]

Leaving aside the question of who is to blame, it is difficult not
to acknowledge a wider anxiety about a decline over the past
decades in the total amount of time that parents spend with children. Both Penelope Leach and Amitai Etzioni anxiously quote
research that shows that the total time parents spend with their
children has dropped by 40 per cent in a generation.[34] This is a
dark, dark subject. Everyone has an opinion and a survey to back
it up, but despite all the controversy there is only minimal long-
term research on the effects on children who are obliged to pass
most of their waking hours with those who are paid to look after
them. There is research that indicates that substitute childcare
does no damage (and can even enhance children's prospects)
whilst other research, used by Patricia Morgan of the Institute of
Economic Affairs, is emphatic that mother is best, pointing to
unsatisfactory outcomes from the majority of day care.[35] And
Morgan points out that even those who conclude that day care for

young children is fine are only talking about high-quality, stable childcare, which is beyond the reach of most parents.

Some of the time budget studies say there is nothing to worry about. According to long-term data on how households pass their time, children are getting more attention than ever, because we have smaller families and social conditions mean that we have to be more cooped up with them. An analysis of time use reflects the different and not always satisfactory ways that children are reared – like the alarming statistic that we now spend nine hundred million hours a year on school runs! The idea that children are receiving more parental attention than ever is, however, only the view of the optimistic minority. There are many more surveys and statistics that support the view that parents are not there and that alternative childcare may not always suffice.[36]

Teachers, who are in a good position to judge the issue, have become particularly concerned about the effects of substitute care on children whose high-flying parents do not spend enough time with them. Tony Evans, as chairman of the Headmasters and Headmistresses Conference[37] (a group of 240 independent schools) invented the phrase 'opulent neglect' to describe the fact that some children received insufficient emotional support from busy, distracted parents too wrapped up in work to pay them sufficient attention. 'I am very sceptical about quality time. Children just need time and you cannot legislate for when they will need it. You have to recognize children have crises outside carefully regimented hours.' In an article entitled 'Working Mothers', a fellow headmaster did not bother with gender-neutral language, stating that the problem lay with mothers who worked, because househusbands could not offer the same emotional support. Allegedly there are even private schools who prefer to select the children of non-working mothers, or at least mothers who do not work full-time.

According to the family therapist Gwyn Daniel, the question of how children's needs can be met if both parents work 'has become a taboo area. Professional childcare can create the illusion that the workplace can be protected from the needs of families. How do children transmit the message that their needs come first. What control do children have over when the quality time takes place?'[38] The whole American myth of quality time is beginning to crumble. *Newsweek* ran a cover story on the subject in 1997 which concluded, 'Children don't do meetings. You can't raise them in short scheduled bursts.'[39] That is the problem with quality time – it is directly translated from the concepts of the workplace where everything can be efficiently slotted into place and problems are ultimately soluble through careful diary management. Quality time is like achieving greater productivity at work, the same results in fewer hours. But the reason children don't do meetings is that their needs are forever unpredictable and shifting. Maybe the parents of small children can keep them up late and adjust their sleep patterns to make them available for quality time, but older children can never be fitted into such a framework. Indeed, sometimes young children do the adjusting for themselves. The childcare expert Miriam Stoppard, who kept herself maniacally busy during the daytime, remarked that after eight continuous years of disrupted nights she realized her children had sensibly calculated that the only way they could be assured of her time and attention was in the middle of the night.

A teenager may not make a nocturnal appearance in the parental bed but requires unstructured chat and discursive unwinding in their own time. Often the needs of older children do not present themselves with the urgency of a work deadline, or even a crying baby. Baroness Brigstocke, who was for many years the high mistress of St Paul's Girls School, found that in her experience 'it is the

teenagers who need home support most of all. Despite the flounc-
ing, the grumbling, the criticism, the rebelling, teenagers definitely
want and need large slabs of time and attention from their parents.'[40] So parents who think they can regularly breeze in late and
have a neatly timetabled session of 'Tell me about your problems'
may be hopelessly naïve. The conventional wisdom was always
that mother ought to be there when children are little but that she
can wander back to work once they are at school. Only the theoreticians really believe that. In practice it can be easier to rely on a
kindly, competent stranger to change nappies and produce imaginative shapes with Play-doh; older children need their parents'
attention and no alternative will do. Countless energy is expended
upon the question of substitute care for babies and toddlers – what
are the effects of day care and how much is too much? The far
more complicated but less commonly considered question is, What
do much older children need and are they being given enough?

Children not only need vast quantities of time, but they need
this from adults who are not preoccupied elsewhere, mentally or
physically, and who do not view parenting as a series of childcare
crises. Psychologists point out that children develop high self-
esteem through the feeling that someone is really interested in
them and that they really matter. Even when their parents are
preoccupied for the best of motives, children may be resentful.
Gillian Slovo wrote a gripping memoir about her parents Joe Slovo
and Ruth First, ANC activists and architects of the modern South
Africa who dedicated their lives to political struggle, often at the
expense of their children.[41] She describes the Soweto funeral in
1995 at which 60,000 people paid tribute to her father. 'My anger
at my parents was essentially because they had a passion in their
life and it wasn't me, it was South Africa . . . at the funeral I
realised that was his family.' Gillian was not alone. When Nelson

Mandela came to offer condolences he told her sadly of the time
when he had tried to hug his grown-up daughter and she had
flinched from him and burst out, 'You are the father to all our
people, but you never had the time to be a father to me.' He told
Slovo his greatest and perhaps only regret was the price his children and the children of his comrades had had to pay for their
parents' commitment. 'So there it was – the one against the other:
their work, our needs, their commitment, our lives, there was no
squaring the circle.' This is a far cry from parents who are merely
preoccupied with late meetings, paperwork, antisocial shifts or
business trips, but no matter how noble the cause neglect feels the
same to a child. According to One Plus One:

> In very busy homes . . . parents and their children aren't
> actually talking at an age when the child becomes more
> difficult to penetrate and when peer groups become more
> important. . . . if you want to keep the lines of
> communication open you have simply got to be there.
> Moreover busy and preoccupied parents may not pass on the
> values which got them to the top and the kids are rejecting
> them and saying 'I don't want to be like you, I want to have
> time for relationships'.[42]

Young and Willmott were already worrying about these difficulties in 1973 when they wrote *The Symmetrical Family*. They
looked at the new employment patterns that were emerging, combined with the constant pursuit of economic growth, and warned
that 'Children coming from homes fragmented by new triumphs
of technology and feminism might fail to develop into the kind of
people capable of making a centre of peace in the homes that they
in turn will establish for their children to be reared in.'[43]

When a study of 600 teenagers in east London was interpreted by the BBC *Panorama* programme in January 1997, the conclusion was that the children of mothers working full-time did less well at school. 'Missing Mum' caused an extraordinary uproar throughout the media. Never mind that the study was flimsy and the commentary inaccurate – in fact the children of non-working mothers did worst of all and there was no control for socio-economic status or types of childcare – while a much larger study undertaken at Essex University at the same time showed quite contrary results.[44] None of this was perceived as relevant: the programme had exposed a raw nerve and so caused major ripples. Even the most secure and confident working mother shuddered and made a mental note to rethink her life and her priorities, when she had a moment; not for the first time she wondered secretly how much parenting was good enough. The programme was not of course titled 'Missing Dad': father's input is considered an optional bonus. It is ironic that the original research that *Panorama* had so selectively reported was initially part of a project to examine father's roles in family life, but this aspect was not of interest. Maternal employment is a perennial focus of anxiety and controversy. The effect of paternal employment or even paternal neglect on children is accepted, like a law of nature.

What Is To Be Done?

The social value of caring and who is doing it is critical in the rearrangement of family time. If men do not assume their share of responsibility and find an identity in the private sphere, then nothing else will change. Similarly these shifts must be addressed on a communal level. So long as the onus remains with the individual, the issue will not become a public question about the redistribution of work and caring between and within families. Boys must feel that society as a whole is offering role models of caring, both at home and in the workplace, regardless of gender. This kind of reinforcement needs to start from the earliest years both in private and in public, challenging the stereotypes and occupational segregation that persist. One route into breaking down the 'reproduction of mothering' would be to extend substantially the scope of parental leave for new parents, as in Scandinavian countries, which offer flexible, partly paid, leave schemes that can be taken by either parent until the child is eight.[45] Crucially some portion of this leave must be non-transferrable between parents so that the father will be more inclined to take it. A few days' paid leave or a few weeks' unpaid leave are not effective substitutes.

Men working in childcare or primary education have become a rare and exotic species, and as such are frequently the object of suspicion. Most nurseries and many infant schools have no male teachers at all. Men account for a mere 17 per cent of teachers for the under-eights, and the Teacher Training Agency forecasts that they will disappear altogether from primary schools by 2010 if this trend continues.[46] Of course the underlying assumption is that men will not become primary school teachers or childcare workers while the financial rewards remain at the level of 'women's work'. Explaining the feminization of their profession, the teaching unions say, 'It is fine as a second income in a family but not a first income.' Yet even when salary is not an issue, conventional attitudes mean that mothers are still far more involved in primary school life than fathers – including those couples where both have a similar position in the labour market. Encouraging fathers to be involved in the education of the very young costs almost nothing at all. An enterprising Hampshire primary school with an all-female staff made a special plea for fathers (and grand-fathers) to become reading volunteers because the boys were noticeably falling behind the girls. The head was delighted at the results.[47] In the USA, parent–child centres managed to encourage fathers to become involved by offering a cooperative car mainte-nance programme, which became the basis for them to participate with their children. If raising the next generation in today's soci-ety is probably more difficult and unsupported than at any previous period, it is crucial that young people are prepared and equipped in advance for the complexities and responsibilities of parenting. Perhaps boys should be learning, from male teachers, about parenting and emotional literacy whilst they are still at school. This would help boys who are currently underachieving to see a wider spectrum of options available to them as men.

In some European countries there has been a proactive cam-paign towards trying, at least at the margins, to change attitudes and stereotypes. The Austrian government has supported a £2 million public advertising campaign called 'Halb Halb' (half and half) aimed at persuading Austrian men to do their fair share in the home. There are proposals to enshrine housework equality in Austrian law, albeit without any penalties for transgression. The Belgian Equal Opportunities Council started blitzing clubs and cafés with posters showing twentysomething males in atypical poses – ironing or feeding the baby – and asking 'Is there a law against it?' In Sweden there was a campaign to persuade men to make use of the parental leave they were legally entitled to take. This followed the realization that simply having something avail-able on the statute book or in the company equal opportunity handbook was not enough to make it happen.

Family-friendly working is often held up as the smart new improvement for women, and as a solution to the problems of women in the labour market.[48] The government's Women's Unit has made this one of its key policy objectives – but that is part of the problem. For the Women's Unit, as its title suggests, is authorized to look at making work more accommodating from a woman's perspective. But as a civil servant sceptically pointed out:

> The battle is lost if we are identifying the pressure point for changing labour market and workplace policies as a women's matter. Men are then conveniently let off the hook on child rearing because it is a women's issue. Unless there is a shared understanding with men that it is in our mutual interest to have family-friendly workplaces we are never going to get anywhere.

If 'family-friendly' translates into mother-friendly working it will be meaningless. And most of the organizations operating these schemes report that the take-up by men is minute. In that case family-friendly working is simply offering the individual woman a private solution to rearrange her burdens – what Americans call the 'mommy track'. Both private and public sector organizations disclaim responsibility for the fact that few men request job sharing, part-time working or a career break. The policies are there but the male employees do not ask. Yet if 'family-friendly' were genuinely mother- and father-friendly, it would mean a culture in which men did not feel socially stigmatized if they asked to treat their family as visible and wanted to share in its future domestically and emotionally.

Family-friendly working in practice, as with so many similar initiatives, diverges radically from the official and considered policy of the handbook. Even in the civil service which is supposedly in the vanguard of such innovations, those who have tried to apply the policy, especially at higher levels, say that it only goes skin-deep. It might be satisfactory for junior staff charged with more routine tasks, but anyone else asking for concessions – especially if resources become stretched – is often perceived as shifting unfair burdens onto their immediate colleagues and can be ominously labelled as 'lacking commitment'.

A study entitled *Best Companies for Women* reported on the different initiatives for flexible working, maternity policies and childcare provision, but ultimately concluded that 'it is far easier for companies to deal with the demands motherhood makes on women by instituting flexible hours, career breaks or even workplace nurseries than to deal with the very real problems that women are not getting promoted in any great numbers'.[49] If the solution is perceived as implementing some special concessions for individual mothers, there will never be any meaningful change. This extends into the wider issue of all equal-opportunity initiatives that so often look only at the symptoms but not at the root causes of the problem – such as the structures of the workplace or lopsided responsibilities at home. Patricia Hewitt points out quite simply that 'equal opportunities in employment is inconsistent with the male organisation of working time'.[50]

Once again this strikes at the heart of the equality-versus-difference debate. Should women forgo any changes that bring short-term amelioration on the grounds that if they do not redistribute power and change attitudes between the genders they are just reinforcing the status quo? The distinguished American sociologist Christopher Lasch believed ardently that

> . . . a strategy more consistent with the original aims of the feminist movement would challenge the prevailing definition of success. It would challenge the separation of home and the

workplace, it would seek to remodel the workplace around
the needs of the family. It would not make a pay check the
only symbol of accomplishment. It would demand a system
of production for use rather than profit. It would insist that
people need self-respecting, honourable callings, not
glamorous careers that carry high salaries but take them away
from their families. Instead of seeking to integrate women
into the existing structures of the capitalist economy, it
would appeal to women's issues in order to make the case for
a complete transformation of those structures.[51]

For some feminists the idea of admitting to differences is like the
disingenuous slogan of 'separate but equal' which blacks confronted for so many years. (The path to advocating racial equality
seems relatively straightforward compared with the minefield of
sex equality, as only an extreme minority still argue that there are
any meaningful racial differences whereas the scope for arguing
significant biological differences between the sexes is still wide
open.) In the United States, the National Organization of Women
failed to support the legislation requiring employers to grant
parental leave. This dismayed Christopher Lasch:

> More flexible working is not part of its agenda because it
> believes that women take more advantage of such leaves than
> men and a parental leave policy would perpetuate the division
> of labour that assigns women the primary role in child care
> and thus inhibits their professional advancement. In the
> highly competitive world of business and the professionals
> those who stray from the careerist path pay a heavy price . . .
> those who allow their children to slow them down lose out in
> the race for success.

This is a logical although extreme position and completely at odds with attitudes in continental Europe, which abounds in measures aimed to make work more compatible with parenting, which invariably means mothering.

The debate continues to rage between entrenched positions on either side.[52] Of course the complicated but confusing truth is that there are elements worth preserving in both approaches. The most useful tactics depend upon the period and the issue involved, and it is too simplistic to pursue either course to the exclusion of the other. Emphasizing difference can lead down a blind alley, but stressing only equal rights within the male status quo can bring empty victories – not everyone is thrilled about women in the boxing ring or shrunken maternity provision. Unfortunately Britain, rather than synthesizing the best of both worlds, has failed to provide many of the European protections and benefits for women. And it has also failed to realize all the advantages of the go-getting US model, where opportunities and potential for advancement are greater through the uncompromising but often harsh pursuit of equal rights. The most satisfactory compromise is to maximize the best in both approaches. A world in which women just become more and more like men and men stay much as they have always been is hardly a vision of nirvana.

Childcare is a good example of the dilemma between equality and difference. If the goal is straightforward equality with the life that men lead, then one of the principal needs is to provide more and more childcare, thereby removing women's traditional burdens. The logic goes that if children are taken care of for the working day, then women can come to compete in the workplace on an equal footing. The high demand for day care in the United States (combined with unwillingness to pay very much for it) has led to provision in some cases that is far below the standards that regulations would allow in Western Europe. There are stories about miserable 'kennels' for young children, with inadequate staffing and facilities.[53] Whilst in the most advanced European countries, although there is satisfactory day care there is also provision for mothers to do their own caring in early years and not lose a foothold in the labour market.

The reality may be more complicated than simply 'Childcare, childcare, childcare' and the visions of the twenty-four-hour nursery. Unquestionably there are parents who urgently want more affordable and quality childcare, and organizations like the Daycare Trust tirelessly point out the hopelessly inadequate shortfall in UK provision. Yet other research shows that most mothers who are currently at home and 'economically inactive' do not necessarily want that much more commercially provided childcare so that they can go to work.[54] Indeed many women work only through financial necessity and would much prefer to be at home instead of using childcare. This evidence supports Catherine Hakim's central argument that it is not the straightforward absence of childcare which is a barrier to working.

One highly paid professional who gave up her job to look after her small children herself said she was not responding to a childcare crisis. 'In the end I was fed up with feeling that my home resembled Grand Central Station.' At the other end of the social scale the much-repeated claim that a majority of lone mothers are anxious to work – childcare permitting – is very ambiguous. Only one quarter of those eligible are turning up to be interviewed for the New Deal for Lone Mothers. The more detailed responses to the question of working tend to show that a substantial number of lone mothers would like to work, but only at some future point when their children are less dependent. In the meantime they want to provide their own childcare, even if it means financial hardship.[55] Many women right across the social spectrum do not want more farming out of their children to others – they simply want a society where bringing up children can be incorporated into the rest of life; they want an end to the feeling that having children means being pushed into a backwater for ever, with the prospect of returning only to low-status work. And they do not necessarily want the 'homemaker' model that Catherine Hakim describes either. There is another alternative, which is to harmonize work and caring within partners' lives rather than accept the strict segregation of work and childcare because this generates the highest income.

Of all the models of contemporary childcare this seems the most difficult to put into practice. We are familiar with the workless household where children face poverty, or the strictly segregated household where childcare is the responsibility of one partner, or the subcontracting model where childcare is paid for outside to enable parenting to fit around the rhythms of work, and where parental time with children is at a premium. In many ways the trickiest model of all is for two partners to provide a high proportion of the care themselves and for each to sustain a reasonable position in the labour market – without having to resort entirely to weatherhouse-style in-and-out parenting and antisocial shifts. For many people the ideal of two parents working part-time, say half or three quarters time, and participating in their family growing up, is the least economically efficient model, because two part-time jobs do not usually add up to a full-time wage.

Rethinking Time

Those who can achieve some kind of balance, sharing work and care, need to have the right financial and professional circumstances, and they need also be temperamentally suited to the challenge. Such domestic arrangements mean going against the currents of the labour market and against the culture of 'he who works the longest is the most important' or 'my clients/job might disappear tomorrow so I had better give them everything I can, just in case'. The man who accepts all the familiar female constraints of leaving work on time to pick children up from school, taking days off for the sick child, will suffer if he doesn't learn the deceptions that women are familiar with – the Houdini acts of disappearing, the highly imaginative excuses. A secretary was routinely instructed to tell clients that her female boss was in a meeting around 3.30, when in fact she had nipped out for the school run. This was fine until her client was another part-time mother who said suspiciously, 'Are you sure she is not out of the office picking up her children?' Dr Wendy Greengross, who was a female medic long before it was commonplace, admits, 'I never took a day off for the children. If I was late I'd say it was the car. Always give the man's excuse, never the woman's excuse.'[56] But what excuse can the man give if he wants to be involved at home?

Those who can most easily avoid the pressures of 'presenteeism' and the invisible family are the self-scheduling workers who have control over their time and who are able effectively to regulate their portfolio existence. The post-industrial life, if it works, could become like the pre-industrial time when home-centred work was interspersed with child rearing in a seamless round of activity, so that children are not seen as an intrusion on working time. It is often commented that work can easily be brought home but children are not welcome in the adult workplace – office or factory.

Noelle Walsh was fired as an editor from National Magazines and then set up a successful home-based company with her hus-

band. She has adapted and is one of the lucky ones to live a version of that lifestyle.

> There is a certain amount of work that I have to achieve and I
> try to do some of it in the evening. I do all the things I *have* to
> do in office hours but if I need to go to the school I can easily
> fit that in. I can plan the children's lives a bit more around
> ours and our work lives a bit more around the kids. When I
> used to leave early in the morning and get back after they had
> to have their homework done I wouldn't know what they were
> up to . . . we used to keep the kids up until nine or ten o' clock
> at night just so that we could see them. This way I now know
> all their friends. I work from a barn connected to the house by
> a conservatory and they come in through the conservatory
> and we keep the door open so we see all the people who are to
> do with their lives. We know them almost as much as we
> would if we weren't working. So we really have the best of
> both worlds.

It was not always like that, though: Noelle says the self-scheduling, self-employed ideal is not as easy as it looks. 'The first two to
three years we weren't the best parents: we were always short-
tempered, we were pretty poor, and we spent up to seven days a
week on the business. We worked every night and usually a day
each at the weekend. So the kids got neglected.'

When things do work out and a satisfactory balance is struck,
the people involved are rare and lucky enough to have tran-
scended the work-rich/time-poor versus work-poor/time-rich
conflicts. Anyone in this position is consciously swimming
against the economic tide and taking a new approach to the politics of family time. In one sense, they have taken the route that

was supposed to be everyone's destiny – until the labour market veered off in another direction putting time and money on an extreme collision course. The fashionable description for this new approach is 'downshifting' or 'voluntary simplicity'. These are the people who trade money and high status for more time and control over their lives and less economic reward. The trouble with downshifting is that it is really a euphemism for describing what mothers have always done: returning to a lower-status, part-time job after children. 'Downshifting' may be the best marketing gimmick since estate agents transformed the humble bedsit into a 'studio apartment'. Crucially, the concept of 'downshifting', just like the 'family-friendly' label, is of little interest or value if it is only relevant to women. It becomes significant when men, especially fathers, see the non-financial advantages in a different rearrangement of time. The new lifestyle can easily be dismissed as New Age dreaminess – merely an updated version of the sixties dropout. And for others, downshifting is not a choice but a miserable necessity when they are made redundant or, in middle-class parlance, 'become a consultant'. Yet there are also some families that have taken a positive and deliberate decision to rearrange breadwinning and caring between them at the expense of economic gain.

Francesca Foster runs an old people's home part-time; her husband gave up the stress of working as a travelling sales rep and became a part-time council worker providing alarm cover for the elderly and vulnerable. Both look after their daughter and an elderly mother. He took a big drop in salary but 'I've achieved a freedom which other workers just don't have. Freedom to spend a significant amount of time with the family and to do my art.' Francesca notices how much calmer he is. 'I certainly wasn't pushing him to get another full-time job. I'd rather have a happy

smiling husband than one coming home with a permanent frown.'
Sue White is a special needs teacher on Monday and Tuesday
and her husband Colin works for BT on Wednesday, Thursday
and Friday as a trainer. Both used to work full-time. Colin has no
regrets.

We've achieved balance in our lives not just between work
and home but between our roles. I'm also a Relate
counsellor and you find with couples where one is totally
the provider and the other looks after the family that there
can be a lot of resentment. We both have a taste of what it's
like to be home with the kids and to be taking responsibility
for the financial side of things. I work to live. I don't have
any burning ambition to get on. I have missed out on
promotions and status by working this way but when you
put it in perspective, status within a company means
nothing outside – I was with a friend who was terribly
excited because he got promoted to grade 32 and I'm saying
'Wow fantastic grade 32. I never thought you'd make it to
that!' I get satisfaction from other things. The expectation
at work is for you to work harder all the time and to move
forward all the time. There is not much link between family
life and work. I didn't see much of my father when I was
growing up and I didn't want that to be the case with my
children. I'm not sure that a lot of men actually do want to
change the traditional work patterns: they say that it
wouldn't be possible in their line of work, but I'm not
convinced. They don't even want to ask just in case it is
possible and they might have to do something about it.
Having said that, there is a lot of job insecurity about and
pressure to work long hours and that's how you get on. The

main pressure is to keep your job and to be seen to be
serious about it. I think the reason that so few men have
chosen to reduce their working hours is because
fundamentally most men have a deep-rooted image of
themselves as the provider and to give that up would
challenge their role in life.

Deirdre and Tim Powell were full-time solicitors but applied for
a job share when they had their first child. Tim left his job with a
West End practice when he tried to get paternity leave and the
request was treated with derision. At first the job share proposal
got nowhere, but eventually because there was a shortage of assistant solicitors one firm agreed. Tim has no regrets. 'It worked
really well for both of us . . . it has been tremendous being
involved with the children on a daily basis. I have a very close relationship with them, and it was a real revelation that life exists
outside the office on a weekday.' Deirdre is equally satisfied. 'We
made a choice to put time with the children over increased income.
When I stopped working full-time I realized I was enjoying my
work more than ever.' Yet she is pessimistic about such a pattern
becoming commonplace. 'This type of working can only make
progress at a time when you are in a sellers' market. We did this at
a time when there was a real shortage of solicitors and firms were
pretty desperate. But employers seem to go back to a conservative
notion the minute they are not forced to take alternatives and even
employers who have tried it and said that you actually get more for
your money with a job share tend to go back to the full-time
option the moment the part-timers leave.' When Deirdre and Tim
had a second child he worked full-time during the maternity leave
and then they returned to the job share arrangement. A few years
later they set up their own solicitors' practice, but still sharing the

childcare between them so that they take it strictly in turns to stop work early and look after the children. They turn away work, if necessary, in order to keep that arrangement going because it yields such mutual satisfaction. 'To my mind there is no comparison. We have been surviving on one income for eight years and so we live in a small house which needs decorating and we have a small car which needs replacing.' They have friends who are partners in big firms where twelve-hour days are the norm, plus endless trips abroad. 'So they have big houses and gardens and cars and we could have that if we both worked full-time but it doesn't seem so important . . . and often the family has plenty of money but the woman does all the childcare because her husband works such long hours and it's like being a single mum.' According to Deirdre, 'If people can afford to share one job between them then the whole of society benefits because there are more jobs around and their family life benefits.'

Downshifting has gradually become a nineties buzzword. Books appeared on how to do it, with titles like *Your Money or Your Life*. Yet it has never moved far outside the realms of 'fancy that' on the newspaper feature pages. It is a distinctly minority, usually middle-class, pursuit and only relevant to those who have something to shift down from. Anyone near the bottom cannot shift further down. Nevertheless those who have done it, whether or not of their own volition, do raise serious questions about the dominant values of late-twentieth-century capitalism. They are attempting to rearrange the equation between time, spending, caring and work, whilst simultaneously trying to establish a different, more fluid gender identity, where breadwinning and unpaid labour are not the exclusive preserve of one or other partner, and thereby managing to live the elusive 'companionate marriage'.

An increasing number of thinkers, economists, psychologists or even historians have started to challenge the increasing commodification of time. Theodore Zeldin, in his *An Intimate History of Humanity*, describes how the obsessive attitude towards time gradually developed when the first workers were employed in factories. Personal rhythms were destroyed by the Industrial Revolution and the concept of the typical male job. Although the whole pattern of work is changing, it seems impossible to change the assumptions surrounding our use of time. Retirement, for example, is still seen as one long slab which takes place after working life is over – even though it may start as early as fifty. Yet an agreed period out of work, like a sabbatical, may be more desirable for someone in their forties who could make up the time and pension contributions by extending their working life at the end. Zeldin looks forward to a stage when 'the idea of taking a year off appears natural and people will be able to insert family life into a cv without loss of status and without having to justify themselves'.[57]

A new approach to the politics of time, one that gives it an independent value quite apart from the monetary equation, is one route to breaking the work/spend cycle. This way it would be feasible to protect time for those who are unable to pay for it – whether children, the old or those who depend upon the voluntary sector. A new approach to the politics of time means a transformation that would challenge both the relentless march of consumerism and the belief that greater output is the overriding measure of greater success; it would also reverse the prevailing belief that what you do is more important than what you are. Potentially these would be huge shifts, but as we have seen there is widespread unease about elevating the measure of economic achievement above all other social goals. If so-called economic progress is accompanied by increasing inequality, unsatisfactory conditions for large numbers of children, the pervasive 'time famine', and continuing 'gender rancour'[58] about the imbalance between roles at work and home, it may become meaningless. The pattern of ever-increasing individualism and deregulation that offers more apparent choice wears thin without the counterbalance of sufficient social cohesion. And this desire to redirect economic goals is not the preserve of the utopian idealists that it once was. Moderates like the veteran Social Democrat David Marquand believe in it passionately as a prerequisite for a civilized society:

> We must abandon the illiterate assumption – not held, it should be noted, by any of the great economists of the past – that GDP per head is to be equated with well-being. The object of public policy should be to maximise well-being, not to achieve the highest feasible rate of growth in GDP per head.[59]

Downshifting is likely to remain a minority fad, but it is churlish to dismiss any sincere attempt to reorganize the prevailing relation between work, time and money, as this is one of the best available routes to real progress. It is only through a wider political recognition of these relationships at their most fundamental level that women's lives will ever really change. The high level of optimism and expectations amongst young women, all the talk about a new feminism – which means if we ask nicely, inequality will be ameliorated – is pointless without a wider understanding of those structures that are often pulling in a very different direction.

The deliberate obstacles women face in fulfilling themselves may have all but disappeared. Fifty years ago there were still marriage bars which excluded married women, let alone mothers, from the workplace. That concept today sounds like something from the Dark Ages, as does the idea that it could be legal to pay women less for performing identical tasks to men. With the formal barriers dismantled, the problem now is to deal with the unintended consequences of a deregulated market economy which according to the capitalist imperative urges ever more consumption. A society that values paid work above all else, that prizes flexible labour markets, and that has seen ever-widening inequality, where children remain a largely private responsibility and where expectations of parenting are high but support is scarce, will need to rearrange its priorities before women (or men) will be able to live fully rounded lives.

Notes

Introduction

1 Fay Weldon and Polly Toynbee, 'Debate: What Women Want', *Prospect*, June 1998.

1   Great Expectations

1 2020 Vision survey of 10,000 young Britons (aged 12–25) for the Industrial Society, 1998.
2 Interview with Ofsted inspectors, November 1997.
3 *The Gender Divide: Performance Differences between Boys and Girls at School*, Joint report by Ofsted and the Equal Opportunities Commission, HMSO 1996.
4 Bernard Carl Rosen, *Women, Work and Achievement: The Endless Revolution*, Macmillan 1989.
5 Sue Sharpe, *Just Like a Girl: From the Seventies to the Nineties*, Penguin 1994.
6 Women at the Millennium research project (supported by The Body Shop), *The Can-Do Girls: A Barometer of Change*, Dept of Applied Social Studies, Oxford 1997.
7 Naomi Wolf, *Fire With Fire*, Chatto and Windus 1993.

8 ICM Research, Genderquake Survey conducted for the Barrass Company, April 1996.

9 *Superwoman Keeps Going: Understanding the Female Web, A Survey of Women's Lives and Expectations*, National Council of Women of Great Britain, 1992.

10 Joan Clanchey (former head of North London Collegiate School), 'If You Want It, Go and Get It', *Independent*, 26 March 1997.

11 Research by Helen Lucey, Goldsmiths College; see Sue Innes, *Making It Work*, Chatto and Windus 1996, pp. 273–4.

12 Interviews with Dr Wendy Greengross and Dr Elizabeth Shore in Valerie Grove, *The Compleat Woman*, Chatto and Windus 1988.

13 Michael White, Steve Lissenburgh and Alex Bryson, *The Impact of Job Placement Schemes*, Grantham Books 1997.

14 *Employment Audit*, Issue 8, Employment Policy Institute 1998.

15 Interviews with pupils from Plumstead Manor and Camden School for Girls.

16 Marilyn French, 'Changes in the Women's Room', in *Wayward Girls and Wicked Women*, Virago 1997. Launch of 'V' Imprint on 25th anniversary of Virago.

17 Julia Neuberger, *Whatever's Happening to Women?*, Kyle Cathie 1991.

18 Helen Wilkinson and Geoff Mulgan, *Freedom's Children*, Demos 1995.

19 Wolf, *Fire With Fire*, Chapter 15.

20 Susan Harkness, analysis of the British Household Panel Survey, wave 5, 1997 (unpublished). In 1998 Women in Journalism (sponsored by Tesco) produced a report, *The Cheaper Sex*, which reinforced this conclusion. Young, childless female journalists earned more than their male colleagues.

2 Danger Ahead!

1 Labour Force Survey 1997 figures and the Employment Audit of the Employment Policy Institute estimate the gender pay gap across all workers as 74 per cent.

2   *National Management Salary Survey*, Remuneration Economics 1997.

3   Sylvia Hewlett, *A Lesser Life: The Myth of Women's Liberation*, Michael Joseph 1987, Chapter 3 and International Labour and Organization, *Breaking through the Glass Ceiling: Women in Management*, ILO, Geneva 1997.

4   Summary in *Equal Opportunities Review*, no 69, September 1996.

5   Paul Donovan, *All Our Todays: Forty Years of Radio 4's Today Programme*, Jonathan Cape 1997.

6   Gary Becker, 'Human capital, effort and the sexual division of labour', *Journal of Labour Economics*, vol 3, no 1, 1985. Becker pioneered the area of New Home Economics.

7   Susan Harkness, 'Explaining Changes in the Relative Earnings of Part-Time Female Employees', Centre for Economic Performance, LSE 1996, makes reference to research on the wage penalties received by women in smaller workplaces; citing Frances Green, Stephen Machin and Alan Manning, *The Employer-Size Wage Effect*, Oxford Economic Papers, 1996, vol 48, pp. 433–53.

8   Jack Irvine, speech to Women in Journalism, reported in *UK Press Gazette*, 10 January 1997.

9   The case of Deborah Banks *v.* (1) Tesco Stores Ltd and (2) Secretary of State for Social Security is winding its way up the legal tree. (She originally went on maternity leave in 1994 and the Tribunal case was in 1997.)

10 *Equal Opportunities Review*, 72, March/April 1997. The exact measurement of the gender pay gap varies a little depending upon which source is used and precisely who is included.

11 There are many comprehensive studies of this; see, for example, Angela Coyle and Jane Skinner, *Women and Work*, Macmillan 1988; Harriet Bradley, *Men's Work, Women's Work*, Polity Press 1989; Eva Figes, *Because of her Sex*, Macmillan 1994.

12 Margaret Mead, *Male and Female: A study of the Sexes in a Changing World*, Victor Gollancz 1949. Quoted in Nickie Charles, *Gender Division and Social Change*, Harvester Wheatsheaf 1993.

13 Cynthia Fuchs Epstein, *Woman's Place: Options and Limits in Professional Careers*, University of California Press 1970.

14   Interview with Baroness Brenda Dean, February 1997.

15   See Ann Phillips and Barbara Taylor, 'Sex and Skill' in Feminist Review, *Waged Work: A Reader*, Virago 1986 and 'Women in the Labour Market: results from the spring 1995 Labour Force Survey', *Labour Market Trends*, March 1996, Office for National Statistics.

16   Feminist Review, *Waged Work: A Reader*, Virago 1986.

17   Bradley, *Men's Work, Women's Work*. A 1998 study by the Policy Studies Institute, *Gender Inequalities in Nursing Careers*, found that the small number of men in nursing were twice as likely to be in the highest grades.

18   Baroness Shirley Williams series on BBC Radio 4, 1997, *Is There a Woman in the House?*

19   S. Dex, H. Joshi and S. Macran, 'A Widening Gulf Amongst Britain's Mothers', *Oxford Review of Economic Policy*, vol 12, no 1, 1996.

20   *New Earnings Survey*, April 1997.

21   Francine Blau and Lawrence Kahn, 'The Gender Earnings Gap: Some International Evidence', *American Economic Review*, vol 82, 1992.

22   Michael Moore, *Downsize This! Random Threats from an Unarmed American*, Boxtree 1997.

23   Alissa Goodman, Paul Johnson and Steven Webb, *Inequality in the UK*, Oxford University Press 1997.

24   This imaginary parade was originally described in J. Pen, *Income Distribution*, Allen Lane 1971.

25   Family Expenditure Survey 1995/6. Amongst full-time working women, 28 per cent earned over £15,000 in 1995/6 compared to 53 per cent of men.

26   Anthony Giddens, *Beyond Left and Right*, Polity Press 1994, p. 161.

27   *Euromoney*, April 1997.

28   'The 300 Most Powerful People in Blair's Britain', *Punch*, 28 June 1997.

29   Rosalind Miles, *Danger! Men at Work*, Futura 1983.

30   Coyle and Skinner, *Women and Work*. See also EOC figures published in *Facts about Women and Men in Great Britain*, EOC 1997.

31   Anthony Giddens, *Sociology*, 3rd edn, Polity Press 1997.

32   See Hilary Metcalf, *Half Our Future*, Policy Studies Institute 1998.

Good summaries of the other reports may be found in Fiona M. Wilson, *Organisational Behaviour and Gender*, McGraw-Hill 1995.

33   'Women on Top', special investigation by *Supermarketing*, 22 March 1996.

34   International Labour Organization, *Breaking through the Glass Ceiling: Women in Management*, ILO, Geneva 1997.

35   Marilyn French, *The War Against Women*, Hamish Hamilton 1992, p. 40.

36   Paul Gregg and Stephen Machin, *Is the Glass Ceiling Cracking?*, National Institute Discussion Paper, 1993.

37   Report of the Hansard Society Commission on *Women at the Top*, 1990.

38   Yvonne Roberts, *Mad about Women*, Virago 1992.

39   Susan McRae, *Women at the Top: Progress after five years*, King-Hall paper no 2, Hansard Society 1996. (This was the follow-up Report to the Hansard Society Commission on *Women at the Top*.)

40   Christine Wenneras and Agnes Wold, 'Nepotism and sexism in peer-review', *Nature*, vol 387, May 1997.

41   Edward Balls and Paul Gregg, *Work and Welfare*, IPPR Commission on Social Justice 1993.

42   Gerhard Sonnert, *Who Succeeds in Science?*, Rutgers University Press 1995.

43   Interview with Pat Dade, January 1997.

44   Pat Dixon, *Making the Difference: Women and Men in the Workplace*, Heinemann 1993, p. 2.

45   Kay Graham, *Personal History*, Weidenfeld 1997.

46   Trudy Coe, *The Key to the Men's Club*, Institute of Management, 1992.

47   Interview with John Viney, Chairman, Heidrick and Struggles, February 1997.

48   Judi Marshall, *Women Managers: Travellers in a Male World*, John Wiley 1984, and *Women Managers Moving On*, Routledge 1995.

49   B. Alimo-Metcalfe, 'Waiting for Fish to Grow Feet! Removing the organisational barriers to women's entry into leadership positions', in Morgan Tanton (ed.), *Women in Management: A Developing presence*, Routledge 1994.

50 'Fifty Most Powerful Women in Britain', *Guardian* series 26, 27, 28 May 1997. The same conclusions about the difference in male and female approaches to management are drawn in a paper by Jane Sturges of Birkbeck College to the British Psychological Society occupational psychology conference, 1998.

51 D.J. Swiss and J.P. Walker, *Women and the Work/Family Dilemma – How Today's Professional Women are Confronting the Maternal Wall*, John Wiley 1993, p. 24.

52 Prof. Susan Greenfield, interviewed in the *Independent*, 7 June 1997.

53 Beverley Stone, contribution to workshop at Demos conference, 'Tomorrow's Women', 7 March 1997.

54 B. M. Brooks-Gordon, 'Assertions of masculinity in London's financial markets', *Proceedings of the British Psychological Society*, vol 4, no 1, 1995, p. 55.

55 Swiss and Walker, *Women and the Work/Family Dilemma*.

56 Professor Lotte Bailyn, quoted in 'The Myth of Quality Time', *Newsweek*, 19 May 1997.

57 Liz Forgan, speaking at the Demos conference, 'Tomorrow's Women', 7 March 1997.

58 Interview with Dame Pauline Neville-Jones, February 1997.

59 Coyle and Skinner, *Women and Work*.

60 Interview with Dawn Airey, March 1997.

61 Coyle and Skinner, *Women and Work*.

3   What Is Happening to Work?

1 Anthony Giddens, *Sociology*, 3rd edn, Polity Press 1997, pp. 317–8.

2 William Bridges, *Jobshift: How to Prosper in a World Without Jobs*, Nicholas Brealey 1995, Chapter 2 'The Rise and Fall of the Good Job'.

3 Ibid., pp. 57–8.

4 Charles Handy, *The Empty Raincoat: Making Sense of the Future*, Hutchinson 1994, p. 9.

5 Juliet Schor, *The Overworked American: The Unexpected Decline of Leisure*, Basic Books 1991.

6　See, for example, Catherine Marsh, *Hours of Work of Women and Men in Britain*, Equal Opportunities Commission, HMSO 1991. A study of managers by Jane Sturges of Birkbeck College, presented to the British Psychological Society occupational psychology conference in 1998, reached the same conclusions.

7　This finding is reported frequently, in academic research and in lifestyle publications (see *Top Santé*, March 1998, which featured a survey conducted with BUPA, or *Management Today*, June 1998, which ran a survey on 'The Great Work/Life Debate'). In 1994–5, 46 per cent of full-time women wanted to work fewer hours (Women in Employment/British Household Panel Survey). Amongst full-timers in the professions the figure is even higher at 55 per cent. See Susan Harkness, 'Explaining Changes in the Relative Earnings of Part-Time Female Employees' mimeo, Centre for Economic Performance, LSE 1996.

8　*Accountants with Attitude*, Institute for Employment Studies 1997.

9　European Commission Figures 1995.

10　National Child Development Study, reported in Elsa Ferri and Kate Smith, *Parenting in the Nineties*, Family Policy Studies Centre 1996.

11　David Cohen, 'Rich Man, New Man?' *Independent*, 4 March 1997.

12　Professor Anthony Clare interviewed in the *Independent*, 9 September 1997.

13　'Is Your Family Wrecking Your Career?' *Fortune*, 17 March 1997.

14　Interview with Professor Andrew Samuels, April 1997.

15　See Robert Lindley (ed.), *Labour Market Structures and Prospects for Women*, EOC 1994, and Angela Coyle, *Women and Organisational Change*, EOC 1995.

16　Coyle, *Women and Organisational Change*.

17　Jane Humphries and Jill Rubery (eds) *The Economics of Equal Opportunity*, EOC 1995.

18　Jay Ginn et al., 'Feminist Fallacies: A Reply to Hakim on Women's Employment', *British Journal of Sociology*, vol 47, no 1, March 1996.

19　Harriet Bradley, *Men's Work, Women's Work*, Polity Press 1989.

20　Pauline Matthews, 'Flexible Working – opportunity or ghetto?',

1995 *Employment Law Briefing*, Pearson Professional 1995, pp. 100–3.

21 Patricia Hewitt, *About Time: The Revolution in Work and Family Life*, IPPR/Rivers Oram 1993.

22 'Job-share Victory Breaks Glass Ceiling', *Independent*, 28 August 1997.

23 Paul Gregg, *Jobs and Justice*, IPPR Commission on Social Justice 1993.

24 Matthews, 'Flexible Working . . .

25 Heather Joshi, Pirella Paci and Jane Waldfogel, *The Wages of Motherhood: Better or Worse?*, Welfare State Programme discussion paper 122, 1996. A number of studies have highlighted the 'family gap', for example Jane Waldfogel, 'Women Working for Less: A Longitudinal Analysis of the Family Gap, Welfare State Programme Discussion Paper 93, 1993.

26 Paul Gregg and Jonathan Wadsworth, 'Gender Households and Access to Employment', in Humphries and Rubery, *The Economics of Equal Opportunity*.

27 Matilda Quiney, 'Women Need the Work', *New Economy*, vol 1, no 3, Autumn 1994.

28 Susan Harkness, Stephen Machin and Jane Waldfogel, *Evaluating the Pin Money Hypothesis: The Relationship between Women's Labour Market Activity, Family Income and Poverty in Britain*, LSE Welfare State Programme paper 108, 1995.

29 John Prescott, quoted in the *Guardian*, 24 June 1994.

30 'Households Below Average Income', Office for National Statistics 1997.

31 D. J. Swiss and J. P. Walker, *Women and the Work/Family Dilemma: How Today's Professional Women are Confronting the Maternal Wall*, John Wiley 1993, Chapter 4.

32 Carol Dix, *Working Mothers: You, your career, your child*, Unwin 1989.

33 'Policies for families: Work, poverty and resources' published proceedings of seminar 'Families Working at Home and at Work', Family Policy Studies Centre, Rowntree Foundation 1995. Discussion on home-working, p. 28.

34   Joan Bakewell, 1996 Fawcett Annual Lecture. 'Women and the Media', delivered 16 October 1996.
35   'Flexible Working: The Impact on Women's Pay and Conditions' (review of EOC reports), in *Equal Opportunities Review*, no 65, January/February 1996.
36   In May 1998 eight trade unions – AUT, Unison, MSF, TGWU, GMB, EIS, Nafthe and AEEU – launched a campaign to 'rebuild job security in higher education', opposing 'exploitative flexible working practices'.
37   Coyle, *Women and Organisational Change.*

4   No Change at Home

1   Jan Morris, *Conundrum*, Faber 1974, p. 138.
2   R. J. Perelberg, 'Equality, Asymmetry and Diversity: on Conceptualisations of Gender', in R. J. Perelberg and A. Miller (eds) *Gender and Power in Families*, Routledge 1990, p. 42.
3   Penelope Leach, *Children First: What Society Must Do – And Is Not Doing – For Our Children Today*, Michael Joseph 1994, pp. 14–15.
4   Taking all families of prime working age (24–55) – but excluding households of just single men – the proportion of 'traditional male breadwinner' households is only 15 per cent. Susan Harkness, Stephen Machin and Jane Waldfogel, *Journal of Population Studies*, vol 10, 1997. According to the General Household Survey, amongst two-parent families with dependent children the proportion of 'male breadwinner' families was 29 per cent in 1991. Ten years earlier it had been 47 per cent. However, since only 78 per cent of families with dependent children are two-parent families (Office for National Statistics, *Trends in One Parent Families*, 1998), the proportion of families with children that are male-breadwinner/nonworking-woman households drops to only 22 per cent.
5   Royal Society of Arts, Eve and Adam series, 'Women and Men in Conversation about their Roles, Relationships and Communication', 24 March 1997.
6   Eileen McNamara column in the *Boston Globe*, October 1997.

7   Women in Journalism research report, *Women in the News: Does Sex Change the Way a Newspaper Thinks?* July 1996.

8   Helen Fielding, *Bridget Jones's Diary*, Picador 1996.

9   Sheila Rowbotham, *A Century of Women*, Viking 1997, p. 561.

10 Rhona Mahoney, *Kidding Ourselves*, Basic Books 1995, pp. 9, 164–7.

11 Joan Smith, *Different for Girls: How Culture Creates Women*, Random House 1997; Margaret Mead, *Male and Female: A Study of the Sexes in a Changing World*, Victor Gollancz 1949, p. 7.

12 M. Young and P. Willmott, *The Symmetrical Family*, Routledge 1973, p. 278.

13 Elsa Ferri and Kate Smith, *Parenting in the 1990s*, Family Policy Studies Centre (Joseph Rowntree Foundation) 1996.

14 Interview with Penny Mansfield, One Plus One, January 1997.

15 Report on a paper by Professor George Akerlof for the *Economic Journal*, *Independent*, 9 March 1998.

16 Ann Oakley, *Housewife* (Allen Lane 1974), Pelican 1977, Chapter 9.

17 Arlie Hochschild, *The Second Shift*, Avon Books 1989.

18 British Household Panel Survey 1997, Economic and Social Research Council.

19 Tables on time use in Patricia Hewitt, *About Time: The Revolution in Work and Family Life* (IPPR/Rivers Oram 1993), Chapter 3 and interview with Jonathan Gershuny about data on changing time use.

20 Julia Brannen and Peter Moss, *Managing Mothers: Dual Earner Households after Maternity Leave*, Unwin 1991.

21 Sue Newell, 'The Superwoman Syndrome: Gender Differences in Attitudes towards Equal Opportunities at Work and Towards Domestic Responsibilities at Home', *Work, Employment and Society*, 1993, p. 283.

22 Ibid., p. 283.

23 Bob Tyrell (chief executive of the Henley Centre for Forecasting), 'Time in Our Lives', in *Demos Quarterly*, no 5, 'The Time Squeeze' 1995.

24 Office for National Statistics, *Household Satellite Accounts*, HMSO October 1997.

25 Duke University study reported in the *Independent on Sunday*, 27 July 1997.

26 Arlie Hochschild, *The Time Bind: When Work Becomes Home and Home Becomes Work*, Metropolitan Books 1997.

27 J. Walter Thompson research on attitudes to Christmas. Reported in the *Independent*, 22 October 1997.

28 Margery Spring-Rice, *Working Class Wives*, Penguin 1939 (republished by Virago 1981), p. 108.

29 Rebecca Abrams, *The Playful Self: Why Women Need Play in their Lives*, Fourth Estate 1997.

30 Kate Millett, *Sexual Politics*, Virago 1977.

31 Hewitt, *About Time . . .*, p. 61.

32 BBC audience research/Gershuny figures in Hewitt, Chapter 3. Also Hewitt refers to British Social Attitudes 1988, Gower, Aldershot.

33 Jonathan Gershuny, 'Economic Activity and Women's time use' in Iris Nieni (ed.) *Time Use of Women in Europe and North America*, United Nations 1995.

34 Ferri and Smith, *Parenting in the 1990s*, p. 22.

35 Mahoney, *Kidding Ourselves*, pp. 182–9.

36 'Odd Man Out: Notes on Full-time Fathering in Switzerland', *Mothering Matters*, February 1998.

37 James Leith, *Ironing John*, Doubleday 1995, p. 161.

38 Peter Mandler, 'No Sex War, Please! We're British', *Jewish Quarterly*, Spring 1997.

39 Interview with Cynthia Cockburn in Sian Griffiths (ed.), *Beyond the Glass Ceiling. Forty Women Whose Ideas Shape the Modern World*, Manchester University Press 1996.

40 Professor David Piachaud made this calculation in *Round about 50 Hours a Week: The Time Costs of Children*, CPAG pamphlet, no 64, 1984.

41 Newell, 'The Superwoman Syndrome . . .', p. 286.

42 Gary Becker, 'A Theory of the allocation of Time', *Economic Journal*, September 1965, pp. 493–517; *A Treatise on the Family*, Harvard 1981; and 'Human capital, effort and the sexual division of labour', *Journal of Labour Economics*, vol 3, no 1, 1985. For a critique of 'efficient specialisation' see Susan J. Owen, 'Household

Production and Economic Efficiency: Arguments for and against domestic specialisation', *Work, Employment and Society*, vol 1, no 2, pp. 157–178, June 1987.

43   Gill Cappuccini and Ray Cochrane, study of 100 couples before and after first child. Presented to the British Psychological Society conference, Strathclyde 1996.

44   Penelope Leach, *Who Cares? A New Deal for Mothers and Their Small Children*, Penguin 1979, pp. 89–90.

45   Penelope Leach, *Babyhood*, Penguin 1983.

46   Leach, *Children First . . .*, pp. 41–8.

47   Leith, *Ironing John*, p. 7.

48   Nancy Chodorow, *The Reproduction of Mothering*, University of California Press 1980.

49   Mahoney, *Kidding Ourselves*. See also Colette Dowling, *The Cinderella Complex: Women's Hidden Fear of Independence*, Michael Joseph 1981 and Rosalind Coward, *Our Treacherous Hearts*, Faber 1992.

50   Susan Harkness, Stephen Machin and Jane Waldfogel, 'Female Employment and Changes in the Share of Women's Earnings in Total Family Income in Great Britain', in Paul Lawless, Ron Martin and Sally Hardy (eds), *Unemployment and Social Exclusion: Landscapes of Labour Inequality*, Regional Studies Association, Jessica Kingsley 1998.

51   Mahoney, *Kidding Ourselves*, Chapter 10 'A Future World'.

52   Charles Handy, *The Age of Unreason*, Random House 1989, pp. 154–64.

53   Howard Glennerster, *Paying for Welfare: Issues for the Nineties*, Welfare State Programme Paper WSP/82, London School of Economics 1992.

54   'The Value of a Mum' was a survey commissioned by Legal and General to coincide with Mother's Day. It was intended to show (for insurance purposes) what it would cost to replace Mother's domestic efforts.

55   Interview with Henry Neuberger, Office for National Statistics; also Household Satellite Accounts, May 1998.

56   Sue Himmelweit, *The Discovery of 'Unpaid Work': The Social*

Consequences of the Expansion of 'Work', Open Discussion Papers in Economic No. 6, Open University 1995.

57 *Genderquake* series produced by the Barrass Company for Channel 4, July 1996.

5 Men Holding the Line

1   Simone De Beauvoir, *La Deuxième Sexe*, Gallimard 1949.

2   Robert Bly, *Iron John: A Book About Men*, Addison-Wesley 1990. This book appeared in the US bestseller list for thirty-five weeks.

3   Andrew Samuels, 'Retraining the Psyche', *Round Table Review*, May/June 1995.

4   Peter Senge, *The Fifth Discipline: The Art and Practice of the Learning Organization*, Century Business 1992.

5   Pamela Meadows (ed.), *Work Out – or Work In? Contributions to the Debate on the Future of Work*, Joseph Rowntree Foundation 1996, p. 11. Refers to J. Schmitt and J. Wadsworth 'Why are 2 Million Men Inactive? The Decline in Male Labour Force Participation in Britain', Centre for Economic Performance Working Paper 338, 1994.

6   Frank Field, 'The Onward March of Women', speech to the Low Pay conference, Accrington, 4 February 1994.

7   Paul Gregg and Jonathan Wadsworth, *Unemployment and Non-employment: Unpacking Economic Activity*, Employment Policy Institute 1998.

8   Christina Beatty and Stephen Fothergill, 'Registered and Hidden Unemployment in the UK Coalfields', in Paul Lawless, Ron Martin and Sally Hardy (eds) *Unemployment and Social Exclusion: Landscapes of Labour Inequality*, Regional Studies Association, Jessica Kingsley 1998.

9   'On the Sick', BBC *Panorama*, 9 February 1998.

10 Will Hutton, *The State We're In*, Jonathan Cape 1995, and Paul Gregg, 'More Work in Fewer Households' in *Policies for Families: Work, Poverty and Resources*, Family Policy Studies Centre, 1995. Both calculate figures of true unemployment.

11 Labour Force Survey quoted in *Equal Opportunities Review*, no 74, July/August 1997.

12 Eric Miller, 'Implications of the Changing World of Work' in David Kennard and Neil Small (eds) *Living Together*, Quartet Books 1997.

13 *Young People and Crime*, Home Office research and planning unit report, 1996. The report was derived from 2,500 interviews with young people aged 14–25.

14 William Julius Wilson, *The Truly Disadvantaged*, University of Chicago Press 1987.

15 Edward Humes, *No Matter How Loud I Shout*, Simon and Schuster 1996.

16 Steve Biddulph, *The Secret of Happy Children*, Angus and Robertson (HarperCollins) 1984. This was his original self-help manual, which became a best-seller, reprinted many times. His approach was summarized in 'Superdad', *The Times*, 5 May 1998.

17 Adrienne Burgess, *Fatherhood Reclaimed: The Making of a Modern Father*, Random House 1997.

18 Roger Jowell et al., *British Social Attitudes*, SCPR 1993.

19 Margaret Mead, *Male and Female: A Study of the Sexes in a Changing World*, Victor Gollancz 1949, p. 189.

20 Derek Coombs, 'The Moral Minority', *Prospect*, May 1997.

21 Francis Fukuyama, *The Great Disruption* (forthcoming from Profile Books 2000).

22 Robert Bly, *The Sibling Society*, Hamish Hamilton 1996.

23 Warren Farrell, *The Myth of Male Power: Why Men are the Disposable Sex*, Fourth Estate (British edn) 1994.

24 The meeting of the UK's Men's Movement was described in various press reports. See Neil Lyndon, 'Man to Man', *Independent*, 20 January 1997, or Stuart Millar, 'Here Comes Trouble', *Guardian*, 13 February 1997.

25 National Association of Probation Officers report, *Women and Crime*, 1997.

26 Richard Gott, 'Can Women Give Blokes What They Want?' *New Statesman*, March 1997.

27 Susan Faludi, *Backlash: The Undeclared War Against American Women*, Crown 1991, p. 62.

28 Thomas Edsall Jr, quoted in Alexander Cockburn and Ken Silverstein, *Washington Babylon*, Verso 1996.

29 Field, 'The Onward March of Women'.

30 Interview with Baroness Brenda Dean, February 1997.

31 ICM Research Genderquake Survey, for the Barrass Company, April 1996.

32 Miller, 'Implications of the Changing World of Work'.

33 *Social Trends* 27, Stationery Office (January 1997); '*Social Focus on Families*', Office for National Statistics 1997; and a survey by the advertising agency Mellors Reay March, 1998, 'The State of Men'.

34 Francis Fukuyama, *The End of Order*, Social Market Foundation/ Profile Books 1997, pp. 116–21.

35 *Genderquake* series produced by the Barrass Company for Channel 4, July 1996.

36 Jill Rubery (ed.), *Women and Recession*, Routledge 1988.

37 Joan Bakewell, 1996 Annual Fawcett Lecture, 'Women and the Media', delivered 16 October 1996.

38 Interview with Fay Weldon in Valerie Grove, *The Compleat Woman*, Chatto & Windus 1988.

39 Fukuyama, *The End of Order*, p. 55.

40 Robert Frank and Philip Cook, *The Winner Take All Society: How more and more Americans compete for ever fewer and bigger prizes, encouraging economic waste, income inequality, and an impoverished cultural life*, Free Press 1995.

41 Edward Balls and Paul Gregg, *Work and Welfare*, IPPR Commission on Social Justice 1993.

42 Alissa Goodman, Paul Johnson and Steven Webb, *Inequality in Britain*, Oxford University Press 1997.

43 Mariah Burton Nelson, *The Stronger Women Get, the More Men Love Football: Sexism and the Culture of Sport*, Women's Press, 1996.

44 Angela Phillips, *The Trouble With Boys: Parenting the Men of the Future*, Pandora 1993.

45 Dorothy Dinnerstein, *The Rocking of the Cradle and the Ruling of*

the World, Harper and Row 1987, p. 76. This book was first published in 1976 as *The Mermaid and the Minotaur*.

46 Ann Oakley, *Housewife*, (Allen Lane 1974), Pelican 1977, p. 89.

47 Demos debate, 'Men the Weaker Sex?' 1997.

6   Choice, What Choice?

1   Even though the tax credits for childcare will change this in 1999 it
    will not help women in a household which is above the limits – so
    there may be greater equality between households but not neces-
    sarily within them.

2   Swedish Ministry of Labour, quoted in Sylvia Hewlett, *A Lesser
    Life: The Myth of Women's Liberation*, Michael Joseph 1987.

3   John Gray, *False Dawn: The Delusions of Global Capitalism*, Granta
    1998.

4   Quoted in Marilyn French, *The War Against Women*, Hamish
    Hamilton 1992.

5   Stephen Machin and Jane Waldfogel, *The Decline of the Male
    Breadwinner: Empirical Evidence on the Changing Shares of the
    Earnings of Husbands and Wives in Family Income in the UK*, LSE
    Welfare State Programme paper 103, 1994. See also Susan
    Harkness, Stephen Machin and Jane Waldfogel, *Evaluating the Pin
    Money Hypothesis: The Relationship between Women's Labour
    Market Activity, Family Income and Poverty in Britain*, LSE Welfare
    State Programme paper 108, 1995.

6   Betty Friedman, *The Feminine Mystique*, Penguin 1963.

7   Interview with Margaret Cook, broadcast in the ITV series
    Westminster Women on 11 January 1998.

8   Amitai Etzioni, *The Spirit of Community*, HarperCollins 1993,
    Chapter 2.

9   Betty Boothroyd, in Central TV documentary *Madam Speaker*,
    broadcast 17 December 1996.

10 Charlotte Perkins Gilman, 'The Passing of Matrimony', *Harpers
    Bazaar*, June 1906, quoted in Dolores Hayden, *The Grand Domestic
    Revolution*, MIT Press 1981, pp. 197–8.

11 Transcript of an interview with Elizabeth Lutyens reprinted in Jenni Murray, *The Woman's Hour*, BBC Books 1996, p. 70.

12 Penelope Leach, *Children First: What Society Must Do and Is Not Doing for Our Children Today*, Michael Joseph 1994, p. 15.

13 Harriet Harman, *The Century Gap*, Random House 1993, p. 115.

14 *Guardian*, 26 September 1997.

15 Interview with Penny Hughes, March 1997.

16 Catherine Hakim, 'Five Feminist Myths about Women's Employment', *British Journal of Sociology*, vol 46, no 3, September 1995.

17 Jay Ginn et al., 'Feminist Fallacies: Reply to Hakim on Women's Employment' and Irene Breugel, 'Whose myths are they anyway?' *British Journal of Sociology*, vol 47, no 1, March 1996.

18 Catherine Hakim, 'The Sexual division of Labour and Women's Heterogeneity', *British Journal of Sociology*, vol 47, no 1, March 1996 and 'Diversity and Choice in the Sexual Contract: Models for the 21st Century' from Geoff Dench (ed.), *Rewriting the Sexual Contract*, Institute for Community Studies 1997.

19 Kathleen Gerson, *Hard Choices: How Women Decide about Work, Career and Motherhood*, University of California Press 1985, p. 213.

20 D. J. Swiss and J. P. Walker, *Women and the Work/Family Dilemma – How Today's Professional Women Are Confronting the Maternal Wall*, John Wiley 1993.

21 Hewlett, *A Lesser Life*, p. 261.

22 Margaret Forster, *Significant Sisters*, Secker and Warburg 1984, p. 320.

23 Germaine Greer, 'We Fought for Freedom – But Now We Just Fight', *Financial Times*, 27 December 1997.

24 Elizabeth Perle McKenna, *When Work Doesn't Work Anymore*, Simon and Schuster 1997.

25 Forster, *Significant Sisters*, p. 321.

26 Terri Apter, *Why Women Don't Have Wives*, Macmillan 1985, p. 103.

27 Gerson, *Hard Choices* . . .

28 Virginia Ironside, 'Forget the Classroom and Take Pride in Teaching Your Own Children', *Independent*, 1 February 1998.

29   Helen Marshall, *Not Having Children*, OUP 1993.

30   W. B. Miller and L. F. Newman, 'Voluntary Childlessness as a mirror of parenthood' in *The First Child and Family Formation*, Carolina Population Centre, North Carolina 1978. Quoted in Cary L. Cooper and Suzan Lewis, *The Workplace Revolution*, Kogan Page 1993.

31   Office for National Statistics fertility projections, 'Percentages of Childless Women by Age and Year of Birth of Woman', table C in *Birth Statistics 1996: England and Wales*, The Stationery Office.

32   Cited in Jane Bartlett, *Will You be Mother? Women Who Choose to Say No*, Virago 1994.

33   Cited in Murray, *The Woman's Hour*, p. 257.

34   Annily Campbell, *Sterilized Women* (forthcoming) Cassell.

35   Joan Smith, *Different for Girls: How Culture Creates Women*, Random House 1997, pp. 79–92, 'The Selfish Jean'.

36   The General Household Survey 1991, table 11.11, analyses differential reproductive rates of women with and without A levels. (Larger families, of more than two children, are most common amongst the least educated (and poorest), although at the other end of the social scale they are also frequent amongst the better off. I am grateful to Kathleen Kiernan of the LSE for this point.)

37   Nick Pettigrew, Richard Paterson and Janet Willis, *Television Industry Tracking Study The First Year: An Interim Report*, British Film Institute 1995. According to this research, in the industry as a whole 71 per cent of women and 34 per cent of men were childless. This changed to 53 per cent and 15 per cent for those aged over forty.

38   Trudy Coe, *The Key to the Men's Club*, Institute of Management 1992.

39   *Wall Street Journal*, 30 October 1984.

40   Yvonne Roberts, 'The Lone Rangers', *Harper's and Queen*, October 1997.

41   Figures from Office for National Statistics 1998; *Birth Statistics 1996: England and Wales*, and 'One Parent Families and Dependent Children in Great Britain', *Population Trends* 91, March 1998.

42   Nicholas Eberstadt, 'Too Few People?' *Prospect*, December 1997.

43   ONS op. cit. Table E, International Comparison of total period fertility rates, 1981–96.

44 Mario Pirani, 'Di chi è la colpa del "anti-baby boom"?' ('Who is to blame for the anti-baby boom?'), column in *La Repubblica*, reviewing the book by Chiara Valentini, *La donne fanno paura* (*Women are Worried*), Il Saggiatore 1997.

45 Agneta Stark, 'Combating the Backlash: How Sweden Won the War', in Ann Oakley and Juliet Mitchell (eds), *Who's Afraid of Feminism?*, Hamish Hamilton 1997. Stark discusses the high rate of female labour force participation and the high proportion of women with low qualifications who work in Sweden.

46 Brit Fougner and Mona Larsen-Asp (eds), *The Nordic Countries – a Paradise for Women?*, Nordic Council of Ministers 1994.

47 It is more likely that the generous childcare provision is a necessary but not sufficient condition for maintaining fertility rates – for when universal childcare disappeared from East Germany after 1989 the total fertility rate dropped lower than ever to 0.84 in 1995 – less than one birth per woman per lifetime. See Table E, International Comparison of total period fertility rates, ONS op. cit.

48 Leach, *Children First. . .*, p. 228.

49 Muriel Jolivet, *Japan: The Childless Society*, Routledge 1997, pp. 144–68.

50 Ibid.

51 Ibid., p. 44.

52 BBC Radio 4, *In the Psychiatrist's Chair*, featuring Ann Widdecombe, first broadcast on 6 July 1997.

53 *Independent on Sunday*, 16 November 1997.

54 Naomi Wolf, *Fire With Fire*, Chatto and Windus 1993, p. 236.

55 'The Guru's Guru', BBC radio interview with Peter Drucker, 19 October 1997.

7   The Black Hole of Policy

1 Nexus virtual debate on the third way, internet site http/www.netnexus.org, February 1998.

2 Tony Blair, speech in Cape Town, 14 October 1996.

3 *Homework: Guidelines for Primary Schools* issued by DfEE in April

1998. They start with a recommendation of 20 minutes a day for four-year-olds and the guidelines stress 'it is the involvement of parents and carers in joint activities . . . which is the most valuable in promoting children's learning'.

4   1997 general election manifesto, *New Labour Because Britain Deserves Better*.

5   *1997 National Survey of Volunteering*, National Centre for Volunteering, showed a decline in volunteering by the young.

6   Denis MacShane, 'Won't Anyone Stand Up for Housewives?', *Daily Mail*, 3 March 1998.

7   Nexus third way internet debate.

8   Reference to Anna Coote in Melissa Benn, *Madonna and Child*, Jonathan Cape 1998, pp. 182–3.

9   Penelope Leach addressing conference entitled 'Manifesto for Maternity' held on 15 October 1996 by the National Childbirth Trust, Maternity Alliance and Royal College of Midwives.

10   Charlotte Adcock, *What Women Want on Politics*. This was a detailed guide to what each of the political parties was saying on issues of interest to women in the period preceding the election, published by the Women's Communication Centre 1997.

11   See BBC *Newsnight* interview with Harriet Harman, 24 March 1998.

12   'Where Wisconsin Goes, Can the World Follow?', *Economist*, 1 November 1997.

13   Institute for Fiscal Studies response to Labour's March 1998 budget proposals. (Also reported in the *Guardian*, 19 March 1998.)

14   'The Honeymoon is Over', *Towards Equality*, Fawcett Society, Winter 1997/8.

15   Welfare round-table discussion reported in *Prospect*, March 1998.

16   Sheila Rowbotham, *A Century of Women*, Viking 1997, pp. 571–2.

17   *The Childcare Gap*, Daycare Trust 1997.

18   Family Policy Studies Centre seminar on 'Families and work', January 1996.

19   William Hague, 'Freedom and the Family' speech to the Social Market Foundation, 29 January 1998.

20   Interview with Penny Mansfield of One Plus One; she estimated

the total costs were £3 billion in 1991. According to Parliamentary answers to Malcolm Wicks MP, the total soared to £4 billion in 1996 (£3.3 billion in social security benefits, £120 million in social services, £320 million legal aid and advice including court costs, £138 million in tax allowances and £190 million in health service costs).

21   See Peter Hennessy, Rosaleen Hughes and Jean Seaton, *Ready Steady Go! New Labour and Whitehall*, Fabian Society 1997.

22   Association of Chief Police Officers Crime Committee, *Report on Juvenile Crime*, 1998.

23   Shirley Dex and Robert Rowthorn, 'The Case for a Ministry of the Family', in Geoff Dench (ed.), *Rewriting the Sexual Contract*, Institute of Community Studies (Rowntree) 1997.

24   Patricia Hewitt, 'Reinventing Families', Mishcon Lecture, University College London, May 1993.

25   Patrick Jenkin, BBC *Man Alive* discussion, quoted in A. Coote and B. Campbell, *Sweet Freedom*, Blackwell 1987.

26   Family Expenditure Survey 1995/6 figures (Households Below Average Income). (These are the figures used by the Health Visitors Association to conclude that one in three children live in poverty.)

27   'Money Can Help to Buy Love', *Guardian*, 12 February 1998.

28   Frank Field, 'Welfare: New Labour Markets and Fiscal Reform', Annual Lecture to the Institute of Directors, February 1997.

29   Michael Young and A. H. Halsey, *Family and Community Socialism*, IPPR 1995. (This was a paper dissenting from the conclusions of the Commission on Social Justice. In many ways it went much further than the commission in calling for a parental wage, and yet it has much in common with traditional conservative ideas – showing the inadequate scope of traditional political boundaries in a period when ideas for 'conserving' social institutions have often come from the left.)

30   Denis MacShane, *Sunday Times*, 25 January 1998 and 'Taxing the Family to Death', *New Statesman*, 4 April 1997.

31   Amitai Etzioni, *The Spirit of Community*, HarperCollins 1993 (Chapter 2) and *The Parenting Deficit*, Demos 1993.

32 Demos debate at the London School of Economics, 'Men: the Weaker Sex?', April 1997.

33 Hamish McRae, *The World in 2020*, HarperCollins 1994, p. 113.

34 William Mattox, 'The Family Time Famine' in *Family Policy*, vol 3, no 1, 1990 (Family Research Council) and 'The Parent Trap', *Policy Review*, Winter 1991, pp. 6–13.

35 Patricia Morgan, *Who Needs Parents?* IEA 1996, quotes the evidence against non-parental care. Ann Mooney and Anthony Munton, *Research and Policy in Early Childhood Services: Time for a New Agenda*, Thomas Coram Research Unit, Institute of Education 1997, summarizes the research in favour and reassures parents that day care and quality, stable substitute care causes no harm and can even enhance young children's development. Despite the enormous amount written and said on this contentious topic there remains very little reliable, longitudinal data in the UK so the jury is still out.

36 See, for example, Diane Ehrensaft, *Spoiling Childhood: How Well Meaning Parents Are Giving Children Too Much but Not What They Need*, Guildford Press, USA 1997. This is one of several contemporary books pointing to the unease about 'hurried' children who need more parental time. Steve Biddulph, the childcare guru, believes that two-thirds of child discipline problems arise because of lack of parental time. At the extreme, a National Commission on Child Abuse (established by the NSPCC), which reported in 1996, included as a specific category of impairment 'middle-class parents working excessive hours'. Yvonne Roberts, 'Save the Children', *New Statesman*, 25 October 1996.

37 *The Times*, 9 March 1996.

38 Gwyn Daniel, contribution to the Family Policy Studies Centre seminar on 'Families at Work', January 1996.

39 'The Myth of Quality Time', *Newsweek*, 19 May 1997.

40 Baroness Heather Brigstocke, 'Educating Women', Third Fawcett Library Lecture, November 1997.

41 Gillian Slovo, *Every Secret Thing: My Family My Country*, Little, Brown 1997, p. 214.

42 Interview with Penny Mansfield, One Plus One, January 1997.

43 M. Young and P. Willmott, *The Symmetrical Family*, Routledge 1993, p. 280.

44 John Ermish and Marco Francesconi, *Family Matters*, ESCR Research Centre on Micro-social change, Paper 97-1, University of Essex 1997.

45 Helen Wilkinson et al., *Time Out – the costs and benefits of paid parental leave 1997*, Demos 1997, argues the case for and in conjunction with the Henley Centre presents concrete proposals for this kind of scheme.

46 1998 survey by the Teacher Training Agency and National Union of Teachers into sixth form boys' and girls' attitudes towards a career in teaching. Forty per cent of girls but only 9 per cent of boys favoured a teaching career.

47 *The Times*, 12 December 1997.

48 The expression 'family-friendly' has become a political catch-phrase and there is little conception of what it really means beyond superficial rearrangement. Suzan Lewis and Jeremy Lewis (eds), *The Work–Family Challenge*, Sage 1996, takes a clear look at some of the obstacles.

49 Scarlett MccGwire, *Best Companies for Women*, Pandora 1992.

50 Patricia Hewitt, *About Time*, IPPR/Rivers Oram 1993, p. 103.

51 Christopher Lasch (edited by Elisabeth Lasch-Quinn) *Women and the Common Life: Love, Marriage and Feminism*, Norton 1997, p. 119.

52 See Ann Oakley, 'A Brief History of Gender', in Ann Oakley and Juliet Mitchell, *Who's Afraid of Feminism? Seeing Through the Backlash*, Hamish Hamilton 1997.

53 Sylvia Ann Hewlett, *A Lesser Life: The Myth of Women's Liberation*, Michael Joseph 1987, p. 181, describes the appalling childcare 'kennels' that some American parents are forced to use.

54 Dex and Rowthorn, 'The Case for a Ministry of the Family'. Their analysis of British Household Panel Survey concludes that fewer than one in twenty women at home (3–5 per cent) are hampered from working by the unavailability of full-time childcare.

55 Reuben Ford, *Childcare in the Balance: How Lone Parents Make*

Decisions about Work, PSI 1996; also *Guardian* panel, March 1998, conducted by Opinion and Leader Research.

56 Dr Wendy Greengross, interviewed in Valerie Grove, *The Compleat Woman*, Chatto and Windus 1988.

57 Theodore Zeldin, *An Intimate History of Humanity*, Sinclair-Stevenson 1994, Chapter 20.

58 This was the phrase used by Oliver James, author of *Britain on the Couch*, Century 1997.

59 Contribution to Nexus third way online debate.

Select Bibliography

Abrams, Rebecca, *The Playful Self: Why Women Need Play in Their Lives*, Fourth Estate 1997

Apter, Terri, *Why Women Don't Have Wives*, Macmillan 1985

Balls, Edward and Paul Gregg, *Work and Welfare*, IPPR Commission on Social Justice 1993

Bartlett, Jane, *Will You be Mother? Women who Choose to Say No*, Virago 1994

Benn, Melissa, *Madonna and Child. Towards a New Politics of Motherhood*, Jonathan Cape 1998

Biddulph, Steve, *The Secret of Happy Children*, HarperCollins 1984

Biddulph, Steve, *Raising Boys*, Thorsons (HarperCollins) 1998

Bly, Robert, *Iron John: A Book About Men*, Addison Wesley 1990

Bradley, Harriet, *Men's Work, Women's Work*, Polity Press 1989

Bridges, William, *Jobshift: How to Prosper in a Workplace Without Jobs*, Nicholas Brealey 1995

Burgess, Adrienne, *Fatherhood Reclaimed – The Making of the Modern Father*, Random House 1997

Charles, Nickie, *Gender Division and Social Change*, Harvester Wheatsheaf 1993

Chodorow, Nancy, *The Reproduction of Mothering*, University of California Press 1978

Coe, Trudy, *The Key to the Men's Club*, Institute of Management 1992

Cooper, Cary and Suzan Lewis, *The Workplace Revolution: Managing Today's Dual-Career Families*, Kogan Page 1993

Coote, Anna and Beatrix Campbell, *Sweet Freedom*, Blackwell 1987

Coyle, Angela, *Women and Organisational Change*, EOC 1995

Coyle, Angela and Jane Skinner, *Women and Work. Positive Action for Change*, Macmillan 1988

Coward, Rosalind, *Our Treacherous Hearts*, Faber 1992

Crosby, Fay J., *Juggling: The Unexpected Advantages of Balancing Career and Home for Women and Their Families*, Free Press 1991

Davidson, Marilyn and Cary Cooper, *Shattering the Glass Ceiling: The Woman Manager*, Paul Chapman 1992

Dench, Geoff, *The Frog, The Prince and the Problem of Men*, Neanderthal Books 1994

Dench, Geoff (ed.), *Rewriting the Sexual Contract*, Institute of Community Studies 1997

Denfeld, Rene, *The New Victorians: A Young Woman's Challenge to the Old Feminist Order*, Simon and Schuster 1995

Dinnerstein, Dorothy, *The Rocking of the Cradle and the Ruling of the World*, Harper and Row 1987

Dix, Carol, *Working Mothers: You, Your career, Your child*, Unwin 1989

Dixon, Pat, *Making the Difference. Women and Men in the Workplace*, Heinemann 1993

Dougary, Ginny, *The Executive Tart and Other Myths*, Virago 1994

Drucker, Peter, *Post-Capitalist Society*, Butterworth-Heinemann 1993

Ephron, Nora, *Heartburn*, Heinemann 1983

Epstein, Lewis, *Coaching for Fatherhood – Teaching Men New Life Roles*, New Horizon Press, 1996

Etzioni, Amitai, *The Spirit of Community*, HarperCollins 1993

Faludi, Susan, *Backlash: The Undeclared War Against American Women*, Crown Books 1991

Farrell, Warren, *The Myth of Male Power. Why Men are the Disposable Sex*, Fourth Estate 1994

Feminist Review, *Waged Work: A Reader*, Virago 1986

Ferri, Elsa and Kate Smith, *Parenting in the 1990s*, Family Policy Studies Centre 1996

Fielding, Helen, *Bridget Jones's Diary*, Picador 1996

Figes, Kate, *Because of Her Sex*, Macmillan 1994

Ford, Reuben, *Childcare In the Balance. How Lone Parents Make Decisions About Work*, Policy Studies Institute 1996

Forster, Margaret, *Significant Sisters*, Secker and Warburg 1994

Fougner, Brit and Mona Larsen-Asp (eds), *The Nordic Countries – A Paradise for Women?* Nordic Council of Ministers 1994

Frank, Robert and Philip Cook, *The Winner Take All Society*, Free Press 1995

Fredman, Sandra, *Women and the Law*, Oxford University Press 1997

Freely, Maureen, *What About Us? An Open Letter to the Mothers Who Feminism Forgot*, Bloomsbury 1995

French, Marilyn, *The War Against Women*, Hamish Hamilton 1992

Friedan, Betty, *The Feminine Mystique*, Penguin 1963

Friedan, Betty, *The Second Stage*, Michael Joseph 1981

Fukuyama, Francis, *The End of Order*, Social Market Foundation/Profile Books 1997

Gerson, Kathleen, *Hard Choices: How Women Decide about Work, Career and Motherhood*, University of California Press 1985

Giddens, Anthony, *Beyond Left and Right*, Polity Press 1994

Giddens, Anthony, *Sociology*, 3rd edition, Polity Press 1997

Gieve, Katherine, *Balancing Acts: On Being A Mother*, Virago 1989

Gilligan, Carol, *In a Different Voice*, Harvard University Press 1982

Gilman, Charlotte Perkins, *Herland*, Women's Press 1979

Goodman, Alissa, Paul Johnson and Steven Webb, *Inequality in Britain*, Oxford University Press 1997

Gray, John, *False Dawn: The Delusions of Global Capitalism*, Granta 1998

Gregg, Paul and Jonathan Wadsworth, *Unemployment and Non-employment: Unpacking Economic Inactivity*, Employment Policy Institute 1998

Griffiths, Sian (ed.), *Beyond the Glass Ceiling*, Manchester University Press 1996

Grove, Valerie, *The Compleat Woman: Marriage, Motherhood, Career: Can She Have It All?*, Chatto and Windus 1988

Handy, Charles, *The Age of Unreason*, Century Business 1992

Handy, Charles, *The Empty Raincoat*, Hutchinson 1994

Handy, Charles, *Beyond Certainty*, Hutchinson 1995

Hardyment, Christine, *The Future of the Family*, Phoenix 1998

Harman, Harriet, *The Century Gap*, Random House 1993

Hayden, Dolores, *The Grand Domestic Revolution*, MIT Press 1981

Hewitt, Patricia, *About Time. The revolution in work and family life*, IPPR/Rivers Oram 1993

Hewlett, Sylvia, *A Lesser Life. The Myth of Women's Liberation*, Michael Joseph 1987

Hill, Dave, *The Future of Men*, Phoenix 1997

Hochschild, Arlie, *The Second Shift*, Avon Books 1989

Hochschild, Arlie, *The Time Bind: When Work Becomes Home and Home Becomes Work*, Metropolitan Books 1997

Horlick, Nicola, *Can You Have It All?*, Macmillan 1997

Hornby, Nick, *High Fidelity*, Victor Gollancz 1995

Humphries, Jane and Jill Rubery (eds), *The Economics of Equal Opportunity*, EOC 1995

Hutton, Will, *The State We're In*, Jonathan Cape 1995

Innes, Sue, *Making It Work: Women, Change and Challenge in the 90s*, Chatto and Windus 1995

James, Oliver, *Britain on the Couch*, Century 1997

Jolivet, Muriel, *Japan: The Childless Society*, Routledge 1997

Katz, Adrienne, *The Juggling Act*, Bloomsbury 1992

Kennard, David and Neil Small (eds), *Living Together*, Quartet Books 1997

Lasch, Christopher (ed. Elizabeth Lasch-Quinn), *Women and the Common Life: Love, Marriage and Feminism*, Norton 1997

Lawless, Paul, Ron Martin and Sally Hardy (eds), *Unemployment and Social Exclusion*, Regional Studies Association, Jessica Kingsley 1998

Leach, Penelope, *Who Cares?*, Penguin 1979

Leach, Penelope, *Children First: What Society Must Do – and Is Not Doing – for Our Children Today*, Michael Joseph 1994

Leith, James, *Ironing John – Men who care for children*, Doubleday 1995

Lewis, Suzan and Jeremy Lewis (eds), *The Work–Family Challenge*, Sage 1996

Lindley, Robert, (ed.), *Labour Market Structures and Prospects for Women*, EOC 1994

Lowry, Suzanne, *The Guilt Cage*, Hamish Hamilton 1980

McAllister, Fiona, and Lynda Clarke, *Choosing Childlessness*, Family Policy Studies Centre 1998

MccGwire, Scarlet, *Best Companies for Women*, Pandora 1992

McRae, Hamish, *The World in 2020*, HarperCollins 1994

McKenna, Elizabeth Perle, *When Work doesn't Work Anymore*, Simon & Schuster 1997

McLoughlin, Jane, *Up and Running – Women In Business*, Virago 1992

Mahoney, Rhona, *Kidding Ourselves – Breadwinning, Babies and Bargaining Power*, Basic Books 1995

Malos, Ellen, *The Politics of Housework*, Clarion Press 1995

Marshall, Helen, *Not Having Children*, OUP 1993

Mead, Margaret, *Male and Female: A Study of the Sexes in a Changing World*, Victor Gollancz 1949

Meadows, Pamela (ed.), *Work Out – or Work In? Contributions to the Debate on the Future of Work*, Joseph Rowntree Foundation 1996

Miles, Rosalind, *Danger! Men at Work*, Futura 1983

Mill, John Stuart, *The Subjection of Women*, Longman 1869

Mitchell, Susan, *Icons, Saints and Divas: Intimate Conversations with Women Who Changed the World*, HarperCollins 1997

Morgan, Patricia, *Who Needs Parents?*, Institute of Economic Affairs 1996.

Morris, Jan, *Conundrum*, Faber 1974

Murray, Jenni, *The Woman's Hour*, BBC Books 1996

Neuberger, Julia, *Whatever's Happening to Women*, Kyle Cathie 1991

Nelson, Mariah Burton, *The Stronger Women Get the More Men Love Football; Sexism and the Culture of Sport*, Women's Press 1996

Oakley, Ann, *Housewife*, Allen Lane 1974

Oakley, Ann and Juliet Mitchell, *Who's Afraid of Feminism? Seeing Through the Backlash*, Hamish Hamilton 1997

Perelberg, Rosine Jozef, and Ann C. Miller (eds), *Gender and Power in Families*, Routledge 1990

Phillips, Angela, *The Trouble with Boys: Parenting the Men of the Future*, Pandora 1993

Rifkin, Jeremy, *The End of Work: The Decline of the Global Labour Force and the Dawn of the Post-Market Era*, G. P. Putnam 1995

Roberts, Yvonne, *Mad About Women: Can there ever be fair play between the Sexes?*, Virago 1992

Rosen, Bernard Carl, *Women, Work and Achievement: The Endless Revolution*, Macmillan 1989

Rowbotham, Sheila, *A Century of Women*, Viking 1997

Royal Society of Arts report, *Redefining Work*, 1998

Rubery, Jill (ed.), *Women and Recession*, Routledge 1988

Schor, Juliet, *The Overworked American: The Unexpected Decline of Leisure*, Basic Books 1991

Segal, Lynne, *Is the Future Female? Troubled Thoughts on Contemporary Feminism*, Virago 1987

Segal, Lynne, *Slow Motion: Changing masculinities, changing men*, Virago 1990.

Sharpe, Sue, *Just Like a Girl*, Penguin 1994

Slovo, Gillian, *Every Secret Thing: My Family, My Country*, Little, Brown 1997

Smith, Joan, *Misogynies*, Faber 1989

Smith, Joan, *Different for Girls: How Culture Creates Women*, Chatto and Windus 1997

Sommers, Christine Hoff, *Who Stole Feminism? Why Women Have Betrayed Women*, Simon and Schuster 1994

Spring-Rice, Margery, *Working-Class Wives*, Virago 1981 (originally published by Penguin 1939)

Swiss, D. J. and J. P. Walker, *Women and the Work – Family Dilemma*, John Wiley 1993

Tanton, M. (ed.), *Women in Management: A Developing Presence*, Routledge 1994

Walsh, Mary Roth (ed.), *Women, Men and Gender: Ongoing Debates*, Yale University Press 1997

Walter, Natasha, *The New Feminism*, Little, Brown 1998

White, Barbara, Charles Cox and Cary Cooper, *Women's Career Development*, Blackwell Business 1992

Wilkinson, Helen, *No Turning Back: Generations and the Genderquake*, Demos 1994

Wilkinson, Helen and Geoff Mulgan, *Freedom's Children*, Demos 1995

Wilkinson, Helen et al., *Time Out: The costs and benefits of paid parental leave*, Demos 1997

Wilson, Fiona M., *Organizational Behaviour and Gender*, McGraw Hill 1995

Wilson, William Julius, *The Truly Disadvantaged*, University of Chicago Press 1987

Wolf, Naomi, *Fire With Fire*, Chatto and Windus 1994

Yeandle, Susan, *Women's Working Lives*, Tavistock 1984

Young, Michael and Peter Willmott, *The Symmetrical Family*, Routledge 1973

Zeldin, Theodore, *An Intimate History of Humanity*, Sinclair-Stevenson 1994

Index